Knaus has hit the bull's-eye! From a horde of scientific studies and his own extensive experience, he has distilled an accessible, easily assimilated, pragmatic, and schematic approach to dealing with "parasite" anxieties. Readers can work through this program in small bites to gradually advance their control over their destructive anxieties.

—Joseph Gerstein, MD, FACP, Harvard Medical School

In The Cognitive Behavioral Workbook for Anxiety, *Knaus condenses cognitive and behavioral skills to combat parasitic fears and anxieties into a clear, orderly, and concise process. Read this book, work through its exercises, and save yourself from the abyss of needless pain and suffering.*

—Elliot D. Cohen, Ph.D., author of *The New Rational Therapy*

This is a great book. It's an extremely well-written guide to action for those suffering from various conditions from anxiety and depression to severe procrastination. But it's far more than just another self-help book. Instead, this prescription for happiness and health is based on scientific evidence. Between these covers there is a complete course in psychology. I only wish my graduate psychology students had as much genuine knowledge of our field as is found in this book.

—Richard Sprinthall, Ph.D., professor emeritus, American International College

Today, fear and anxiety are almost as prevalent as the common cold. But we have to wait for a cold to run its course before we feel better. This well-written, detailed, and informative book offers immediate, practical, and tested strategies that we can apply to get results right away!

—Sam Klarreich, Ph.D., C. Psych., author of *Pressure Proofing* and president of the Berkeley Centre for Effectiveness in Toronto, ON, Canada

Every once in a while, a self-help book appears that is so reader-friendly and thorough that I feel compelled to insist that my patients acquire it. The Cognitive Behavioral Workbook for Anxiety *is such a book. Its innovative and powerful strategies will reduce the suffering of many. I predict it will quickly become the standard in scientifically sound assistance for anxious and fearful individuals.*

—Barry Lubetkin, Ph.D., ABPP, director of the Institute for Behavior Therapy in New York, NY

Knaus has written an engaging book filled with practical strategies for defeating anxiety based on sound scientific principles. I recommend it highly for the millions who are plagued by unnecessary, pleasure-robbing fears.

—Joel Block, Ph.D., ABPP, assistant clinical professor of psychiatry at Einstein College of Medicine

Knaus digs deep into his years of clinical experience to provide both practical and powerful ways to eliminate the fears and worries that compromise one's quality of life. Each chapter is filled with useful ideas, tips, and strategies that move a person from anxiety to peace of mind. My hope as a practicing clinical psychologist and workshop leader is that those who want to substantially lessen their anxiety as well as those who want to increase their well-being will give themselves the gift of this book.

—Russell Grieger, Ph.D., clinical psychologist, adjunct professor at the University of Virginia, and organizational consultant

This book is solidly researched and based on proven helping methods. The analyses of cases clearly show how to break down problems and provide ways to develop alternate views and behaviors. Forms and exercises provide guides for readers to examine their concerns. The complex cases demonstrate how clients can increase their tolerance for negative emotions and use self-management techniques to develop self-control. Only a person with decades of clinical practice could write a book of this depth and quality.

—Robert E. Arthur, professor emeritus of psychology at the University of Wisconsin—La Crosse

Knaus uses the term "parasite" to describe the impact of fear on behavior to vividly illustrate how it directs our lives. The Cognitive Behavioral Workbook for Anxiety not only shows one "how to," but, of equal importance, "why to" address one's fears. Knaus' emphasis on prevention is further reason why a copy of this book is a must for students and families.

—George Elias, professor emeritus of psychology at Assumption College

Anxiety is one of the most debilitating emotions that we have to deal with. It prevents us from having a better life in many areas and restricts us from reaching our full potential. In The Cognitive Behavioral Workbook for Anxiety, one of the field's most rational and insightful minds takes readers on a journey of discovery into the heart of anxiety and shows how to largely eliminate this emotional plague from our lives.

—Vincent E. Parr, Ph.D., president of the Center for Rational Living in Tampa, FL

The Cognitive Behavioral Workbook *for* Anxiety

A STEP-BY-STEP PROGRAM

WILLIAM J. KNAUS, ED.D.

New Harbinger Publications, Inc.

Publisher's Note

Distributed in Canada by Raincoast Books

Copyright © 2008 by Bill Knaus
New Harbinger Publications, Inc.
5674 Shattuck Avenue
Oakland, CA 94609
www.newharbinger.com

Cover design by Amy Shoup
Text design by Tracy Carlson
Acquired by Jess O'Brien
Edited by Brady Kahn

Printed in the United States of America

Library of Congress Cataloging-in-Publication Data

Knaus, William J.
  The cognitive behavioral workbook for anxiety : a step-by-step program / William J. Knaus.
     p. cm.
  ISBN-13: 978-1-57224-572-3 (pbk. : alk. paper)
  ISBN-10: 1-57224-572-7 (pbk. : alk. paper) 1. Anxiety. 2. Rational emotive behavior therapy. 3. Cognitive therapy. I. Title.
  RC531.K63 2008
  616.85'2206--dc22
                            2008029812

14   13   12

15   14   13   12   11   10   9

Contents

PART II
Intensifying Your Campaign Against Fear

Foreword

Worry gives a small thing a big shadow.

—Swedish proverb

My grandparents, who emigrated directly from Sweden, had many sayings (like the one above) that I learned as a child. Most of these sayings did not have much meaning for me until later in life. Much of our learning occurs in this fashion from our families and cultures. This is the type of learning that seems second nature, the kind that seems invisible because we don't even know how or what we know. Many positive as well as negative habits are transferred to us through this transgenerational learning. Some learnings help us to cope with life while others tend to be destructive and include fears, anxieties, worries, and phobias.

Alfred Adler explained that fears, anxieties, worries, and phobias have a function or purpose. Anxiety is a safeguarding mechanism that causes people to frighten themselves out of doing things. They could simply decide not to do these things, but then they might have to face their complexes and admit them. With anxiety as a mechanism, they claim they are too afraid to try (Carlson, Watts, and Maniacci 2006). These patterns are frequently acquired without our direct awareness or conscious intent.

It has been reported that anxiety impacts one-third of the population at one time or another. In researching this topic, I found that Google had over nearly 60 million entries for anxiety alone. The various listings described the many strategies purported to provide relief for anxious mood. These ranged from various drugs to biblical passages to diets to folk cures.

This book is different in that it has strategies that have been researched and proven to be effective. They do not promise a quick fix but, rather, teach us how to take responsibility for our own lives. Too many people blame others for their personal challenges. As Bill Knaus states, "Blame, like the air, is everywhere." This book provides three basic prescriptions to help conquer the problem of anxiety:

1. Educate your reason to oppose parasitic thinking and reacting. (Change your thoughts.)

2. Learn to build emotional tolerance. (Strengthen your emotions.)

3. Behaviorally engage the fear and desensitize yourself to it. (Take action.)

These interventions integrate thinking, feeling, and acting modalities. This allows individuals to utilize their strengths and preferences.

I have had the good fortune to travel to many different cultures. In my work with indigenous people, I learned that it is not possible to feel anxious while breathing abdominally. This is often the best first step, as it not only provides relief from anxiety but also increases awareness. The quickest way to clear anxiety out of your body is to take a few deep belly breaths. Chest breathing seems to be wired into anxiety production, while belly breathing is connected to anxiety reduction. If you are anxious, you can wait until you are not anxious and your breathing will slow down. But if you are in a hurry to clear out the anxiety, you can slow down your breath consciously and watch the anxiety go away.

By concentrating on our breathing, we can learn to accept the fact of fear, learn to feel fear fully, and act so that fear does not interfere with life choices. As David Riccio (2008, 21–22.) states, "We all feel afraid sometimes. This is an appropriate feeling and can be a signal of real danger and threat. At the same time, we sometimes feel afraid without reason. Our guesses and fantasies about what might happen keep us afraid of events and experiences that may never befall us. It is useless to attempt to eliminate fear altogether, whether it be ritualistic or imagined."

This book provides an impressive collection of techniques that can be used to provide the courage necessary to face anxieties and fears. All of the strategies have their roots in the work of the great psychologists Alfred Adler, Aaron Beck, Albert Ellis, and Arnold Lazarus and have withstood the test of time. They can be used to help change transgenerational learning patterns by developing courage and self-control.

As I read through this exceptional resource book, I was reminded of the power of the mind. Bill Knaus has clearly presented many effective strategies that will allow readers to solve their own problems. This type of solution will lead to greater psychological hardiness and self-efficacy of the population. It is now possible to go beyond the many self-imposed prisons that we place ourselves within. Eleanor Roosevelt perhaps said it best: "You must do the things you think you cannot do."

—Jon Carlson, Psy.D., Ed.D., ABPP
   Distinguished Professor
   Division of Psychology and Counseling
   Governors State University

I want to thank my wife, Nancy, for her review and comments on the manuscript, and my friend Ed Garcia for his many thoughtful contributions to the book. I also want to thank the following people for commenting on or contributing ideas to specific chapters: Gayle Rosellini, David Cowles, Bob Forester, Rina Cohan, Will Ross, Diana Nadeau, George Morelli, and Michael Edelstein. Last, but certainly not least, thanks goes to my copyeditor, Brady Kahn, for helping to improve the clarity of this book.

This book is the first in a tribute book series to honor Dr. Albert Ellis, the founder of rational emotive behavior therapy. It is dedicated in his memory and in acknowledgment of his enormous contribution to the field of psychotherapy as the grandfather of the currently popular cognitive behavioral therapy methods. General editors for the series are Dr. Bill Knaus, Dr. Elliot Cohen, and Dr. Jon Carlson.

Introduction

Look into the rearview mirror of your life. Do you worry too much? Do you wade through a world with terrors at every turn? If you want freedom from fear, read on!

From time to time, everyone experiences feelings of fear or apprehension. It's only natural. In the face of present and overwhelming danger, or an omen of real danger, avoidance or flight is adaptive. But some anxieties and fears are both needless and largely psychological. I call these fears *parasitic anxieties and fears*, for like parasites, they drain you of energy and leach precious resources, offering nothing in return. An overwhelming fear of failure can block success. The thought of making a public-speaking error can evoke high anxiety and cause you to freeze up in the spotlight. While such anxieties and fears may be fictional in many respects, they may feel paralyzing. In these cases, avoidance or flight normally does more harm than good. This book will demonstrate how to overcome these and many other needless anxieties and fears.

Parasitic fears and anxieties are among the most dreaded of human psychological experiences. They include fears of snakes, being alone, darkness, open spaces, social gatherings, rejection, competition, confrontation, discomfort, making mistakes, loss, evaluation, and fear of the feeling of fear. And even when you recognize that what you fear is not life threatening—and sometimes may be silly—your fears can continue as if they have a life of their own.

If you count yourself among the millions affected by such needless anxieties and fears, you have reason to feel optimistic. You can overcome them by (1) educating yourself to oppose parasitic thinking and reacting, (2) learning to build emotional tolerance, and (3) behaviorally engaging your fear and desensitizing yourself to it. Following these three basic prescriptions, you can dramatically tip the odds in favor of reducing or eliminating these terrors and stopping them from coming back.

RELIEF FROM FEAR

Can applying ideas from a psychology self-help book help reduce unwanted fears and anxieties? The answer is yes. A book that emphasizes evidence-based methods can be as effective as individual counseling (Hirai and Clum 2006). *The Cognitive Behavioral Workbook for Anxiety* contains many ideas, tips, and exercises that will help you address your problem. In this book, you'll learn how to break fear habits and increase your chances for happiness and health. By educating yourself and applying what you learn, you can make progress against the fears that haunt you.

This book contains 260 pages of information on how to deal with your anxieties and fears, which suggests there's a lot to learn and do. The handy workbook format allows you to take in all this information and apply it at your own pace. Working at your own pace is important, for it normally takes time to digest new ideas, choose exercises, design your responses to fear, test your design, and make revisions based on what you've learned.

Defeating anxieties and fears is a process. This is something that takes place over time, where you make adjustments as you go. Through this process, you gain progressive mastery of the techniques that can help you reduce or vanquish needless fears.

You will decide how to pace yourself. So instead of feeling overwhelmed by all the possibilities, you can feel optimistic about the opportunities. Stretch a bit to see what you can do.

A NO-BLAME APPROACH

Blame, like the air, is everywhere. Blame can be useful at a social level, such as dispassionately assigning accountability. If left at this level, we'd all be better off. But as practically everyone knows, blame can be punitive.

We live in a blame culture. There are three "e" factors in a blame culture. We have blame excesses (complaining, nitpicking, faultfinding), blame extensions (downing and damning), and blame exonerations (denials, excuses, and shifting the blame). Of these, extensions of blame are ordinarily the most destructive.

Blame extensions involve (1) condemnation for any real or imagined rule violations, (2) debasement or dehumanization for the error, and (3) punishment that exceeds the level of real or imagined damage.

Extending blame to yourself can follow a pattern of magnifying your own foibles and faults, fearing blame for real or imagined faults, and, finally, blaming and downing yourself. When this double-trouble blame thinking dominates, you can feel considerable psychic pain.

You can break a blame-anxiety connection by recognizing blame when it pops into mind. Taking responsibility for blame thinking opens opportunities to rid yourself of this kind of stress. A kindly, self-accepting attitude of mind helps mute the cries of parasitic anxieties and fears. With fewer extensions-of-blame moments, you can more ably put your attention on addressing your fears.

You can develop self-kindness through reflection, reason, and by drawing upon your natural sense of compassion. A self-accepting view rolls the dice in favor of a happier and healthier lifestyle. You are also more likely to take prudent risks when your mind and emotions are not jolted by blame beliefs. You can more easily question frightening assumptions.

This book takes a blame-free approach. The focus here is on solving problems.

DEALING WITH COEXISTING ISSUES

Do you sometimes feel overwhelmed by pressures and fears? Does it seem that one misery follows another? Do you feel overwhelmed by powerful feelings of depression? When you are anxious, do you tend to procrastinate? Do you hold to lofty ideals and feel anxious when you fall short?

You're not alone. Most people who suffer from parasitic anxieties and fears tend to find themselves challenged by depression, perfectionism, and self-doubt. These coexisting conditions include these features:

■ Unpleasant or stressful emotions and sensations

■ Faulty beliefs

■ Unrealistic self-perceptions

■ Intolerance for discomfort

■ Threat sensitivity

■ Self-defeating behaviors

Effectively addressing any one issue will help you address other issues. Dealing with self-doubts can help defuse parasitic anxieties and fears. The methods you use to defeat powerlessness thinking in anxiety apply to defeating powerlessness thinking in depression. Developing an optimistic outlook can undo many forms of distress based on unrealistic pessimism. Becoming less of a perfectionist removes reasons for feeling anxious. Threat sensitivity cuts across all forms of anxieties and fears (Bar-Haim et al. 2007). Learn to tolerate your sensitivity to threat, and you may soon find less reason to feel threatened. In short, cognitive behavioral techniques that are useful for addressing anxiety often are useful in addressing coexisting conditions (McEvoy and Nathan 2007).

You can reduce the negatives in life by building positive resources, such as your power of reasoning, your tolerance for emotional discomfort, and the will to engage in productive actions. It's also important to keep your eyes on the positive goals that your anxieties and fears block. These goals can give you an incentive to go beyond your fears. If you exclusively focus your efforts on overcoming the negatives, and you succeed, then what do you have? Relief, of course. But there is more to life than that, especially if you want to stop parasitic anxieties from coming back.

A BOOK WHERE SCIENCE AND PRACTICE MEET

The Cognitive Behavioral Workbook for Anxiety describes many ways to reduce needless fears and anxieties and to build positive experiences into your life. The knowledge contained in this book draws on a number of different sources. The scientific and clinical literature on anxieties and fears is extensive. I've selected examples from both classical and recent thinking on the subject. I've included many references to the most recent research, as well as to older work that still applies today.

This book also draws from my forty years of experience as a psychologist and psychotherapist. It represents an *awareness-and-action* approach. This approach draws from the broad field of psychology, psychotherapy practice, philosophy, and related resources. It's an approach that the most effective therapists take, regardless of their particular persuasion. The goal is to help promote realistic understanding and awareness and to serve as a catalyst for effective problem solving.

The awareness-building process comes from monitoring your thinking, getting new information, playing with paradoxes, making insightful connections between present and past patterns, separating realistic from fanciful views, recognizing what can trigger both negative and positive reactions, and so on. The action process includes developing new habits and consciously directed behaviors to counter your fears. It involves acquiring some new skills. It also involves helping you recognize your aptitudes and talents. In the context of breaking free from needless fears, the goal is to make positive changes. Most of the time, in the process of quelling needless fears, your emotions blend with awareness-and-action experiences to motivate constructive action.

Awareness-and-action techniques are normally *evidence-based*, or capable of being tested. These techniques are definable, doable, and measurable. They can give order to what can sometimes seem like a chaotic inner process of fear. But other techniques are metaphorical and can titillate awareness at a more creative level. Some techniques involve paradoxes and their resolution. Some involve experimentation. Rather than look for evidence to support your view—as you would if you prepared for a debate—in an experimental mode, you look for exceptions as well as evidence, to broaden your perspective. Using this awareness-and-action process to defeat needless anxieties and fears, you direct your efforts to reduce negatives and build positives.

Throughout, you'll learn to be your own coach and to do what effective therapists tend to do: help promote realistic awareness and serve as a catalyst for constructive actions. This awareness-and-action approach weaves throughout the book.

The Cognitive Behavioral Workbook for Anxiety highlights the contemporary work of many great thinkers. Within these pages, you will find ideas and methods from Albert Ellis's rational emotive behavioral therapy (REBT), Arnold Lazarus's multimodal therapy, Aaron Beck's cognitive therapy, Joseph Wolpe's behavior therapy, and psychologist Albert Bandura's work on self-efficacy, as well as currently popular cognitive behavioral therapy concepts and techniques.

From a historical standpoint, techniques for dealing with parasitic forms of anxieties and fears are continuing to evolve. You'll find many new ways to examine and address anxieties and fears within these pages. You'll find ideas that you can use to understand your fears and to feel better about yourself. You'll find solid ways to defuse parasitic anxiety-and-fear thinking. You'll discover how to build resilience against your fears. In short, you will discover many sound reasons for optimism.

Does this book cover everything? No book can. There is currently a knowledge explosion going on in the area of anxiety. Part of this explosion involves the use of magnetic imagery devices that record pictures of brain activity onto a computer screen. As a result, we are improving our understanding of how the brain works when in a state of anxiety and fear. Soon we will be able to use magnetic imagery to see how cognitive behavioral therapy affects anxious thinking and the brain. Such an approach can help streamline what we do.

HOW THIS BOOK IS STRUCTURED

The Cognitive Behavioral Workbook for Anxiety provides step-by-step guidance for addressing parasitic anxieties and fears. It offers multiple ideas and exercises to address them. Which exercises you decide to do will depend on your preferences, circumstances, and readiness to act.

This book follows a stepping-stone approach. Exercises from earlier chapters provide ideas as a foundation for later chapters. As you become more skilled in the use of these ideas, the odds are that you'll find new ways to apply them.

The book breaks out into two parts. Part I focuses on helping you develop a perspective about your fears, build self-observant skills, deal with fears of fear, map a program for positive change, take a multidimensional approach to defeat fear, and learn to decrease the negatives in your life by advancing your positive interests through five phases of change.

Part II offers advanced techniques to deal with parasitic anxieties and fears and coexisting conditions. This part starts with training your mind to shut off parasitic anxieties and fears. You'll learn how to build and sustain emotional tolerance. You'll learn behavioral methods to quell your fears. Then you'll learn to manage common coexisting challenges that commonly accompany anxiety. You'll learn how to break the procrastination-fear connection, deal with the anxiety-and-depression connection, and address worry. Then you'll learn how to deal with the perfectionism, harmful inhibitions, self-worth problems, and social evaluation fears that can artificially limit your social life and career. You'll learn how to defeat panic. In the final chapter, you'll learn how to preserve and advance your gains, and thus reduce your risk for relapse.

KEY IDEAS AND ACTION PLAN

Without a photographic memory, it would be difficult to remember all the ideas and exercises in this book. Using a highlighter may help. But the best way to focus your attention on what you can do to progressively master your fears is to keep a record of ideas that catch your attention and write down actions you plan to take.

In each chapter, starting with this introduction, you will find a Key Ideas and Action Plan section. Here you will choose the ideas that you found most meaningful in each chapter. You will decide the actions you will take and record the results.

A word of warning: Preparing to take action can pay off in many ways, including boosting your personal sense of command over the manageable parts of your life. But there are possible barriers. For example, if you think you need to be fully prepared before you can act, you'll be waiting a long time.

So it's time to get started. Here's how to put this Key Ideas and Action Plan to use:

1. What are three ideas from this introduction that you believe you can use to help yourself overcome your parasitic anxieties and fears? Write them down.

2. What actions can you take to begin addressing your fears? Write them down.

3. Test the plan and record the results. Use the results to decide what to repeat, modify, or drop.

Key Ideas

1.

2.

3.

Action Plan

1.

2.

3.

Results from Actions Taken

1.

2.

3.

POSTSCRIPT

Parasitic fears and anxieties can seem like formidable foes, but these are foes that exist within you and nowhere else. When these fears and anxieties hobble you, you may feel like your body is wrapped in wet leather, shrinking in the sun. Decreasing core parasitic beliefs can help you shed the leather. As you free yourself from the fictions and restrictions of parasitic anxieties and fears, you can create a life story based on accomplishments that might otherwise not have happened.

In your battle against needless fears, you've made a start. You've bought this book. You've read the introduction. And you've already begun to apply what you've learned.

PART I

Defeating Fear Through Understanding

- Learn how to recognize handicapping parasitic anxieties and fears.

- Distinguish between parasitic anxieties and fears with a time and proximity analysis.

- Apply cognitive, emotional tolerance, and behavioral methods to defeat needless fears.

- Build your self-observation skills, so you can better assess needless fears and free yourself from them.

- Use your intellect, ingenuity, and will to defeat fear.

- Recognize and defeat catastrophic thinking.

- Effectively address secondary distresses that may be part of, and even worse than, your original parasitic anxieties and fears.

- Learn how to unconditionally accept yourself, with or without your fears.

- Create a master plan for defeating your fears.

- Using a powerful multimodal approach, address your anxieties and fears on multiple dimensions.

- Use a five-phase approach to change that will decrease the negatives in your life and promote positive steps toward a healthy and happy future.

CHAPTER 1

Welcome to the World of Parasitic Anxieties and Fears

When fear causes you to escape a life-threatening danger, it is your friend. But some fears have this sordid tale to tell:

> *I am fear. I make your mind spin out of control. I wind your body tight as a drum. You try to hide from me. I will find you. Look over your shoulder. I am behind you. Look forward. My shadow crosses your path. Look into a mirror and you see me sneering back at you. I control your life. You can do nothing to stop me.*

This brash voice of fear has little to do with self-preservation. It's a parasitic fear that feeds off its host and offers nothing of benefit.

In the grip of a fearful state of mind, you likely have trouble concentrating. Your mind goes from one dreaded possibility to another. You worry about making mistakes. You make mountains out of molehills. You second-guess yourself and hesitate when action is the better response. You act out of impulse when reflection is the better response. You may experience difficulties falling asleep, fatigue, headaches, digestive problems, lower-back pains, and other unpleasant physical signs of anxiety. In this turbulent inner world, your demon of fear is ever near. But reasoned explanations can go far to send the demon into retreat.

If you count yourself among those suffering from parasitic fears, you are neither unique nor alone. Twenty-nine percent of the U.S. population will at some time over their lifetimes suffer an intense and persistent fear or anxiety (Kessler et al. 2005). If the population remained constant at 300 million, this would mean that 87 million people would experience a persistent and debilitating anxiety at some time during their lives. This makes parasitic anxieties and fears the most common form of human distress (Mineka and Zinbarg 2006).

Some anxieties are brief. If you have a mild but passing apprehension as you approach someone for a date, it's usually no big deal. Parasitic forms of anxiety are much bigger deals than that. They are intense, persistent, recurrent, and debilitating. Left unaddressed, the more intense forms of anxiety will probably get worse or can lead to distressing coexisting conditions. For example, anxiety commonly precedes depression and substance abuse.

This chapter will turn parasitic anxieties and fears upside down. It's time to mount a spirited attack against them.

Although high anxiety can feel like the most horrifying of experiences, it is a state that you can do much to change. Parasitic anxiety and fears are highly manageable, if you know how to manage them. There are now many tested cognitive, emotional tolerance, and behavioral ways to address and defeat these fears. If one approach doesn't work, you can try another way.

FEARS AND ANXIETIES AS GUARDIANS

Your fears are like alarms that warn of threat and danger. When danger beckons, you automatically freeze or retreat. Your heartbeat quickens. Your blood pressure rises. Blood rushes to your inner organs. You take in more oxygen. This is your natural reaction to threat.

Natural anxiety and fear reactions are a form of life insurance. In fear, your body is almost instantly energized. You startle at sudden and abrupt changes, such as the unexpected appearance of a confusing shadow. You jump back from a snake before you know you are afraid.

Throughout life, you get many more false alarms than alarms for real danger, however. A darting shadow proves harmless. The crackling sound in the tree above is a squirrel, not a leopard. At home alone at night, you startle in response to a creaking sound. Nothing is there. The house has settled a bit more. But if your fear alarm has saved you from injury or death even once, it's done its evolutionary job.

We all learn new ways to experience fear. You'd likely experience an emotional jolt if you saw blue flashing lights on a vehicle coming up behind your car. There is nothing inherently dangerous about blue flashing lights, except the nearly instant meaning you give to the event. Your knowledge of an impending danger is ordinarily sufficient to avoid the situation. Knowing that wood alcohol is poisonous, you don't drink it. Touching an exposed electrical wire can cause a shock. So you don't do it.

Anxiety is natural. Apprehension in unfamiliar circumstances is understandable. You don't know what to expect. You feel wary. Your senses are on alert. You feel poised for action. You find nothing of concern. This preliminary scan costs little more than a few calories. Picking up a threat or danger before it comes into sight has a big survival benefit.

Modern anxieties involve intellectual and experiential understandings that give you a highly advanced signaling system. You know about the danger of encountering a mugger, even if one has never robbed you. So you don't walk alone late at night through a slum neighborhood that's known to be controlled by a crazed drug czar.

PUTTING A FACE ON PARASITIC ANXIETIES AND FEARS

Normal anxieties and fears are not the problem. The problem is the more frequent and persistent parasitic anxieties. If you are among the millions for whom anxieties and fears are both parasitic and persistent, this state can restrict your life. But even parasitic fears can be managed, unlearned, or extinguished.

When I run groups for people with fears and anxieties, I find that most feel relieved when they discover that they are not unique. By revealing their anxious thinking in a safe group atmosphere, few continue to think of themselves as odd. Once out of the shadows, parasitic fears and anxieties are more readily addressed.

John's Panic

John, a group member, was a frequent panicked visitor to his local hospital emergency room. Gasping for air and feeling sharp chest pains, John would arrive provoked by panicked thoughts that he was having a heart attack and was going to die. After twenty-six hospital emergency visits, John came to see his breathing difficulties and chest pains as a bodily expression of anxiety sensitivity and tension-magnifying thinking. He felt relieved to know that most people who learn to use cognitive and behavioral methods to cope with panic make meaningful progress. John aimed to join them.

Elaine's Silence

Social pressures are part of the dynamics of any social group. Social anxieties about violating group norms can cause you to curb impulsive behaviors. But you may become a social casualty. With an exaggerated fear of censure, you can figuratively hand-cuff yourself in social situations. Elaine wore these handcuffs.

Elaine was the most silent member in her group. She became petrified at the thought of saying something foolish. After eight weeks of saying very little, she confessed that if the others really knew her, they'd force her out. She calmed down when she learned that this fear of rejection said more about her own self-doubts than the views of any other person in the room. Based on group feedback, she figured out that what she thought others thought about her could not possibly be true. Different people tend to have different opinions. The group members did not all have to think alike.

Larry's Stress

Larry told group members that he became stressed easily. He had moments of panic where he had trouble breathing, felt dizzy, and his heart beat like crazy. He said that this panic occurred when he was "stuck in one place with a lot of people in a small area." Larry went on to say that he had bad headaches. He was afraid that he might have a brain tumor.

Larry was in a rotating procrastination pattern. He'd start to deal with one stress and then put off the resolution by skipping to another. Because his problems kept recycling, he felt overwhelmed. He said, "This is too much for me. I can't handle it." But what was "too much" was his internal monologue. He exaggerated the fearsomeness of his tensions. At the same time, he minimized his capacity to cope. When he focused on stopping the rotating procrastination pattern by dealing with one fear at a time, he found he had fewer fears to handle.

Joy's Apprehension

Practically everybody experiences at least mild apprehension when faced with an upcoming situation he or she finds stressful, such as preparing for an important test, being uncertain about the causes of an illness, or preparing to deliver a public speech. When these tensions spur constructive actions, they serve a useful purpose. But you can also go overboard with parasitic anxieties and fears. Joy went overboard.

Joy felt anything but joyful. She told her group that she was a dim light in a brightly lit world of intelligent people. Then she got blunt. She described herself as stupid. She argued that she makes a lot of mistakes. She dreaded the thought that people might catch on to her and discover that she was a fake.

Joy was finishing her second year of graduate school. She reported that she pondered over her studies until she had a reasonable chance of succeeding. She said, "It takes me three times as long as anyone else to pass the courses." Although Joy had a high grade-point average and received praise from her professors for the quality of her work, she claimed that she had fooled them all. When asked, "How can a dull light fool bright lights?" at first she seemed baffled. Then Elaine pointed out that the main reason Joy felt like a dim light was because she held a dimmer switch and refused to turn up the light. And Joy said, "I never thought about it that way before." With a changing self-view, she was in a better position to benefit from her achievements.

Tom's Fear of Complacency

Tom was convinced that the only reason he kept going was because of his fears. He said his fears drove him to achieve.

Tom suffered from a fear of complacency. He hated his fears. But he saw himself on the horns of a dilemma. If he eased up, he believed he'd do nothing and "go down the tubes." Tom's all-or-nothing thinking about the driving force of fear meant that he was going to be either driven by fear or slump into complacency. He began to rethink this position when asked, "What is in between?"

In the spirit of an observation by *Dune* novelist Frank Herbert (1965), Tom realized that after fear was gone, he remained. He could harness the power that was previously driven by fear to meet challenges rather than avoid fictional threats.

John, Elaine, Larry, Joy, and Tom cannot be easily pigeonholed under a label, such as an "anxious" or "nervous" person. No single label describes each person's complexities, hopes, wishes, and dreams. Yet they do share a common problem: parasitic anxiety and fear habits.

Parasitic anxieties are a part of your thoughts, emotions, and behaviors. You can partially to completely eliminate your anxieties and fears by making changes in your thinking, developing emotional tolerance, and taking problem-directed behavioral actions. This one-two-three punch can be the parasite's coup de grâce.

ANXIETY AND FEAR ARE RELATED BUT DIFFERENT

In ancient Greece, terror and dread were the work of two capricious gods of war. Phobos was the spirit of fear, panic, and flight. Deimos infected the mind with dread. These gods symbolized the human ability to respond when confronted with an overwhelming danger and to anticipate threats beyond the horizon.

Putting the fable of the two gods aside, the ancients got it right: fear and anxiety are both related and different. Normal anxiety and fear are separate processes (Perkins, Kemp, and Corr 2007; Davis 1998).

Buried in the limbic region of the brain is an almond-shaped area called the amygdala. This is the center for fear and some forms of anxiety (LeDoux 1998). When you sense danger, the sensory information goes first to your amygdala and then to your higher mental processes. The amygdala activates stress hormones that trigger arousal sensations, such as rapid heartbeat and hyperventilation. The second signal takes a roundabout route to the cortex. Conscious thoughts follow. This process involves filling in details, judging what is happening, and deciding the degree of the danger.

Fear is immediate, perceptual, and reactive. Anxiety reflects a future threat. Although fear and anxiety have joint connections in the brain, they also track along different circuits. This distinction between fear and anxiety is important.

Although the ways to deal with parasitic anxieties and fears overlap, you typically do better taking behavioral action to deal with fear. Parasitic anxiety alarms are triggered by fearsome beliefs and imaginary dreads. You can deal with them through counteracting your parasitic thoughts and by knowledgeably engaging in fear-related behaviors. In dealing with both fears and anxieties, reducing or eliminating nonexistent threats also involves developing emotional tolerance.

PROXIMITY AND TIME DIMENSIONS

You can identify fear and anxiety by the dimensions of proximity and time. When in a state of natural fear, an overwhelming danger is happening now. Anxiety is on a time dimension; the threat comes later, but you know about it now. If you are unable to avoid the threat, anxiety switches to fear, when time and proximity converge.

You can accept a danger to life and limb as a legitimate reason to react with flight. But parasitic fears reflect a false alert about fictional dangers. There is a big difference between feeling fear when a bear crosses your path and standing before a group holding a microphone. I know of no one planted six feet under for, say, making a mistake before a group. Yet many would rather spend a year in a dungeon than speak in public.

A natural anxiety alerts you to a real and impending future danger that is yet to happen. A parasitic anxiety also operates on a time dimension. But this form of anxiety involves worries and troubles over fictional or magnified events related to exaggerated concerns.

Natural Fear on a Proximity Dimension

Fear involves proximity. At a comfortable distance, you may observe a grizzly bear with curiosity. You see the bear a mile away through a telescope and feel fascinated by what you see. There is no danger. You and the bear exist in the same time dimension, but not in close enough proximity to where the bear poses a threat.

On the other hand, if you see the animal directly in your path on its hind legs with bared fangs, you and the bear are in the same time and space together. That proximity is an obvious danger for you. You don't need a textbook to learn what to do. Your automatic preservation responses take over.

Parasitic Fears on a Proximity Dimension

In a parasitic fear situation, the moment is now. You are in it. You touched a dirty rag. You fear contamination. You panic at the thought of billions of invading germs saturating your body with toxic chemicals. It all happens in a twinkle. Several coworkers plan a surprise party for you at a local restaurant. You're afraid to eat at the restaurant because you (1) feel self-conscious in public places, (2) fear crowded places, or (3) fear being seated too far from an exit door. You discover the surprise as they lead you to the restaurant door. You're not in danger for your life, but it feels that way. Most people feel frustrated about fears that they know come from parasitic threats that don't make sense and that feel inhibiting.

Natural Anxiety on a Time Dimension

Anxiety exists on a time dimension. The dreaded event is in the future. The distance between you and the feared situation is measured by the hands on a clock. Still, your tension over the anticipated event is in the present moment.

When you feel anxious, the threat is not yet there. You still have time to avoid it or to figure out how to cope if the threat is unavoidable. Say you've been told you need an operation that has a 20 percent risk factor. The operation is scheduled for two weeks from now, and you are concerned about the outcome. The operation is unavoidable since you have no meaningful chance without it. To cope with your anxiety over the 20 percent risk factor, your goal would be to emphasize the 80 percent survival rate.

Parasitic Anxieties on a Time Dimension

A parasitic anxiety exists on a time dimension in which you think about a disastrous event that could happen. You fear slipping on a wet floor and looking like a klutz. You anxiously believe that your currently devoted mate will eventually abandon you, leaving you devastated. You fear for your unborn great-great-great grandchildren, whom you worry may die in a catastrophic collision between Earth and a giant asteroid. These and other parasitic anxieties serve no adaptive purpose. Instead, they promote pessimism, powerlessness, and psychic pain without meaningful gain.

Dread can center on anticipation: fearing fear; worrying about looking like a fool, appearing incompetent, or getting rejected; or confronting other parasitic threats. It's not a question of whether these events will happen or not. They can happen. The main issue is the meaning you give to what often amounts to unprovable assumptions about improbable events.

Suppose that you are petrified at the thought of attending your best friend's wedding. You know you feel self-conscious at formal events. You dread the social fears that you expect to flower at that time. As you worry about the wedding, you invent dire possibilities, such as fainting in public. These possibilities escalate your level of anxiety. You now have two problems. The first one is anxiety over the upcoming wedding. The other problem is the fear you may experience at the wedding. The American humorist and author Mark Twain understood these phantom fears well. He once said he had a great many troubles in his life but that most of them never happened.

COGNITIVE, EMOTIONAL, AND BEHAVIORAL INTERVENTIONS

This book offers cognitive, emotional tolerance, and behavioral interventions for parasitic anxieties and fears. A change in belief can influence how you feel and what you do. Emotional tolerance can buffer you against higher doses of tension. Behavioral activities that evoke tolerable levels of discomfort can aid in building emotional tolerance. Throughout this book, I'll show you how to apply these three prescriptions for freedom from parasitic anxieties and fears.

The Cognitive Approach

The cognitive approach involves educating your reason and using this educated reason to disable parasitic thinking. This approach is important because parasitic fears and anxieties involve erroneous interpretations and evaluations.

In a perfectionist state of mind, for example, parasitic anxieties and fears can be stirred by beliefs that other people are evaluating and judging you for not measuring up to what you assume they think are acceptable standards. This is what psychologist Charles Horton Cooley (1902) described as the *looking-glass effect*. You imagine what others think about you, you think the worst, and you conclude that they think what you think they think.

This kind of thinking has a cast of thought characters who disseminate such thoughts as "I don't want to do what I fear right now to do" (procrastination) and "I can't change" (defeatist thinking). These are samples of parasitic thoughts that can run through your mind.

Instead of raising the white flag to your fears, you can take a radically different direction with a thought-clarification process. The thought-clarification process starts with definitions.

Using the above "I can't change" thought as an example, you can ask yourself to define what you mean by "I can't change." You may discover that what you really mean is that unless the change is pleasant, you won't do it. That sets up an interesting paradox. If you don't want to continue to experience parasitic anxieties and fears, and yet you don't want to act to change unless this can be comfortably done, you have two opposing agendas. Agenda one is to bust the fear. Agenda two is to avoid discomfort in this process. When agenda two dominates, where does this leave you?

Since anxiety is on a time dimension, you have time to address a parasitic anxiety and to prepare to deal with what you fear. As a rule of thumb, fearful anticipations can be addressed by examining and questioning parasitic fear thinking. This *cognitive rethinking* approach can be especially useful when you have reason to believe that your fears are imaginary or when you have no objective proof to support them.

Along the time dimension of anxiety, you can do many things. Four sample actions follow:

1. Separate possibilities that could or might happen (worries) from probabilities. What is the chance of an event happening? The idea is to disrupt fearful thinking with enough authority to impeach its credibility.

2. Recognize and act to challenge highly speculative parasitic projections by considering alternative probabilities. For example, if you worry that a friend who didn't meet you at an

agreed-upon time has died in an accident, consider the more likely possibility that he or she got a late start or forgot your appointment.

3. Remind yourself—as many times as it takes—that a parasitic fear is a temporary, passing thought.

4. Work to unconditionally accept yourself despite your parasitic fears. This means accepting yourself as a person with multiple talents, abilities, and experiences who is so much more than the fear(s) that paralyze you.

The Emotional Tolerance Approach

Natural anxieties and fears are typically situational and of short duration, whereas parasitic tensions can come about through invention, attach to many nondangerous situations, and linger. Building tolerance for tension typically involves experiencing what you fear. I know this part of the solution may not seem so attractive. But a conscious willingness to endure unpleasant moods, sensations, and emotions can boost your emotional tolerance. You'll be less tyrannized by what you feel.

The idea here is that tolerating less distress is better than tolerating greater amounts of distress. The goal is to reduce the amount of needless emotional tension you experience so that you have less stress to tolerate. The emotional tolerance approach is based on the idea that discomfort won't kill you. Stress is temporary. Unpleasant emotions eventually go away.

I have found that people with high emotional tolerance tend to accomplish more and seem healthier and happier. This doesn't mean that you can't achieve at high levels if you have low-tension tolerance. You could feel driven to achieve. You could have special talents. High production can come naturally despite a tendency to get easily upset.

Nevertheless, knowing that you can tolerate what you don't like makes you less vulnerable to parasitic anxieties. With this knowledge, you view yourself as able to accept tension. You are less likely to fear what you can accept. If you don't feel distressed over parasitic feelings, you are less likely to panic over them.

Emotional tolerance includes accepting reality. If you're tense, you're tense. That's it! This does not mean capitulation. Indeed, there is much you can do to contain parasitic thoughts so that they do not rage unattended.

The following four questions and answers can put tension tolerance into perspective:

How can you learn to stop magnifying tension? If you do not fear the sensations of discomfort associated with parasitic beliefs, you are less likely to magnify them. If you don't magnify them, you are less likely to experience them in the first place.

What alternative ways do you have to stop magnifying tension? Instead of putting a magnifying glass onto the discomfort, take a closer look at your ideas behind your fear of discomfort. For example, you may hear yourself saying that you can't stand the feeling. But are you not already putting up with what you don't like?

What happens when you show yourself that you can tolerate tension? By showing yourself that you can tolerate sensations of parasitic anxiety and fear, you transform dread into an unpleasant emotional state. A 10 percent gain in tolerance can make a big difference.

Are there any special benefits in developing higher levels of tension tolerance? People with high-tension tolerance are likely to get further faster than those who shrivel up at the first sign of tension. This is because the focus of the higher-tension tolerance group is on pushing aside impediments between where they currently are and where they would like to be. By reducing parasitic stresses, you'll have more time to manage the ordinary and extraordinary stresses of life, as well as to increase your chances of experiencing more of life's pleasures.

The Behavioral Approach

Conquering parasitic fears normally takes more than recognizing fearful thinking, seeing the fallibility of parasitic beliefs, and learning to tolerate them. Breaking a parasitic-fear habit includes squarely facing the fearful situation and living through the tension. You choose the time, place, and method.

Although the primitive fear center of the brain learns quickly when it comes to imprinting a new fear, this area is a slow learner when it comes to dumping a parasitic fear. But by engaging in designed behavioral exercises, you can teach yourself to calm down.

A classic behavioral exercise involves doing what you fear. But you don't have to swamp yourself. You can break your fear down into digestible bits. You can talk yourself through the paces. Here are some ideas:

■ If you fear speaking before a group, join an organization that is designed to help people curb their public-speaking fears. You start with a thirty-second comment and gradually increase the amount of time in which you speak.

■ If you fear going on the elevator, get on an elevator and get off at the next floor up. Count this and each additional flight as an accomplishment. If you hear a whining inner voice asking, "What if the elevator breaks down?" challenge yourself by asking, "So what if the elevator breaks down?"

■ If you have a strong parasitic fear, such as a snake phobia, and this fear restricts what you do, you might start by looking at pictures of harmless snakes until you feel comfortable with viewing the pictures. Then move to the next level, such as viewing a stuffed snake behind a glass barrier at a natural history museum. After going through tolerance-building steps, you may successfully end this process by handling a harmless snake.

Exposure exercises train the primitive parts of the brain to *habituate* to the feared but nondangerous situation. This means getting used to the situation so that it no longer feels troublesome. As the old saying goes, repetition dulls the senses.

When you follow a behavioral approach, it is important to finish what you start. If you start to address a fear, feel discomfort, and then back away, you can reinforce the fear. That reinforcement signals the reptilian areas of the brain that relief comes easy through avoiding or escaping discomfort. But by taking on smaller parts of the challenge, you are likely to reinforce a sense of accomplishment as you move toward progressive mastery of your fear.

A COGNITIVE-EMOTIVE-BEHAVIORAL MATRIX FOR MANAGING TIME AND DISTANCE

How might you use time and proximity dimensions to handle your parasitic anxieties and fears? The following matrix describes cognitive, emotional tolerance, and behavioral ways to defang parasitic anxieties and fears. Use this matrix as a guide for completing your own matrix plan in the following exercise.

Parasitic Threat:	Anxiety	Point of Merging	Fear
Cognitive	"What can I do to put the feared situation into a reasoned perspective? What can I do to shorten the proximity between anticipation and the feared event to get practice in experiencing and facing the fear?"	"How might I think when the fear is not yet here but is in the process of becoming? If the event is exaggerated or a phantom, how can I cope, at the transition point between anxiety and fear?"	"As I experience the fear, what can I tell myself about the situation and sensations to defeat fear-magnifying ideas?"
Emotional Tolerance	"What do my physical feelings of anxious tension feel like? What can I do to tolerate the physical feelings of anxiety? If the anxiety is about a speculative event, how can I establish perspective? What life experiences did I survive that I thought I couldn't, and how can I use those strengths?"	"To promote tolerance for the sensations of a parasitic anxiety or fear, what actions (thoughts, behavior) can I take at the point when an anxious anticipation blends into the experience of fear?"	"Can accepting the tension and living through it without bailing out help reduce the future release of fear hormones and their accompanying sensations in similar circumstances?"
Behavioral	"What specific behaviors can I test in advance of a fearsome event to prepare myself to face the event?"	"What behavioral actions can I take to face a parasitic fear at the transition point when anxiety merges into fear?"	"What behavioral actions can I take when in a parasitic-fear situation to avoid retreat and to face the fear?"

YOUR MATRIX PLAN

Now, it's your turn to fill in the blanks. Write down the particular parasitic threat that you want to defang. Then complete this worksheet describing cognitive, emotional tolerance, and behavioral interventions to defeat this parasitic threat.

Parasite Threat:	Anxiety	Point of Merging	Fear
Cognitive			
Emotional Tolerance			
Behavioral			

AWAKENING THE FORCE WITHIN

Ridding yourself of needless anxieties and fears can involve multiple challenges to gain emotional freedom. It's a search for what mythologist Joseph Campbell (1967) might call the hero within. Hero myths involve a search that often comes about accidentally due to extraordinary circumstances. According to Campbell, hero myths have common features. There is a sheltered life. There is a change that impels action. There is a quest. There are multiple challenges to face. There is the emergence of the hero within. There is self-discovery through action. There is a resolution. This basic story can be told in infinite ways.

In *The Wonderful Wizard of Oz*, by L. Frank Baum (1960), Dorothy is beset by a disaster and is transported to a place where she does not want to be. She learns that to find her way home, she needs to follow the yellow brick road to the Wizard of Oz. Along the way, Dorothy meets a tin man, a cowardly lion, and a straw man who seek to discover what they think that they lack. In her trek to Oz, Dorothy encounters the forces of the Wicked Witch of the West, which represent furies of fear that distract Dorothy from her quest. When she finally meets the wizard, she discovers that he has no magic. But he does have a wise observation: all along, Dorothy had the capability to return home, but that capability awaited discovery. In confronting the Wicked Witch of the West, Dorothy discovered her own strengths and ingenuity, and, in the process, found her way home.

You too are on a challenging quest. The extraordinary condition here is that of facing an ancient enemy: a tenacious, unyielding, parasitic anxiety or fear. And like Dorothy, you are seeking the hero within. In facing your own anxieties and fears, you face a formidable battle. Fearsome thoughts unsettle your life. You decide to fight back. In the process, you discover that you are not helpless against what can first seem like an uncontrollable force. Indeed, you can learn to effectively contest parasitic threats through cognitive, emotional tolerance, and behavioral means.

Engaging fear represents an act of courage. It is through this engagement that you can discover powerful antidotes for fear, as well as discover your strengths. By engaging needless and imaginary fears, there is a potential payoff in the form of self-discovery, freedom from fear, and emergence of the hero from within.

In the journey that lies before you, I won't wish you luck. That leaves too much up in the air. Instead, I wish you the will to persevere. Through willfully acting against your fears, you are likely to learn a great deal about yourself and the resources you have available to uncouple parasitic threats from the unpleasant arousal of fear.

KEY IDEAS AND ACTION PLAN

What key ideas from this chapter can you use to rid yourself of your parasitic anxieties and fears? What's your action plan? Write it down. Test it out. Record what happened.

Key Ideas

1.

2.

3.

Action Plan

1.

2.

3.

Results from Actions Taken

1.

2.

3.

POSTSCRIPT

In his 1932 presidential inauguration address, Franklin D. Roosevelt described what he saw as our paralyzing fears: "The only thing we have to fear is fear itself: nameless, unreasoning, unjustified terror, which paralyzes needed efforts to convert retreat into advance." He proposed bold initiatives against unjustified terrors.

You can put this thinking to use to counter your parasitic fears. By facing your parasitic fears, you can strip away negative fear thinking, tolerate unpleasant fear sensations, and engage in productive pursuits that you previously avoided because of unpleasant sensations of fear. Throughout this process, you can remind yourself that even the most devastating parasitic fear has at least one vulnerable point and a beginning, middle, and end.

CHAPTER 2

Developing Your Self-Observant Skills

You have the ability to profit from what you observe about yourself. Say you were trying to control food cravings to avoid becoming overweight. If after eating an unusually large meal on Monday, you found that you had an increased craving for food on Tuesday, you could use this information. As you make the connection between one day's feast and the next day's craving, you are in a position to know the cause of your craving, put the craving into perspective, and wait out the craving until it passes.

Making the connection between parasitic beliefs and distress helps put your distress into perspective. You can make this connection through self-observation. As you begin to see the connections between your stressful thinking and distressful feelings, you can start to make positive choices that you may not have considered before. You can make different choices about fearful views of situations, thoughts, and feelings, for you are in a position to try a new way.

LOOKING INWARD AND OUTWARD

In self-absorbed fearful thinking, you focus on suffering and desperation. In this self-absorbed state of mind, you will tend to worry, fixate on your feelings of stress, and occupy yourself with events you attach to your fears. Through periodic fiery downdrafts of fear, you may feel as if you were collapsing under the heat of many burdens. At those times, you are likely to try to get rid of the tension through any means.

To get your mind off your fears, you may find diversionary pursuits appealing. These activities include playing computer games for, say, forty hours a week or using up your spare time sitting glassy-eyed before a television set. These deflective activities provide specious temporary solutions. Like the proverbial ostrich with its head in the sand, you limit your view with these diversions. The answers lie elsewhere. The more productive solution is typically that of eliminating the source of the downdraft.

In a self-observant state of mind, you can seek rational understandings and corrective solutions. You can examine the thoughts behind needless fears, take corrective actions, look at what results, and make adjustments to improve your performance. In a self-observant state of mind, you may act in paradoxical ways. For example, you may decide to think stressful thoughts. By exercising this choice, you are in a position to observe the results. You might find that by choosing to think a scary thought, the thought has no emotional value.

The degree to which you can profit from self-observation largely depends upon the accuracy—or inaccuracy—of your observations. If you were to play guitar and practice using false feedback, you'd likely get better at playing sour notes. On the other hand, a guitar player can significantly improve performance through breaking a practice down to scale playing, chord playing, song playing, and using self-observation to monitor his or her progress. Breaking down and observing your cognitive processes, emotions, and behaviors, likewise, can lead to positive change. In the area of cognitive processes, observing and monitoring inner speech helps to promote self-awareness. Over 2,000 studies show that irrational types of inner speech connect to inner turmoil.

Self-observation can also include a backward look to see how your beliefs connect to emotions that motivate known outcomes. You can use this form of observation to gain clarity, weed out erroneous thoughts, and reinforce reasoned perspectives.

Part of self-observation involves anticipating your feelings and behaviors, but this anticipation is different from the self-absorbed variety of thought. Here's an example: "If I believe such and such, how is this likely to affect how I feel and what I do? Are their plausible alternative views? How might these views affect my emotions and behavior?"

INTELLECT, INGENUITY, AND WILL

Through enlightened self-observation, you intentionally look to see what results when you apply three of your most powerful capabilities to liquidate your anxieties or fears. These capabilities are your intellect, ingenuity, and will. We are probably the only species on earth with the awareness to apply our intellect, ingenuity, and will to meet short-term challenges and achieve long-term goals.

Say you found yourself in danger of being swept away in a flood; what could you find in your bag of survival tricks? Plenty!

Intellect enables you to recognize and avoid danger. Through ingenuity, you may find a novel way to survive. A will to endure can make all the difference. If you have a higher purpose for survival, such as living for your family or fulfilling an important mission in life, your survival chances are substantially improved. Such a purpose gives you the persistence to tolerate emotional discomfort. While getting caught in a flood doesn't happen every day, you can strengthen your gifts of intellect, ingenuity, and will by applying them to daily challenges. Learning to respond effectively to pushy people, for example, can involve a practical application of all three.

When absorbed by anxieties and fears, you do not lose your intellect, ingenuity, or will. But sometimes these precious faculties become distorted. You use your intellect to turn out excuses; through ingenuity, you find diversions to duck your fears; you employ your will in a stubborn refusal to face your fears. Still, you can turn these gifts around to question excuses, come up with novel ways to address your fears, and teach yourself to put up with stresses and inconveniences when dealing with parasitic dread.

A PRACTICAL APPLICATION FOR INTELLECT, INGENUITY, AND WILL

Here's a question: how would you use your intelligence, ingenuity, and will to handle *phrenophobia*, the fear of going mad?

At times, anxiety can feel so intense and disorienting that you take the experience to mean that you will have a "nervous breakdown" or "lose your mind" or lose your "self." Through the use of your intellect, ingenuity, and will, you can put fears like phrenophobia into a calming perspective. The following worksheet shows how you might do this.

Target parasitic anxiety or fear: phrenophobia, or fear of a nervous breakdown

---

Knowledge translated through intellect to confront the anxiety or fear: 1. Nerves don't break down. This euphemism is a cultural folktale. 2. A fear of "something" doesn't mean that the fear will turn into reality. 3. At the height of a phrenophobic fear, the worst has already happened. 4. The fear of going crazy is real enough, because you feel it. By labeling the fear as *phrenophobia*, you know what you are dealing with. 5. People with phrenophobia are highly unlikely to go crazy.

Use of ingenuity to defeat the anxiety or fear: 1. Play with paradoxes. View the fear as normal and as evidence that your mind is inventive. 2. Extend the paradox by creating a phrenophobia jingle, such as, "Phrenophobia is so much fun that I hope it will never be done." 3. Reduce the fear to something comedic: Draw a picture of the fear and dress it up in a clown's costume. Animate the fear by making it into a squeaky mouse hiding behind a screen, pushing emotional buttons, yelling "danger" through a megaphone. 5. Evaluate the fear, not yourself.

Ways to will a change: 1. Envision yourself chipping away at phrenophobia until it becomes a faint whisper from the past. 2. Refuse to accept that you are having a nervous breakdown or losing your mind. 3. Recognize that your body can take a flood of fear hormones for just so long before it goes into a resting phase. 4. Remember the difficult changes that you have already made that you once thought you couldn't make. 5. Respect your emotional strength.

Now it's your turn to fill in the blanks.

YOUR INTELLECT, INGENUITY, AND WILL PLAN

Come up with a plan, using your intellect, ingenuity, and will, to defeat your anxiety or fear. First write down your target anxiety or fear. Then list the ways you will confront it, using your intellect, ingenuity, and will.

Target anxiety or fear:
Knowledge translated through intellect to confront the anxiety or fear:
Use of ingenuity to defeat the anxiety or fear:
Ways to will a change:

The feedback you get from the above exercise is part of a self-observant process where you watch what you do and examine the results. Through routinely engaging in this process, you can approach that often-elusive goal "to know thyself."

DIRECTIONS FOR POSITIVE CHANGES

Practically everyone who suffers from their anxieties and fears can benefit from accurately monitoring their thoughts, emotions, physical sensations, and actions. This self-observant approach boils down to taking the extra step to examine your anxieties and fears as though you were objectively observing yourself from a distance.

Accurate self-observation provides you with data for directing your actions so you can defuse parasitic thinking or engage in other change-related behavior. Through observing and monitoring a parasitic-fear process, you can do the following:

1. Break down your fear into its critical parts, such as thoughts, imagery, sensations, emotions, and behavior. Doing so puts you in a position to deal with the parts and thereby disrupt the fear as a whole.

2. Develop an alternative perspective, one based upon reason, knowledge, and fact, to counter anxiety-and-fear thinking.

A Journal for Doing Better

Keeping a journal may also help. By recording your anxiety-and-fear thinking, you make the ideas visible. This sets the stage for reflection, where you consider alternative ways of thinking. As you recognize and record your anxiety-and-fear thoughts, you may begin to see them as nonmysterious and more controllable. Here are answers to four common questions about keeping a journal:

How can you make an internal fear dialogue more visible? There are many ways to build accurate self-observation skills to make your anxiety-and-fear thinking more transparent. The most direct way is to educate yourself about this kind of thinking and use this knowledge to cull out this thinking when it occurs. Keeping a journal is a time-tested way to help accomplish this result.

How can you recognize parasitic thoughts for your journal? If a thought recurs when you feel a parasitic anxiety and fear, the chances are that it is parasitic thought. This book gives examples of parasitic fear thinking. You can use these sample thoughts as a guide for your journal.

In keeping a journal, is there a preferred way to log fear thoughts? To keep a record, you can use a handheld electronic recording device, your computer, a notepad, or index cards, among other things. Choose whatever way feels most natural. You are more likely to use a technique if it fits your style.

Is there a preferred way to structure the log? Whatever works best for you is the best choice. Typically, techniques can be divided into free flowing and structured. A free-flowing style means recording the ideas with commentary as the ideas arise; for example, you might write down whether a thought is anxiety provoking, positive, or neutral, and where it leads. This approach may be useful if you like to keep a diary or if you prefer to record information and digest it later. By bringing self-questioning closer to the fear-evoking event, you can nip the anxiety-and-fear process in the bud.

A more structured approach involves putting parasitic self-talk into context. You can do this by organizing information under situations, thoughts, and emotional and behavioral results. This extra step initially takes extra time. But by flowing information into this framework, you can map an important part of the anxiety-and-fear process. You are then in a better position to make connections between situations, beliefs, and emotional and behavioral reactions, and eradicate the parasitic influence.

The following chart illustrates a structured approach to organizing self-information. The example comes from a client, Bob, who daily found something to worry himself about.

Bob took the extra step of organizing his self-observant information into a chart. Through this approach, he found a way to visualize the process between worry situations, cognitions, emotions, and behaviors.

BOB'S CHART OF WORRY SITUATIONS, THREAT COGNITIONS, EMOTIONS, AND BEHAVIORS

Situation	Threat Cognitions	Emotions	Behaviors
Friend overdue	"My friend got into an accident and may have died, and that is horrible."	Worry, anxiety, fear	Pace floor. Call friend's cell phone. Swig down a glass of wine.
Registered letter notice	"Something dreadful is about to happen. I'm going to be sued. The IRS wants to audit my taxes."	Anxiety and panic, and more worry and panic as the dreaded possibilities keep coming to mind	Avoid the notice. Swig down a glass of wine.
Colleague walks by without saying hello	"I must have done something wrong. I'm being rejected. This is awful."	Anxiety	Avoid looking at colleague. Go out of way to avoid colleague. Get back at colleague by bad-mouthing him or her to others. Drink to avoid thinking of the incident.

Bob's review of these three examples was sufficient to convince him that he tended to jump to conclusions and to strain himself without cause. Upon reflection, he noted that he drank excessively when worried. He did this to smother his tensions. That was a problem habit he also needed to address.

Taking the extra step to map a situation, cognitions, emotions, and behaviors puts you in a strong position to change the process and the result.

Examining Alternative Hypotheses

When anxieties and fears come from parasitic threat cognitions, or ideas, you can add an important category: alternative hypotheses. Suppose you receive a notice for a registered letter and have no idea what it is about. You might jump to the frightening conclusion that the letter is from the IRS.

Other hypotheses are worth generating, however. A registered letter may be a public notice that a nearby neighbor has applied for a variance to build a garage. Perhaps you forgot to update your pet's license and are being notified to pay. The letter could be from the executor of the estate of a long-lost relative informing you of an unexpected inheritance. If the letter has come out of the blue, who knows what it's about?

Getting the facts to see which hypothesis, if any, is confirmed, is the next step. Once you know what is happening, you are in a position to decide a course of action.

CATASTROPHIC THINKING

Through self-observation, you can identify one of the more stressful forms of parasitic threats, *catastrophic thinking*. Uncloaking this threat-thinking process starts with knowing what to look for.

New York psychologist Albert Ellis, the founder of the rational emotive behavior therapy (REBT) system, describes catastrophic thinking as a form of magnifying and exaggerating the fearsomeness of events. Ellis finds this type of thinking common among people who suffer from persistent troubling anxieties (Ellis 2003).

Ellis uses the term *catastrophizing* to describe a human tendency to blow situations out of proportion or turn minor threats into calamities; for example, an increase in your heart rate means that you're having a heart attack; an imperfect performance means that you're totally incompetent; not being able to get a song out of your head means you are going crazy; restlessness, fatigue, and lower-back pain are symptoms of a terminal illness. But is any of this true, or are all of the above examples of intellect gone awry?

Say after climbing a long flight of stairs, you experience a slightly unpleasant physical sensation of shortness of breath. You've recently had a physical examination and were given a positive bill of health. But you also find that your heart is beating faster than normal. You start to feel dizzy. You wonder whether your doctor missed something. The thought of a heart attack crosses your mind. In this self-absorbed state, you begin to interpret these sensations as symptoms of a heart attack. Now that you believe you are having a heart attack, your fear can escalate to catastrophic proportion. A frantic trip to the emergency ward is a distinct possibility. But what does this shortness of breath really mean? It could mean you are a little out of shape from climbing a long flight of stairs at the pace you took.

Challenging Catastrophizing

Emotions, behaviors, and thoughts tend to blend together. But you can separate them when it's important to examine the relationship between your catastrophic thinking, stressful emotions, and avoidance behaviors. The aim is to disrupt the process of self-absorption.

In a catastrophic state of mind, you are likely to focus on what's troubling you and to neglect examining your thinking. If you find yourself catastrophizing, then a prime solution is to think about your thinking.

Swiss psychiatrist Paul Dubois saw anxiety as a reflection of the mind's ability to create needless crises. As an intervention, he showed his patients how to use reason to stop feeling anxious. According to Dubois, the *nervous person* "looks at everything through a magnifying glass. The slightest event becomes a catastrophe" (Dubois 1908, 106). Dubois saw the value of using persuasive methods to reeducate reason to combat the magnifying forces of anxiety thinking.

If you find yourself in a catastrophic-thinking trap, here are some questions to help you identify and challenge this thinking:

1. What thoughts do you associate with feeling fearful or anxious?

2. Would an objective observer consider your thoughts to be valid?

3. In what other legitimate ways can you view the same situation without the parasitic threats?

Reasoned answers to these three questions can guide you along a path to liberate yourself from catastrophic-thinking processes.

Identifying Anxiety Self-Talk

A parasitic anxiety often uses threat language to describe experience. By identifying such anxiety self-talk, you may recognize patterns in your thinking that evoke the arousal of distress. "Everyone hates me" is an example of catastrophic threat thinking. Who wouldn't feel threatened if always in the presence of people who hate them? But is the proposition true? Could it be a projection? Is it that you don't like yourself and think others feel the same way about you as you do about yourself?

If Socrates were alive today, he might challenge this "everyone hates me" thinking in this way:

1. Give me a *definition* of "everyone."

2. Give me an *example*.

3. Show me an *exception*.

This simple three-phase challenge process can prove surprisingly helpful in defusing catastrophic thinking. When you focus on exceptions, it is tough to maintain disturbing overgeneralizations.

Even without Socrates over your shoulder, specific catastrophic thoughts normally fizzle out in time. The event doesn't happen. You get distracted. You find a way to cope. But why wait?

If you do decide to wait out a catastrophic parasitic-fear threat, you can add a new twist to your perspective. The next time a catastrophic parasitic-fear thought appears, remind yourself that it's time-limited. Relabeling the fear by reminding yourself that "this too shall pass" can help shift your perspective to one of acceptance.

Watching "What If" Thoughts

Magnifying remote possibilities into probabilities can start a spiral of catastrophic panic.

The phrase "what if" is a common catastrophic thinking trigger for parasitic anxieties. The thought, "What if I fell down and couldn't get up?" can panic some elderly people. Another common thought, "What if the plane I'm on crashes?" can evoke an image of being trapped in the cabin of an airliner as it spins out of control.

In the world of parasitic threats, "what if" questions can have a haunting effect. But "what if" questions are not true questions. The answer is already known: the outcome would be devastating and horrible. Thus, they are statements in disguise.

ASSESSING THE PROBABILITY OF CATASTROPHIC THOUGHTS

"What if" thinking opens another opportunity to take an extra step to bring fear thinking into a different perspective. You can ask, "What are the odds of this happening?" That is, you can calculate the odds using probability theory. Use the following example as a guide for doing this exercise.

Catastrophic "What If" Thought	Probability Assessment
What if the plane I'm going to fly on crashes?	Do the research. Get the numbers. Assess the probability. Discover that the risk is minuscule. Raise the question, with these odds in your favor, why think a crash is a near certainty? Is your fear really that of uncertainty in the face of improbability?

Now it's your turn.

YOUR CATASTROPHIC ASSESSMENT

List three catastrophic "what if" thoughts and do your own probability assessment on each.

Catastrophic "What If" Thought	Probability Assessment
1.	
2.	
3.	

Using a Reduction Approach

A reduction approach can also help defuse catastrophic thinking. This approach involves breaking the issue down to its basics.

Suppose you don't pass an important test. You might tell yourself that your life is finished. Taking a reduction approach to this catastrophic thought, you could ask yourself, "And then what?" You might say that you'll get depressed and hide in a darkened room. And then what? You might then say, "I'll be miserable." And then what? "I'll likely get back to my normal life." And then what? You might say, "I'll study and retake the test." If getting back up and trying again is the bottom line, then why not go directly for that solution and bypass the catastrophic part of the process?

SUBSTITUTING CHALLENGES FOR THREATS

Parasitic anxieties over health are common. This kind of anxiety is sometimes called *health anxiety*. For example, you've had a few more headaches than usual. You wonder if this is the first sign of a brain tumor. In a catastrophic state of mind, you panic at the thought of this possibility. You're now sure that something is wrong with your brain. You're thinking about writing your will before it's too late.

So what do you do? You get checked by different medical specialists. They find nothing. Yet you still feel anxious about having what you believe to be an undetected brain tumor.

Alternatively, you could view a situation as a challenge. This is remarkably different from retreating from the same situation that you define as a threat. In a threat mode, you see the event as uncontrollable and overwhelming. You feel tense following this interpretation. Viewing the same situation as a challenge brings about a more positive mental direction. Instead of assuming that a brain tumor is inevitable, a positive mental direction would be to redefine your belief that you have a tumor as a hypothesis that is not supported by medical fact.

Have you ever accomplished anything of value without challenging yourself? When you face a problem as a challenge (thinking you can actively cope with it or master the situation), you are likely to experience increased myocardial efficiency. This means your heart pumps more efficiently because blood goes through the system with less resistance. On the other hand, a threat outlook, where you see dangers as uncontrollable, leads to vascular constriction. The heart pumps harder to get the blood through the system. Perhaps this is one reason why your heart rate increases when you're anxious. Psychologist James Blascovich and his colleagues have advanced this commonsense challenge-threat theory (Blascovich 2000; Tomaka et al. 1997).

Parasitic anxieties and fears involve shuttering before threatening possibilities and recoiling in fear. Figments of the imagination fog not only your thoughts but also affect your vascular system. Over the years, these restrictions can negatively impact your health as well as your happiness.

A radical shift from a threat to a challenge outlook starts with accurate self-observation. This means recognizing the capabilities you have put to use in meeting prior challenges. These capabilities can include examples of your intellect, ingenuity, and will to persist. They can include a tolerance for frustration or an ability to shift perspective.

CATALOGUE YOUR CAPABILITIES

What capabilities have you used in meeting prior challenges? Which of these positive qualities applies to meeting the challenge of addressing parasitic anxieties and fears?

Tested Capabilities for Meeting Challenges	Capabilities for Meeting the Challenge of Addressing Parasitic Anxieties and Fears

KEY IDEAS AND ACTION PLAN

What key ideas from this chapter can you use to rid yourself of your parasitic anxieties and fears? What's your action plan? Write it down. Test it out. Record what happened.

Key Ideas

1.

2.

3.

Action Plan

1.

2.

3.

Results from Actions Taken

1.

2.

3.

POSTSCRIPT

Where do you want to go with your life? What do you want to experience? What do you observe within yourself that opens opportunities for experiences that support getting what you want out of life? What do you observe within yourself that gets in the way? What do you see as your responsibility to yourself to move past those internal barriers? How might you and society benefit from an exercise of your intellect, ingenuity, and will in the service of stretching to achieve your enlightened self-interests? Your answers to these questions can motivate you to use your self-observant abilities with reasonable consistency.

CHAPTER 3

Overcoming Double Troubles

Having needless anxieties and fears is unpleasant enough. But this situation can get worse. You fear feeling afraid. You worry about feeling anxious. You feel disturbed about feeling distressed. You panic about panicking. You tell yourself something like "I can't stand feeling this way." Now you have what I call a *double trouble*, or two problems instead of one. This double trouble relates to your interpretations of the feelings and physical symptoms of anxiety or fear, as well as to your interpretations of your fear-related behaviors and self-characterizations.

Among a medley of double-trouble miseries, you can wrongly define yourself as helpless and weak because of your fears. In comparison to this added strain, your original fears can seem like feathers floating in the wind.

How common is it to have a double trouble with ongoing anxieties and fears? I can't think of a single anxious person with whom I've counseled who, at one time or another, did not layer this type of secondary problem onto the original anxieties. This added burden can be especially acute among people who suffer from both depression and anxiety, or whose sensitivity for tension is high and tolerance for discomfort is low.

If you focus your attention on your uncomfortable feelings, as many do, you can burden yourself with a double trouble. On the other hand, when you feel threatened by a nondangerous and possibly beneficial event, and you feel anxious, you can learn to accept your feelings for what they are. This will allow you to better concentrate your attention on uncoupling your original anxious thoughts from the situation. Learn to effectively deal with double troubles, and you are well on your way to overcoming a major tension intensifier.

Double troubles are correctable. This chapter will show you how to use your self-observant skills to recognize double troubles. You'll learn how to use your educated reason to unburden yourself from the sort of double-trouble thinking that has the power to suck out your enthusiasm for living. Armed with powerful cognitive, emotional tolerance, and behavioral tools, you can profitably dispense with needless extra tensions.

RECOGNIZING DOUBLE-TROUBLE THINKING

When it comes to the doubly troubling fear of fear, you normally get double the toil and trouble. If you believe that you can't control your oppressive thoughts and emotions, you will be ruled by them. But if you identify tension-magnifying double-trouble thoughts and put your psychological magnifying glass onto them, you can symbolically turn them to cinders. This starts with double-trouble recognition.

Double troubles come in many forms, including fearing the sensations of fear, feeling helpless over feeling helpless, and panicking over the prospect of feeling panicked. A feeling of dizziness, weakness, or a change in your breathing can cause you to think that these sensations predict feelings of terror. When you press yourself by thinking, "I've got to get rid of this feeling, I've got to get rid of this feeling," you can double the despair and fear you want to avoid. In this mental whirlpool, you won't find contentment.

When you feel "sick about feeling sick," you might tell yourself to stop thinking such thoughts. But doing so is likely to be as effective as telling yourself to stop thinking of a pink elephant. By trying to stop thinking about it, you have put your attention onto the very thing you want to stop thinking about. Accepting what's there—not necessarily liking it—makes the process tolerable and the pink elephant's presence less durable.

Here is a sampling of some different ways that people can cause themselves double trouble with their thoughts:

- "I'm killing myself with my fears."

- "I must stop feeling anxious right now."

- "I can't stand feeling afraid anymore."

- "I must feel calm now."

- "I must not feel fear again."

- "This feeling of fear is awful. I can't take it anymore."

- "My fears won't stop."

- "I can't change."

- "My anxieties are destroying my life."

- "I'm free-falling and can't stop."

- "I can't recover."

- "I feel as if I'm living in hell."

- "I'm going crazy."

Some people take this kind of destructive thinking one step further. They blame themselves, telling themselves they should know better than to feel so bad. Blaming yourself for feeling anxious is about as useful in quelling fear as spraying gasoline to put out a fire.

Atlanta psychotherapist Ed Garcia (personal communication) has a useful way to look at this double-trouble issue. He sees it as paying the toll twice: Before accessing the bridge and at the end. Say you are anxious about attending a friend's wedding because you fear feeling out of place. Indeed, when you go to the wedding, you feel uncomfortable and out of place, so you retreat into the background.

In this example, one cost is the anxiety you feel in anticipation of the event. The other cost is the fear you experience at the wedding. Learning to overcome anxiety about fear would eliminate the first toll. When at the wedding, questioning and defusing the idea that you are out of place would go far to limit or eliminate the second toll. With both threats gone, you might even have a good time.

BREAKING THE VICIOUS DOUBLE-TROUBLE CYCLE

Double troubles usually involves two or more of the following five conditions of mind:

1. Problem magnification

2. Overgeneralization

3. Urgency

4. Helplessness and resignation

5. Circular thinking

These conditions typically occur in some combination. But you can examine each one separately. By separating out these troublesome processes, you can better focus your attention on disrupting each part of the double trouble. Here's a look at how this works:

How does problem magnification become activated? In problem magnification, you are likely to concentrate too much on the feared situation or on your tension. Sleep difficulties are common among those who worry at bedtime about what happened the previous day and what could happen tomorrow. If the arousal from worry keeps you awake, then you worry about not falling asleep (you worry about feeling tired the following day), and then you press yourself to fall asleep (and then blame yourself for feeling tense), you have multiple double troubles. You are better off recognizing that if you are anxious, you are anxious. If you can't sleep, you can't sleep. That's the way it is. This acceptance, when genuine, can transform tension into tolerance. And even if you don't fall asleep following this cognitive shift toward tolerance, you still can have a more relaxed and restful night. Relaxation has restorative value.

What is involved in a double-trouble overgeneralization? An overgeneralization is a form of faulty reasoning in which you draw too broad a conclusion. The words "always" and "never," when used to describe relative conditions, typically represent overgeneralizations. Double troubles can reflect exaggerated forms of resignation, such as "I can't change" or "my fears will go on forever." These overgeneralizations translate into this: "I will never change. I will always be the same. I will suffer forever." But if you don't have a crystal ball, then how can you know these predictions will come true? Can there be exceptions?

What triggers urgency to get relief from fear? Double troubles have an underlying message of urgency, such as "I must stop feeling anxious now." The intolerance for tension is unmistakable. However, a clarifying question can shift your attention to solving a problem: "What is the worst thing that could happen if

I don't stop feeling tense immediately?" Among the various possible answers, here is a rational one: you'll likely feel anxious in the next minute and survive what you are surviving now.

What goes into anxious helplessness? Helplessness is a belief that you can't do anything about your situation. An agitated sense of helplessness involves hating fears that you believe you can't change. Hating a feeling that you believe you can't change is worth a second look. If beliefs are a mental product that can be altered by new information and experience, why declare permanent helplessness? Alternatively, you can look for ways to question helplessness thinking. Can you think of times when you have tolerated what you didn't like? Can you act to add benefits to your life? Can you blink your eyes?

Where does thinking in circles lead? In most double-trouble patterns, you think in circles within a compartment. Here are two sample circles. The first goes like this: "Because I cannot change, my fears will go on forever. Because my fears go on forever, I cannot change." The second goes like this: "Anxiety feels awful, and because it feels awful, anxiety is awful." This circularity links one double trouble to the next. Then, round and round you go. But you can step out of a double-trouble circle by taking out the components and defining them as assumptions. In the first example above, "I can't change" is an assumption. So is the statement that "fears will go on forever."

If double troubles arise from certain assumptions and judgments, you can check those assumptions to see if they are valid, and you can question your judgments to see if they are misguided. Instead of accepting your assumptions as fact, you can make a self-observant shift by starting your double-trouble statements with "I assume" or "I believe." For example, "I assume that I'm going crazy" and "I believe that I can't change." These assumptions and beliefs are then subject to methods of scientific inquiry.

EXERCISING YOUR REASON

Stopping double troubles is among the simplest of acts to accomplish. Of course, simple doesn't mean quick or easy. But with thoughtful effort, you can often minimize stealthy double troubles by using scientific methods of inquiry.

Karl Popper (1963) writes that if a statement cannot be tested and *falsified* (shown to be untrue), it pays to be skeptical of it. For example, if you believe that angels dance on the heads of pins, how can you subject this belief to a test to see if you can falsify it? You can't. Therefore, the statement is a fiction.

The circular reasoning in a double trouble is normally easy to falsify. Some form of irrationality is practically always present in circular reasoning.

Take the statement "my anxiety will go on forever because I cannot change, and because I cannot change, my anxiety will go on forever." To properly test this as a theory, you would look for exceptions to the statement that better fit reality. If you can't find ways to disprove the statement, then it probably has a basis in reality. But some fears are not fictional (if someone threatens you with a knife, you have a good reason to feel afraid). In such cases, falsification efforts are foolish.

In applying a falsification test, start by defining your key terms:

1. What does "change" mean?

2. What does "cannot" mean?

3. What does "forever" mean?

Making this clarification usually shows that the key words in a circular statement represent extremist thinking. This type of key-word recognition and definition exercise can end the double-trouble circular-thinking problem.

To add wind to the sails of educating your reason, look for exceptions to the "I cannot change" belief. Ask yourself, "Are there any exceptions to the 'I cannot change' rule?" By identifying exceptions, you've taken a giant step toward falsifying an overgeneralization. By dumping these doubly troubling extremes, you can find relief from their effects.

Are all forms of circular reasoning irrational? No! Some circularity can resist falsification: "I am changing in appearance as I grow older, and as I grow older, I change in appearance." You can independently confirm this statement. It is the irrational type of circular thinking that bears attention.

FALSIFYING YOUR DOUBLE-TROUBLE CIRCLE OF TENSION

The following exercise asks you to examine a double-trouble circular-thinking trap that you may identify in yourself.

1. Describe your primary double-trouble circle of tension (a statement you make to yourself):

2. Identify and define the key terms in the statement:

3. Identify magnifications that can intensify the tension:

Identify exceptions to the belief(s) that propel that part of the circle:

4. Identify any overly generalized ideas:

Identify exceptions to the belief(s) that propel that part of the circle:

5. Describe the results of your falsification effort:

By disabling double-trouble circular thinking, you simultaneously develop and strengthen reasoning skills that you can carry with you over a lifetime.

THREE DIMENSIONS OF ACCEPTANCE

Psychologist Albert Ellis (2003) describes three dimensions of acceptance, or ideals to stretch for in the area of self-development:

1. Unconditional acceptance of self

2. Unconditional acceptance of others

3. Unconditional acceptance of life

You can use the ideas behind these ideals to blunt double-trouble thinking. What are they?

What is the basic idea behind unconditional self-acceptance? Why accept yourself for who you are? Unconditional self-acceptance is discretionary. You have many other choices. The most obvious reason for unconditional self-acceptance is that you are the only you that you will ever be. You will also likely do far better when you accept yourself than when you put yourself down or double-trouble yourself over your fears. While you can accept yourself for who you are, you can still take a forceful approach toward correcting your errors and solving your problems. Another argument is that you are pluralistic, in the sense that your whole life includes countless experiences, emotions, beliefs, and knowledge. You may prefer some of your attributes to others. You may be proud of certain accomplishments. There will be some aspects of your life that you want to change, such as your fears. But you cannot be only one way. Self-acceptance involves acceptance of this plurality principle. But unconditional self-acceptance comes with responsibility. Unconditional self-acceptance, to be functional, involves a philosophy of asserting your personal rights and interests while actively seeking to avoid causing needless harm.

What is the basic idea behind unconditional acceptance of others? Unconditional acceptance of others recognizes that other people are not the same as you, and they have their own complexities. The person who cuts you off in traffic may have a valued job, contribute to the community, and exhibit a broad range of positive characteristics, as well as a fair share of moles and warts. If you can accept yourself as a pluralistic person and accept others as pluralistic, this perspective can strip away a lot of needless troubles, including bothering yourself over what you dislike about the behavior of others. Most people are doing their thing without any intent to cause harm. This doesn't mean that you have to accept the behavior of people who act badly and refuse to take responsibility. The key is to avoid filling your thoughts with hatred, thus giving yourself the special double trouble of (1) disliking and disapproving of an action, (2) insisting and demanding that what happened shouldn't have happened, and then (3) troubling yourself by dwelling on what you don't like. If you can do something constructive to rectify a wrong perpetrated by others, by all means do so. Otherwise, try to accept what you don't like instead of dwelling on the event.

What is the basic idea behind unconditional acceptance of life? Events happen over which you may have no control. You lose your home in a fire caused by lightning. You lose a dear friend through death. You make mistakes, a minority of which will have severe consequences. When you accept life for what it is, you acknowledge that what is, is. This doesn't mean that you have to like what you find troublesome, uncomfortable, or unpleasant. You can act to change what you can, accept what is etched in stone, and figure out what lies in between. What's the point in double-troubling yourself? Is not the original loss and stress sufficient?

These three dimensions of acceptance have one point in common: reality is reality. And what is this reality? Las Vegas psychologist Jon Geis (personal communication) has a simple definition: reality is what is.

Through acceptance, you engage in a tolerance-development process. You acknowledge that your imperfections will sometimes result in harm also but that you can do considerable good and can change and improve. Some people can and do act oppressively. Harmful events occur. But acceptance doesn't mean disabling yourself or stopping yourself from doing anything. You can oppose the oppressive actions of others with force. You can rebuild many things that you lose. You can cope by accepting what you cannot change. You can seek alternatives.

CONTESTING SUFFERING WITH MEANING

Victor Frankl (1959) saw that suffering was part of the human condition. Frankl was incarcerated in several Nazi death camps. There, Frankl's self-observant talents came to the fore. Rather than absorb himself in his fears, he rose above them.

Frankl's frightening experience strongly influenced him in his quest for meaning. Motivated by the idea of a higher purpose or meaning for life, Frankl found ways to survive his death camp ordeal. Thereafter, he went forward to publish many books on his logotherapy system.

Frankl's intellectual contribution is the idea that we cannot avoid suffering. Nevertheless, it remains your responsibility to manage your suffering.

But there is more to life than suffering. We can choose to go forward with our lives with direction and purpose.

An enlightened awareness of the human condition includes the acceptance of anxiety and fear. Through acceptance, you position yourself to develop your personal power to control what you can, to recognize what you probably cannot influence, and to see what lies in between.

Consider this Mother Goose rhyme:

For every ailment under the sun,
There is a remedy, or there is none.
If there be one, try to find it.
If there be none, never mind it.

ELIMINATING FAILURE

Failure can be defined as falling far below a reasonable standard for an action or not achieving a desired result. There can be objective consequences for failure. You don't meet your sales objectives and can no longer maintain your business. So, you can persist and try again, or you can do something different. You don't pass a test to gain entry into a desired profession. You can persist and try again, or you can do something different. If you stuck strictly to this uncomplicated view of failure, you could eliminate a major form of double trouble: fear of failure.

Failure is instructive. The inventor Thomas Edison once faced the question about what material to use to create a durable lightbulb filament. He tested thousands of materials. Each failing filament meant to Edison that he would have to find some other way. Rather than see his initial efforts as failures, Edison saw his experiments as a way to discover what wouldn't work on the path to what would.

The subjective experience of failure in a world of parasitic fears is different from the "so you try again or do something different" attitude, however. In this world, falling below standard can feel devastating. In a double-trouble world, you can feel anxious about failing, then put yourself down in anticipation of something that has not yet happened.

By overcoming fear of failure, you can help open more pathways for success. In the area of self-development, a "no failure" philosophy represents a radically different way of thinking.

From a self-development perspective, you can do much to eliminate a bedeviling parasitic feeling of failure. A major step is to say that what you do in this area represents an experiment. In this experiment, you discover what works, what doesn't, what can be retested, what can be modified, and what lies in between. In this sense, you operate like a scientist.

In following the method of scientific inquiry, you start with a problem that you want to solve, such as finding a way to decrease double-trouble thinking. To go about this, you create a question that you can test: Can fear of failure be contested and tension lessened? Next, you devise an experiment to put your hypothesis to the test. You do the experiment. You assess the results. You use the information to decide your next step. In this dispassionate way, you can determine what works, what doesn't, and what lies in between. Based on what you learn, you can modify what you do. This is usually a far better approach than hand-wringing and stirring up a double-trouble stew, such as by blaming yourself for your imperfections.

Through self-development experiments, you can change double-trouble ideas that are inconsistent with reality. In this evolving process of acceptance, you may discover a more spontaneous you.

The value of taking a scientific, nonblaming, failure-free approach to deal with double-troubles is best understood by engaging the process.

SIX STEPS TO ENDING DOUBLE TROUBLES

You can put an end to your double troubles. By answering the following six questions and acting on your answers that you get, you will be well on your way.

1. What is your most pressuring double trouble?
2. What would your future look like if you were relatively free from double-trouble anxieties and fears?
3. What positive information have you gathered about your potential for addressing your double-trouble anxieties and fears and changing your future?
4. What higher purpose or value in life can you focus on?
5. What concrete steps can you take to uncouple from a double-trouble anxiety-and-fear entanglement?
6. What did you learn from taking these steps?

KEY IDEAS AND ACTION PLAN

What key ideas from this chapter can you use to rid yourself of your parasitic anxieties and fears? What's your action plan? Write it down. Test it out. Record what happened.

Key Ideas

1.

2.

3.

Action Plan

1.

2.

3.

Results from Actions Taken

1.

2.

3.

POSTSCRIPT

Overcoming a medley of parasitic anxieties fears, and double troubles often involves positive cognitive, tolerance, and behavioral efforts. Dousing the fire under the double-trouble mix can cool a hot fear.

There are many events over which you have no control. You may love African impala antelopes, but you can do nothing about the news of a leopard stalking one 3,000 miles away. You have no control over your tendency to think anxious thoughts. But you can apply your intellect, ingenuity, and will to address and subdue your parasitic fears. Separating what you can control, can't control, and what's in-between opens opportunities for doing more than treading water and struggling for emotional survival. Double troubles, a figment of the mind, are controllable through enlightened reason.

CHAPTER 4

Self-Management Techniques to Defeat Fear

One of the best ways to understand a process is to try to change it. This chapter will explore a seven-phase self-management plan for making positive changes. This plan includes analyzing the problem of fear, establishing a mission, setting goals, planning and organizing for action, executing the plan, reviewing results, and revising the plan.

ANALYZING THE PROBLEM

Without analyzing your fears, your efforts to overcome them are likely to be hit or miss. Analyzing your anxiety or fear involves separating out the parts from the whole of the process, examining interrelationships, and reassembling the fear process. You will start by taking an anxiety inventory to pinpoint your anxieties and fears.

TAKE AN INVENTORY OF YOUR FEARS

The following anxiety-and-fear inventory includes a series of statements describing fear situations, fear thinking, coexisting conditions, and physical symptoms of fear. You rate each statement based on how much it applies to you. This inventory is neither a standardized measure nor all-inclusive. Rather, its items represent common features of parasitic anxieties and fears.

You can make copies of this inventory for future use. After taking an inventory of your fears now, you can measure your progress by taking it at a later date. Completing the inventory once a month is a good idea. You can use the results as an early warning system to prevent anxiety-and-fear recurrences.

This inventory uses a scale of 1 to 4 to measure conditions of fear. Here are the points on the scale:

1. If the statement does not represent how you think and feel, circle "not you."

2. If the statement mildly suggests how you feel, circle "somewhat like you."

3. If the statement reflects a more bothersome state, circle "often like you."

4. If the statement represents an ongoing state of fear, circle "just like you."

Circle the point on the scale that represents the statement's general impact in the past month.

	1	2	3	4
"My performances are substandard."	Not you	Somewhat like you	Often like you	Just like you
"I feel self-conscious in public restrooms."	Not you	Somewhat like you	Often like you	Just like you
"I worry about eating in public places."	Not you	Somewhat like you	Often like you	Just like you
"I avoid social events."	Not you	Somewhat like you	Often like you	Just like you
"I'm frightened by snakes."	Not you	Somewhat like you	Often like you	Just like you
"I'm terrified of speaking before a group."	Not you	Somewhat like you	Often like you	Just like you
"I'm afraid of germs and disease."	Not you	Somewhat like you	Often like you	Just like you
"I'm afraid of rejection."	Not you	Somewhat like you	Often like you	Just like you
"I'm frightened by interviews."	Not you	Somewhat like you	Often like you	Just like you

"I'm afraid to leave my home."	Not you	Somewhat like you	Often like you	Just like you
"I feel uncomfortable around people."	Not you	Somewhat like you	Often like you	Just like you
"I'll do practically anything to avoid a conflict."	Not you	Somewhat like you	Often like you	Just like you
"I hold high standards for myself."	Not you	Somewhat like you	Often like you	Just like you
"My inhibitions hold me back."	Not you	Somewhat like you	Often like you	Just like you
"My memories are negative."	Not you	Somewhat like you	Often like you	Just like you
"I am bothered by imperfection."	Not you	Somewhat like you	Often like you	Just like you
"I'm afraid of dying."	Not you	Somewhat like you	Often like you	Just like you
"I think I'm going crazy."	Not you	Somewhat like you	Often like you	Just like you
"I expect the worst."	Not you	Somewhat like you	Often like you	Just like you
"I see myself as inadequate."	Not you	Somewhat like you	Often like you	Just like you
"I can't cope."	Not you	Somewhat like you	Often like you	Just like you
"I can't stand tension."	Not you	Somewhat like you	Often like you	Just like you
"I view myself as weak."	Not you	Somewhat like you	Often like you	Just like you
"I'm afraid of feeling anxious."	Not you	Somewhat like you	Often like you	Just like you
"I easily feel overwhelmed."	Not you	Somewhat like you	Often like you	Just like you
"I often think of what I should have done."	Not you	Somewhat like you	Often like you	Just like you
"I worry about my past."	Not you	Somewhat like you	Often like you	Just like you

"I have thoughts that I can't get rid of."	Not you	Somewhat like you	Often like you	Just like you
"I'm afraid of losing control."	Not you	Somewhat like you	Often like you	Just like you
"I'm afraid of being judged."	Not you	Somewhat like you	Often like you	Just like you
"I procrastinate."	Not you	Somewhat like you	Often like you	Just like you
"I feel both anxious and depressed."	Not you	Somewhat like you	Often like you	Just like you
"I shake when tense."	Not you	Somewhat like you	Often like you	Just like you
"I have trouble breathing."	Not you	Somewhat like you	Often like you	Just like you
"I feel faint."	Not you	Somewhat like you	Often like you	Just like you
"I need to urinate frequently."	Not you	Somewhat like you	Often like you	Just like you
"I have headaches."	Not you	Somewhat like you	Often like you	Just like you
"I feel fatigued."	Not you	Somewhat like you	Often like you	Just like you
"I have trouble concentrating."	Not you	Somewhat like you	Often like you	Just like you
"My stomach feels upset."	Not you	Somewhat like you	Often like you	Just like you
"I feel like I'm choking."	Not you	Somewhat like you	Often like you	Just like you
"My heart pounds and races."	Not you	Somewhat like you	Often like you	Just like you
"I have trouble falling asleep."	Not you	Somewhat like you	Often like you	Just like you
"I have hot or cold sweats."	Not you	Somewhat like you	Often like you	Just like you

The conditions that you rate as "just like you" deserve priority attention. But some deserve more attention than others. For example, having cold sweats commonly coexists with anxiety. So does depression. But whereas having cold sweats may be a nuisance, a joint anxiety-depression condition can seem overwhelming, especially if you view yourself as powerless. So if you suffer from depression, and you also suffer from cold sweats (you rate both as being "just like you"), the coexisting condition of depression is likely to be of greater significance to you.

Some of the items on the scale that you give a lower rating may not represent a big problem area for you. Nevertheless, they can describe conditions that you go out of your way to avoid. If you fear being evaluated poorly if you get before a microphone, you may avoid public speaking, even if doing so limits your chances to get a desired job promotion. You don't feel much public-speaking tension because you avoid conditions that would evoke the fear. Yet if this fear interferes with your interests, it merits addressing.

FOUR QUESTIONS FOR ANALYZING YOUR FEARS

The fear inventory provides information you can use to answer some important questions:

What situations are likely to activate anxiety or fear? Albert Ellis (2000) describes situations that we associate with our anxieties and fears as "activating" or "adverse" events. These events can be external or internal. An external event that can evoke terror might be the act of public speaking, observing a snake in a glass case, or being in an enclosed space that you temporarily can't escape, for example. Internal events can involve scary images, traumatic remembrances, nightmares, and unpleasant sensations that you associate with fear.

What can you tell yourself about these situations that can evoke or intensify fear? Like the Amazon River, thinking flows on uninterrupted. So you will practically always be thinking about something. (Try to stop thinking for the next five minutes and see what happens.) Most people typically don't monitor their flow of thought. But when you think about your thinking, this *metacognitive* ability of yours rises above the flow of thought. From a higher vantage point, knowing what you are looking for, you can detect fear thinking and companion states, such as a double-trouble panic over the prospect of panicking. You can teach yourself to recognize and debunk needless fear thinking.

What coexisting conditions add to your vulnerability for distress? Parasitic anxieties and fears rarely occur independently of other conditions, such as anger, perfectionism, depression, blame, procrastination, impulsiveness, addiction, insecurity, inhibition, and so on. Knowing what coexisting states affect you, and how they operate alongside of anxiety, can give you an edge in your fight against needless fears.

What physical forms do your fears and anxieties take? When you feel bombarded by worries over your health, worries about your future, and dread about feeling tense, you can come to experience physical symptoms that correspond to where you are most physically vulnerable. Muscular tension, chest pains, and gastrointestinal problems can be symptoms of anxiety. Some of these physical factors could reflect a medical problem, so if you haven't done so, it would be wise to have a medical checkup to assure yourself that any persistent anxieties don't have a medication or disease connection. Some medications, such as

Valium (diazepam), used for relaxation, can produce the very anxiety symptoms that they are supposed to reduce. A hyperactive thyroid condition can stimulate anxious feelings and thinking. In the majority of cases, however, parasitic fears and anxieties are psychological issues. If your physical symptoms are extensions of psychological fears, then it makes sense to deal with the fears using techniques that get at fear-related thinking and behavior.

CHART THE DIMENSIONS OF YOUR ANXIETY OR FEAR

Use the following chart to break down your primary anxiety or fear along the dimensions of activating situation, anxiety thinking, coexisting conditions, and physical symptoms.

Primary anxiety or fear:
Activating situation(s) (event, circumstances):
Anxiety thinking about the situation (fear of the feeling, describing the condition in extreme terms):
Coexisting conditions (perfectionism, depression):
Physical symptoms (tense muscles, rapid heartbeat, choking sensations, and so on):

STARTING A MISSION

A mission is a statement of fundamental purpose. For example, World War II President Franklin D. Roosevelt's prime mission was to defeat the Nazi forces to preserve freedom. An advocacy mission might be to contribute resources to protect those who cannot ably protect themselves. A poet's mission might be to develop lyrical verse for others to enjoy. A parent's mission might be to provide love and support for helping children grow into healthy and happy adults. You can have multiple missions. Depending on your stage of life, values, and situation, your missions may change. Here are some sample self-development missions for overcoming parasitic fears:

- Test new initiatives to discover what works and what doesn't.

- Reduce fear through challenging fear thinking.

- Eliminate a fear of spiders in order to walk comfortably along hiking trails.

- Arrest feelings of helplessness by challenging helplessness thinking.

- Build tolerance for tension by accepting unpleasant fear sensations.

- Counteract fearsome images by balancing them with relaxation responses.

- Decrease social fears by developing small-talk skills.

Most missions to overcome a needless fear can be reduced to this simple idea: challenge parasitic thinking to get relief from fear. But to paraphrase the nineteenth-century Prussian general Carl von Clausewitz, simple is not the same as easy (von Clausewitz 1982).

Von Clausewitz observed that you can make simple actions difficult by burdening yourself with misgivings, complications, and meaningless fears. He thought that while preparation was important, action was preferable to theoretical contemplations about the uncertainties and ambiguities of situations. In a nutshell, self-absorbed thinking tends to be less productive than self-observant efforts directed toward achieving a desired outcome.

A mission idea can be simple. But its implementation can take years of effort with no guarantee of success. It is simple to see that we need alternative fuel sources to support national security and economic growth. But developing those sources cheaply and efficiently is a significant and complex challenge. By comparison, dealing with a parasitic anxiety or fear may be complex, but it is a process that is readily manageable.

Atlanta psychotherapist Edward Garcia (personal communication) carries this idea a step further. He points out that while selecting your mission is an intellectual process, implementation is a cognitive, emotive, and behavioral process. The drive is supplied by emotion. Behavior is directed by the intellect.

What is your prime mission when it comes to overcoming a fear or anxiety? Describe it in the space provided.

_____

_____

_____

_____

_____

_____

SETTING REASONABLE GOALS

To reach your mission, you need to set specific, workable goals. Workable goals are relevant, measurable, and achievable.

A mission to overcome a public-speaking anxiety to advance self-interests might lead to your reading a book on effective public speaking or joining an organization to gain practice speaking. Each of these goals is relevant, measurable, and attainable.

Here are some goal-setting guidelines:

- If your goal is relevant and consistent with an objectively positive personal and social outcome, it's probably worth stretching to achieve it. Being able to speak in public is a concrete goal that is relevant if you want to stop feeling afraid of speaking up in groups. You benefit, and others benefit from the information you can impart.

- Focus on measurable goals. If your goal is measurable, you can track your progress. Identifying and changing fear thinking about public speaking is a measurable goal.

- Select desirable and attainable goals. Knowing that a goal is attainable can be motivational. Developing effective public-speaking skills is an attainable goal.

Executing purposeful, measurable, and attainable goals is one of the most reliable ways to obtain positive results. But there is a caveat. A goal to overcome a parasitic anxiety or fear may be secondary to another goal. Thus you have two agendas. One is stated. The other, while hidden, can be more powerful.

Say that you want to overcome a fear of public speaking (your stated goal). Sounds good. However, you may more intensely want to avoid the discomfort of practicing public speaking (your hidden goal), and practicing is part of the solution. If a desire to avoid discomfort is stronger than a desire to overcome a fear, your urges to dodge discomfort are likely to prevail. Now, how do you tip the balance in favor of action rather than avoidance? The answer is simple: redefine your goal. Be sure to state your primary goal. An intent to withstand tension can, in the long run, trump tension avoidance.

WHAT ARE YOUR PRIMARY GOALS?

List your primary goals:

1.

2.

3.

CREATING OBJECTIVES

Your missions and goals map a direction for you to organize and regulate your efforts to overcome your fears. Your mission describes the general direction that you'll go in to get what you want, such as gaining emotional freedom from a public-speaking fear. Your goals clarify and refine that direction. Now, how do you go about achieving your goals? You need objectives. Objectives break down goals into measurable steps.

If your mission is to reduce worry in order to reduce stress, a related goal might be to develop your clear-thinking skills. An objective would be to challenge inner-worry talk, to change it from negative to proactive. If your mission is to develop public-speaking skills so that you can present your views with conviction, a related goal might be to tolerate discomfort in the process of developing that skill. As an objective, you might want to analyze the thinking that fuels your discomfort about speaking before a group. When you break your goals down into attainable and measurable objectives, you improve your chances of producing the results you want.

You can break down your objectives into cognitive, emotional tolerance, and behavioral ones. The following list of objectives describes how you might achieve the goal of practicing public speaking:

■ A *cognitive objective* could be to challenge and neutralize the double-trouble fear of the feeling of fear.

■ An *emotional tolerance objective* could be to get yourself into a position where you are likely to experience public-speaking anxieties, such as taking a public-speaking course at a high school or local college.

■ A *behavioral objective* could be to join Toastmasters International and get practice in formal and informal public speaking.

WHAT ARE YOUR GOALS AND OBJECTIVES?

List your goals and objectives.

Goal 1:	Objective 1:	Objective 2:
	Objective 3:	Objective 4:
Goal 2:	Objective 1:	Objective 2:
	Objective 3:	Objective 4:
Goal 3:	Objective 1:	Objective 2:
	Objective 3:	Objective 4:

ACTION PLANNING

How often have you heard the phrase "we need a plan"? You need a plan to accomplish many things in life. For example, to raise money for a charity, you would need a plan. Your plan to boost charitable funds would probably outline a method that is consistent with your values. Similarly, a sound self-development plan is a framework for outlining your day-to-day actions to execute your objectives.

Your plan defines the steps that you will take and the order in which you will take them. It is the glue that holds the process together. Without an action plan to anchor your efforts, missions, goals, and objectives can vaporize like a summer morning mist.

Action plans typically answer four questions:

Where are you starting from? The answer to this question is likely to be relatively simple. You start with an anxiety or fear, such as a public-speaking anxiety, that you want to minimize or eliminate.

Where are you heading? You are ultimately heading toward speaking before groups with little more than normal apprehension or stage fright and preferably with an excited anticipation for what you plan to convey to your audience.

What do you need to do to get there? Your plan would naturally involve meeting objectives to fulfill goals that support your mission. You'd probably apply cognitive, emotional tolerance, and behavioral practices to manage, minimize, or overcome the fear.

What detours are available if parts of the road are blocked? Expected detours can include dealing with a procrastination habit that is triggered by fear, as well as with lapses in the use of your metacognitive abilities when in the grip of fear. Your plan may include dealing with expected and unexpected detours so that you can stay on track.

Clearing Barriers from Your Path

Alexander the Great grappled with unraveling the puzzle of the Gordian knot. At first, he tried to unravel it, but he soon became frustrated with these efforts. Stepping back, he called out, "What do I care how I untie it?" Instead of trying to unravel the knot by taking it apart strand by strand, he simply cut it in two. The legend was that whoever solved the mystery of the knot would rule the world. Alexander went on to rule the known world.

Oh, if only clearing away the barriers in your path were so straightforward! Few deal with their problems so directly as Alexander the Great did when confronted with the Gordian knot. Distractions and detours are bound to get in the way of even the best-laid plans. Therefore, you need to prepare for such obstacles.

A plan does not serve its purpose unless you put it into action. The payoff comes about through the actions that you take. So it's important to learn to recognize and cope with the known impediments that can get in your way.

If you know the barriers you face, you can do something about cutting through them. Common barriers include the following:

- *Ambivalence*: when you want the change but don't want to experience the doubts and the tension associated with it, so you sit on the fence

- *Reactance*: when you view taking action as interfering with your freedom to stay in a safe haven where you don't have to directly confront your fears

- *Perfectionism*: when you believe that you can't act unless perfectly able to do so

- *Procrastination*: when you con yourself into thinking that later is a better time to start, and then when later comes, you delay some more

- *Emotional reasoning*: when you believe you have to feel comfortable before undertaking something uncomfortable

- *Helplessness thinking*: when you defeat yourself before you start

PLAN TO DEFEAT A TARGET ANXIETY

The following nine-step plan how to deal with a public-speaking anxiety. You can adapt this framework to deal with your own anxieties and fears.

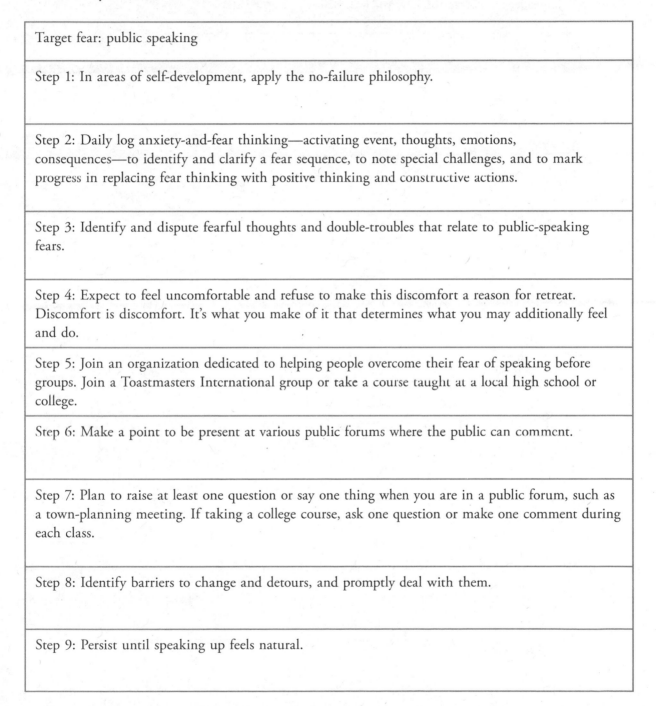

Target fear: public speaking
Step 1: In areas of self-development, apply the no-failure philosophy.
Step 2: Daily log anxiety-and-fear thinking—activating event, thoughts, emotions, consequences—to identify and clarify a fear sequence, to note special challenges, and to mark progress in replacing fear thinking with positive thinking and constructive actions.
Step 3: Identify and dispute fearful thoughts and double-troubles that relate to public-speaking fears.
Step 4: Expect to feel uncomfortable and refuse to make this discomfort a reason for retreat. Discomfort is discomfort. It's what you make of it that determines what you may additionally feel and do.
Step 5: Join an organization dedicated to helping people overcome their fear of speaking before groups. Join a Toastmasters International group or take a course taught at a local high school or college.
Step 6: Make a point to be present at various public forums where the public can comment.
Step 7: Plan to raise at least one question or say one thing when you are in a public forum, such as a town-planning meeting. If taking a college course, ask one question or make one comment during each class.
Step 8: Identify barriers to change and detours, and promptly deal with them.
Step 9: Persist until speaking up feels natural.

Use the following space to chart your own plan.

YOUR PLAN TO DEFEAT A TARGET ANXIETY OR FEAR

Fill in your target fear and describe how you will defeat it, step by step.

Target fear:
Step 1:
Step 2:
Step 3:
Step 4:
Step 5:
Step 6:
Step 7:
Step 8:
Step 9:

It helps to keep an eraser handy. Plans, like goals, can change. And you can always revise or add on to them. For example, by the time you finish reading this book, you might find some worthy additions.

Your Action Schedule

I've heard people say, "I know this is good for me to do, but I just don't have the time." This is another example of the double-agenda problem. It may be more convenient and easier to avoid facing a feared situation than to apply a prime solution, which is engaging the situation and living through the discomfort until you no longer feel excessively tense.

Maintaining your fears robs you of precious time and opportunities. If you are going to address them sooner or later, why not take a step-by-step approach to quell your fears starting now?

EXECUTING YOUR PLAN

A major way to rid yourself of a needless fear is to engage what you fear. I know that overcoming fear through engaging it may seem unpleasant. But that's the point. To rid yourself of fear involves experiencing discomfort or fear as part of the solution. There may be no better or easier way.

Once you confront a feared situation, the odds are that you will experience an unpleasant arousal. A critical part of the execution phase involves staying with your sensations of fear until they subside. By allowing yourself to live through the feelings that you'd ordinarily avoid, you've shown yourself that you can survive them. By repeatedly facing your fears without retreat, you'll likely find that they fade.

EVALUATION AS FEEDBACK AND GUIDE

There are three classic ways to measure progressive mastery over fear:

1. You realize that you are thinking more clearly.

2. You feel better.

3. You see changes in behavior.

Using these guidelines, you can tell how you are doing in meeting your goals to defeat your fears. In evaluating your progress, you can look at your choice of tasks, the time they take, and what you gain through the effort. Here are some questions:

1. Does your mission state a clear purpose?

2. Have you set relevant goals?

3. Have you mapped out your objectives?

4. Does your plan contain sufficient details and organizational directions to accomplish your mission?

5. Have you executed your plan?

6. Are you on track, or are adjustments in order?

After making this evaluation, you may decide that you are on the right track. On the other hand, you may decide that you need to modify your task choice, put in more time, accelerate your efforts, or try a different way.

KEY IDEAS AND ACTION PLAN

What key ideas from this chapter can you use to rid yourself of your parasitic anxieties and fears? What's your action plan? Write it down. Test it out. Record what happened.

Key Ideas

1.

2.

3.

Action Plan

1.

2.

3.

Results from Actions Taken

1.

2.

3.

POSTSCRIPT

You may seize an opportunity to quickly overcome your fear by squarely facing your fear. If you succeed, you have one less problem to face. But overcoming a long-term fear is rarely done quickly. You normally have to figure out how to apply your action plan based on the amount of tension you can tolerate. As your tolerance for tension increases, you can take further steps to master your fear. And so it goes. Self-development is a work in progress.

CHAPTER 5

A Multimodal Attack Against Anxieties and Fear

By educating your reason, boosting your tolerance for tension, and using behavioral solutions, you can decrease your fears. Making a radical shift from a self-absorbed to a self-observant viewpoint, you put yourself in the driver's seat. Once behind the wheel, your intellect, ingenuity, and will to do better come into play. Is there any more to it than that?

So far this book has focused on cognitive, emotional tolerance, and behavioral methods for quelling anxieties and fears. But there are modalities beyond the cognitive, emotional, and behavioral types that feed fears.

Psychologist Arnold Lazarus (1997, 2008) pioneered a multimodal approach that can be applied to parasitic anxieties and fears. He uses the acronym BASIC ID to describe seven *modalities*: behavior, affect, sensation, imagery, cognition, interpersonal, and drugs/biology. This BASIC-ID acronym reminds you of areas to target as you work out your problems.

Lazarus argues that by adding the modalities of sensation, imagery, interpersonal (relationships), and drugs/biology to traditional cognitive, emotional, and behavioral approaches, you broaden your opportunities to successfully work on your fears. He sees this multimodal approach as comprehensive and predicts that using it will promote rapid change and reduce the risk that a parasitic anxiety will return.

Lazarus's *technical eclectic* approach advocates drawing from technically sound methods and theories to address each modality. This distinguishes it from other eclectic approaches that are relatively arbitrary in what they offer.

Here are some definitions of the different modalities:

Behavior refers to what you want to stop doing, such as retreating when tense, or what you want to start doing, such as standing up for your rights.

Affect refers to your emotions. You may want to decrease negative affects, such as a parasitic anxiety or harmful anger. You may want to increase moments of satisfaction and happiness.

Sensations refer to what you see and hear. But they also can refer to generalized tension that you feel throughout your body. These sensations can include headaches, lower-back pain, and gastrointestinal distress that are linked to tension.

Imagery refers to pictures you have in your mind, such as a caricature of yourself, a fantasy, or a self-image.

Cognition includes your beliefs, attitudes, opinions, values, and philosophy.

Interpersonal refers to all the relationships that you have with others. This includes people who are significant to you as well as those with whom you have limited contact, such as a cashier at your local supermarket.

Drugs/biology includes medications you are on, substances you may abuse, health concerns, or biological tendencies toward anxiety or depression.

From person to person and situation to situation, the modalities can vary in their order of importance. For example, you may be sensitive to changes in your sensations. If you have a surprising increase in your heart rate, this sensation can trigger a panic cognition: "I'm having a heart attack and I'm going to die." You can have an image of yourself in an ambulance heading to the hospital. This image can further agitate you and lead to breathing problems. The above combination would be S-C-I-D (sensation, cognition, imagery, and drugs/biology) pattern.

This chapter will look at an example of how to use the BASIC-ID approach. Then you will have a chance to use this approach to quell your own target anxiety or fear.

ANXIETY: A HELPFUL SIGNAL FOR CHANGE

Most parasitic anxieties and fears are complex. Working out these problem habits is rarely a one shot affair. But you can sometimes find an interesting twist where a parasitic anxiety and a natural cause for anxiety blend. When that happens, the parasitic anxiety often fogs the picture. The art is to get rid of the fog and deal with the real fear.

The following story is about Diana's battle with her fears and how she used the BASIC-ID approach. The story begins with a look at Diana's anxieties. Her BASIC-ID program follows.

As you read Diana's story, imagine how you might put it into a BASIC-ID framework. This exercise will help you learn how to organize a multimodal attack against your own parasitic fears.

Diana's Background

Diana was a twenty-three-year-old single woman who complained of severe anxiety and panic. Dwelling on her worries, she often had trouble falling asleep. She did not exercise and often found herself gasping for air when climbing stairs. Otherwise, she was in good health. She did not use drugs or alcohol to deal with her tensions. She was not on any medication. Her weight was normal. Her appearance was attractive. Her demeanor was warm and engaging.

Diana said her anxieties controlled her life. She frequently panicked. She feared losing control and going crazy. She dreaded the feelings and said she would do practically anything to make them go away. She reported that her muscles felt tense and her stomach felt tied in knots. Often she couldn't think straight. She had difficulty concentrating. She was forgetful. She feared doing the wrong thing and being criticized. She was afraid to offend anyone. She felt insecure and riddled with self-doubt. She described herself as a fearful person, and that self-definition partially guided her destiny.

When did her anxieties start? Diana described her early childhood as filled with pleasant memories and largely free of anxiety. Her description of that period seemed reasonable enough.

When she was a young adolescent, her anxiety escalated. She described herself as moody and some-times difficult for others to deal with. At the time, she was hypersensitive about making mistakes, looking like a fool, and getting rejected.

In this awkward adolescent period, she had an insight. She thought that to be liked she would become a *pleaser* and cater to others' interests. Perhaps they wouldn't pick up on her imperfections. Perhaps she could avoid conflict.

On her twenty-third birthday, she became engaged to Jack. She had been involved with Jack only briefly before becoming engaged. Within three months following the engagement, her level of anxiety skyrocketed. Moving in with Jack was the trigger. That move happened soon after they were engaged. Her level of anxiety steadily rose thereafter.

Diana said that prior to the engagement, Jack seemed charmingly jealous, solicitous, and attentive. Sure, he drank a tad too much. He said he needed to knock down a few cool ones to relax. She told herself, "That's a guy thing."

Once she announced a wedding date, Diana moved into Jack's apartment. His jealousy increased. He demanded that she tell him where she was going whenever she went out and keep in touch with him by cell phone. He literally followed her around the apartment. She rarely went to the bathroom without Jack. More than drinking a few cool ones, Jack would drink every night until he was drunk. On the weekends, he centered his life on drinking. After three months of living with Jack, Diana felt confused about her feelings toward him.

Separating Parasitic Anxieties from Natural Anxieties

Diana first denied there was any connection between the rise in her anxiety and her decision to move in with Jack. She attributed it to normal prenuptial tension. Yet she broke into a sweat when she talked about her fiancé's tracking her every move and his uncontrolled drinking.

Doubting herself, she blamed herself. She recalled that at the beginning of their relationship, Jack was pleasant and attentive. Over time, he changed for the worse. It had to be her fault. She said he now knew the real Diana. Knowing her was driving him to drink.

But by taking a self-observant view, Diana admitted that she was in an unhealthy relationship. She recalled pleading with him to trust her. That plea got her nowhere. Jack continued his inquisition about where she went and whom she saw. She couldn't reason with him about his drinking. He told her to stop complaining. He had it under control.

Diana soon figured out that Jack had serious problems that could not be fixed by pleasing or trying to work things out with him. Still, her relationship with Jack represented the lesser of two evils. She feared that no one else would marry her. She would end up alone. She had a bleak image of her future. She saw herself as a wrinkled spinster surrounded by pet cats.

Shifting Perspective

When there is more than one way to view a situation, an *incongruity intervention* can help cause a shift in thinking. Here you contrast a parasitic perspective with a realistic alternative view.

Diana talked about her dating history before Jack entered her life. She was physically attractive. She had an engaging personality. She dated often. Now she faced an incongruity. How could she be doomed to a life of spinsterhood when she previously had many suitors? Diana quickly saw that the spinster image didn't jibe with experience.

Once she had contained one fear, another surfaced. Diana understood that she would never be happy with Jack. But she felt socially embarrassed at the thought of cancelling the wedding. She thought others would see her as a failure. She had already announced to her family and friends that Jack was a wonderful man and that she was very lucky to have found him. Would she sound like a hypocrite? She imagined her friends and family rolling their eyes in disapproval.

Diana faced another incongruity: if her best friend left an unhealthy relationship, she'd see it as a mark of courage. If she could accept that her friend could exit an unhealthy relationship without being a hypocrite and a failure, then why should she see herself as a hypocrite and failure? She concluded that the fear that everyone would see her as a failure was a figment of her imagination.

Diana agreed to a reality check. She asked her mother and two best friends to give her their honest opinion of Jack. Her mother was blunt. Jack's drinking pattern was obvious and serious. She worried about Diana's future with Jack. She had planned to ask her daughter to delay the wedding and preferably to drop the engagement. Diana's two best friends knew about Jack's suspiciousness and drinking habits and said she should drop Jack. That ended her fear of public embarrassment about breaking off the wedding. (Perhaps a more elegant solution would have been for Diana to act on her best behalf independently of what her mother or friends thought. But elegance is in the eyes of the beholder.)

Diana asked her mom and friends why they hadn't expressed their opinions about Jack before. No one had wanted to cause her to feel bad about her choice. That reality check was an eye opener for Diana. She saw that by walking on eggshells around people, you can deprive them of helpful information. At times, she realized, withholding her own opinions could prove harmful to the people she cared about.

Taking Action

In a complex situation, when one parasitic anxiety is debunked, another may take its place. This can be a form of procrastination to avoid discomfort. Unfortunately, such avoidance can have a boomerang effect, when the avoidance bears more discomfort and no resolution. In Diana's situation, a case can be made that her parasitic fears both reflected and sidetracked her from facing her anxieties about confrontation and her fears of rejection. (For more on the procrastination-fear connection, see chapter 10.)

Diana accepted that she could never be happy with Jack. Yet, as is typical for many who are in similar situations, she waded through several weeks of viewing herself as a bad person if she hurt Jack's feelings. She feared that Jack would get angry at her, resent her, and reject her if she called off the wedding. She imagined him towering over her shouting, "How could you do this to us? You promised to marry me!" But she continued to work on the relationship, hoping she could get through to Jack about her wishes to be an independent partner in the relationship. Despite her efforts, he rejected her communications and blamed her for disagreeing with him.

Diana faced another incongruous situation: If she couldn't get through to Jack and he had already rejected her ideas and wishes for an equal partnership, what would be different if she left him? What was there to fear if he had already rejected her? She decided that she could not control Jack's thoughts about her. Once she accepted that idea, she realized with relief that she could probably never please Jack, no matter how hard she tried, especially when he prioritized drinking over their relationship.

Through exploring her fear of rejection, Diana eventually came to see that she probably had a strong fear of confrontation. Her strategy was to duck conflict through appeasement. But that was about to change.

At a crowded restaurant, Diana told Jack that the wedding was off. She had picked the restaurant because she knew Jack was sensitive about making a good public impression. He would not make a scene. Despite her initial firmness, Jack persuaded her to give him a second chance. He told her he would change. She suggested that he seek counseling. He agreed. Rather than make a final break, she agreed to try again.

For a short while, Jack was on his best behavior. He cut down on his drinking. He was less inquisitive about whether she was having liaisons with other men. Within three weeks, he rejected counseling and resumed his old patterns. Diana's anxiety escalated. But this time she recognized that her anxiety was about her future with Jack.

Once she cleared through her parasitic-anxiety clutter, Diana was better able to trust her real feelings. She accepted that her anxiety was a signal that the relationship was not right for her. She made the final break. Her anticipatory anxiety about the marriage ended. She had fewer parasitic anxieties to contend with.

Breaking Down Diana's Experience into Modalities

To augment her change program, Diana used a BASIC-ID approach. The following chart highlights some of the items in Diana's multimodal matrix plan. It illustrates how Diana took emotionally hot material and found solutions. It includes a problem description and a prescription plan.

Since the seven modalities tend to overlap and interact, Diana personalized their organization. She started with cognition.

DIANA'S BASIC-ID MATRIX

Modality	Problem Description	Prescription Plan
Cognition	1. Belief that conflict and rejection can be avoided by pleasing others	1. Incongruity intervention: if you can accept that others won't be 100 percent pleasing, then why can't you accept that different people can have different interests on specific topics, and that's a normal part of life? A sample answer: Unless you grew up in a fanatical cult that indoctrinated all members, differences in opinions, perceptions, and perspective are normal.
	2. "Cancelling the wedding will make me a failure in the eyes of others."	2. Seek opinions from others as a reality check.
Imagery	1. Image of self as wrinkled spinster	1. Picture yourself as a person succeeding and coping effectively. Picture yourself as a heroine. Decide what the heroine would do under trying circumstances and play out the role.
	2. Self-image of a fearful person	2. Write out parasitic-fear talk. Carry on a dialogue in your mind between educated reason and parasitic-fear talk. Log telling points from reason into the BASIC-ID coping matrix on your laptop.
Interpersonal	Avoid conflicts and rejection at all cost.	Risk standing up for your rights. Risk expressing your views and opinions.
Behavior	Actions that get in the way of health and happiness include making up excuses for others' poor behavior.	1. Hold people accountable for destructive behaviors. 2. Avoid taking the blame for other's problem habits. 3. When appropriate, speak up for your rights.

Sensation	Tension, stiff muscles	Get massage. Do stretch exercises. Listen to relaxing music. Take a warm bath. Tighten and relax all major muscle groups in sequence.
Affect	1. Parasitic anxiety	1. Punch holes in parasitic beliefs, such as "I'll be hated if I don't please." Use incongruity intervention: "If my mother and best friends did something I didn't like, would I hate them forever? If not, then why conclude that I have to be 100 percent perfect and curry 100 percent favor or lose all of my primary relationships? Who's to say that if I'm not perfect, I can't enjoy my primary relationships?"
	2. Natural anxieties	2. Heed them as warnings and respond in a timely and appropriate way. Rather than hide and procrastinate, take steps to cope!
Drugs/ biology	1. Lack of exercise	1. Exercise is associated with a reduction in anxiety. Engage in moderate exercise program: bicycle to work each day. Do an aerobic program at health spa.
	2. Delayed sleep	2. Take a warm bath two hours before going to bed. During that time, list the evidence to support worry thinking. Note contradictory facts, information, or beliefs. Evoke that contrary perspective when worry thinking starts around bedtime.

CREATING YOUR BASIC-ID BLUEPRINT FOR CHANGE

To create your own blueprint for change, first focus on a prime parasitic anxiety or fear. Then organize your information around the BASIC-ID framework. Since the categories tend to overlap, you'll have to make judgment calls about what information goes where. The important thing is to put key components of your parasitic anxiety or fear into an organized framework. Then come up with prescriptions of your own invention or from technically sound techniques from this book and other sources. Test the prescriptions and see how they work.

YOUR BASIC-ID

To start your BASIC-ID program, write down your target anxiety or fear and use the following list of questions to gather information. Then build your own matrix.

Target parasitic anxiety or fear: _____

Behavior: What are you doing to get in the way of your own health and happiness? List that. Then list what you would like to start or stop doing. For example, would you like to act more assertive? Would you like to stop trembling?

Affect: What negative emotions, or affects, dominate your psychic life? Are you dealing with anxiety, anger, depression, or some combination? What appears to generate these negative affects? Is it cognition, imagery, interpersonal conflict, or what? How do you act when you feel anxious?

Sensation: What do you like or dislike to hear, see, or experience that links to your fears? For example, are you fearfully affected by someone's angry tone and facial expression? Do you tend to panic when you feel irregularities in your heartbeat?

Imagery: How do you picture yourself when you are in a state of distress? For example, do you see yourself as shriveling and retreating? Do you have haunting nightmares?

Cognition: What are your main beliefs when you feel your target parasitic anxiety or fear? For example, do you think that you can't stand the tension and that it will never end?

Interpersonal: How do you get on with others when in a state of parasitic anxiety? For example, do you see yourself as entitled to their support in easing your tensions? Do you place demands on others? Do you withdraw into yourself and retreat?

Drugs/biology: What do you do to quell your tension? Do you smoke or drink when tense? Do you take a walk to calm down?

Now, take the above information and pencil it into the following matrix. Then, using your own intellect, ingenuity, and will, devise prescriptive plans for each key modality problem. Based on your readiness level, execute the plan on a step-by-step basis.

A precautionary note: If you feel tense, such prescriptions as meditation, massage, and muscular relaxation or deep-breathing exercises may have an initial appeal and be at the top of your list of things to do. Such techniques can be a springboard for action. However, when used as *palliatives*, where you seek to relieve tension without addressing the cause, the same techniques can reflect a special form of procrastination. So be sure to follow your relaxation techniques with cognitive and behavioral actions to attack your anxiety or fear.

YOUR BASIC-ID MATRIX

Modality	Problem Description	Prescription Plan
Behavior		
Affect		
Sensation		
Imagery		
Cognition		
Interpersonal		
Drugs/biology		

If you wish, number each modality according to its importance, or impact. Then address each modality according to its priority.

KEY IDEAS AND ACTION PLAN

What key ideas from this chapter can you use to rid yourself of your parasitic anxieties and fears? What's your action plan? Write it down. Test it out. Record what happened.

Key Ideas

1.

2.

3.

Action Plan

1.

2.

3.

Results from Actions Taken

1.

2.

3.

POSTSCRIPT

Parasitic anxiety-and-fear tensions are complex. When coexisting with a signaling anxiety that presents a legitimate risk, separating the parasitic from the signaling anxiety is a useful process. Remember that making a positive change takes time. You can often accelerate the process if you follow a defined plan for positive change. Chapter 6 will show you how to do just that.

Five Steps for Positive Change

The idea of changing from a more to a less anxious state of mind can seem like a great idea, but personal change involves facing uncertainties. The future is unknown. Uncertainty can lead to more anxiety.

You can feel anxious about what you don't know, and there is much to life to stimulate the imagination about the unknown. If you think you have more than your share of uncertainty, anxieties, and fear, and you want relief, however, the answer is not to retreat.

FACING YOUR FEAR OF UNCERTAINTY

Carrying out a decision to face your fears means facing uncertainty. But if you have an intolerance for uncertainty, you are likely to worry excessively (Buhr and Dugas 2006). For people with more generalized forms of anxiety, uncertainty can quickly translate into a fear of the unknown that worsens anxiety (Dugas et al. 2007).

If you fear events that involve uncertainty, or about which you have gaps in your knowledge, you'll probably feel conflicted and hesitate when facing such situations. You'll want a guarantee before you go forward. In this anxious state, the thought of change—even a positive one—can kick up doubts: "What if I get overwhelmed with fear? What if I can't do it?"

Intolerance for uncertainty can stir catastrophic thinking and anxiety about change (Carleton, Sharpe, and Asmundson 2007). The more catastrophic your beliefs become, the greater the intensity of your negative feelings. In the sweat of catastrophic expectations, the path of least resistance has great appeal.

Starting a journey where you head toward freedom from parasitic anxieties and fears can first seem like entering unchartered waters. You have no guarantee you'll pilot them well. But setting yourself adrift along the shoals means you will take more bumps. Yet all is not bleak: Education about how to correct parasitic thoughts can help ease edginess and doubts. Charting a process for change can demystify it.

If you both fear uncertainty and worry about what you fear, creating a negative forecast is part of what you do. It takes time and effort to break this habit. Ending the forecasting of negative omens involves facing uncertainties with a plan.

The following five-phase change approach is a chart for piloting the rocky waters of uncertainty so that you can get where you want to go.

A FIVE-STEP PROCESS OF CHANGE

When I gave my first talk on my five phases of change approach in 1975, it helped many participants feel more at ease. Personal change was now a process that they could realistically work toward. This idea helped participants ease a general sense of urgency and uncertainty. The five-phase process is a step-by-step chart for change that can help boost your tolerance for uncertainty. Its phases are awareness, action, accommodation, acceptance, and actualization.

Awareness

Awareness is the first step in a process of making positive voluntary changes. This is your sense of consciousness about what is taking place within and around you. Awareness refers to knowing the makeup of your parasitic fears and what you can realistically do to stop feeling afraid. Awareness includes understanding the inevitability of uncertainties, your anti-anxiety capabilities, and how to use them.

By taking a self-observant perspective, you can build a more realistic sense of awareness. Armed with this realistic awareness, you'll have some ideas about how to liberate yourself from an anxiety or fear process. Your insights into how to change can incubate for a while. Then at a point of readiness, you use them to trump fear.

Unless you think about your thinking (the metacognitive approach) in adverse conditions, your level of awareness of the link between your thoughts, emotions, and behaviors is likely to be limited. The following awareness exercise shows how to build a metacognitive awareness of a parasitic intolerance for uncertainty; it came from my case files.

SEVEN-QUESTION AWARENESS EXERCISE

Target situation or fear: Intolerance for uncertainty	
What situations trigger anxious thoughts and feelings about uncertainty?	Practically any situation of personal involvement that is unfamiliar and where there is no guarantee it can be controlled: speaking before a group, joining a club, attending a wedding.
When you experience an intolerance for uncertainty, what do you normally do?	Worry. Give up. Make up excuses. Avoid the occasion.

Other than evocative situations, what self-conditions add to your vulnerability for overreacting to this form of apprehension? Mood? Diet? Season of the year? Conflicts? Finances? Health?	Overweight and lack of exercise. Low income. Unexpected inconveniences, such as car breaking down, an overdue water bill, past poor school grades, gloomy weather. Drinking too much at times.
What ideas, feelings, and behaviors go with uncertainty fears?	*Ideas*: Change is too risky. Can fail. Can look awkward. Will embarrass self. Will fail. Worry that I will never get over these feelings. *Feelings*: Anxiety. Irritation. Anger at times. Depressed. *Behaviors*: Eat, drink, and smoke to calm nerves.
What worsens fears of the unknown? What lessens them?	*Worsens*: Fatigue. Lack of sleep. Wintertime. Boring job. *Lessens*: Exercise. Sleeping well. Doing something to address fears. Challenging worry talk.
What is missing in your life that connects with your fears?	Lack of friendships. Friends are usually people met at bars. Have abilities and college degree, but take low-level repetitive jobs. Quality work is missing. Vehicle is a beater; prefer a new car. Most of all, miss a feeling of stability and self-worth.
Do you have a way to influence an uncertain outcome?	Sit back, reflect, figure out what to do, and then try to do it. But some things happen fast and take quick decisions. Mostly retreat, but when trying to sort things out on the spot, can sometimes work "miracles." Avoiding hesitations and delays seems to help. It's the anticipation of something awful about to happen that feels crushing.

Now it is your turn to use these seven awareness-developing questions to chart your priority fear.

YOUR SEVEN-QUESTION AWARENESS EXERCISE

Write down your target anxiety or fear and answer the following questions to build awareness.

Target situation or fear: _____	
What situations trigger anxious thoughts and feelings?	
When you experience this anxiety, what do you normally do?	
What conditions add to your vulnerability? Mood? Diet? Season of the year? Conflicts? Finances? Health?	
What ideas, feelings, and behaviors accompany your anxiety?	*Ideas:* *Feelings:* *Behaviors:*
What worsens your anxiety? What lessens it?	*Worsens:* *Lessens:*
What is missing in your life that connects with your anxiety?	
In what way can you influence the outcome?	

Action

Awareness without action is like a ball caught in a whirlpool. There is a lot of churning, but nothing else happens.

Action is the process of taking steps to achieve the goal of ridding yourself of burdensome anxieties and fears. If you fear uncertainty, you'd wisely enter that zone of uncertainty for purposes of obtaining clarity and direction about defeating your fear. Clarity born from experience adds a dose of realism to awareness.

When you have gaps in your knowledge, you necessarily have uncertainty. By entering situations with imperfect information, you could step into quicksand. You could fail. And this awareness may stop you from going any further. But what would it mean if you took a learn-as-you-go approach? What if you gained ground in arresting your parasitic anxieties and fears? What if you could eliminate failure?

TURNING FEAR OF FAILURE INTO HYPOTHESES

Chapter 3 looked at how to keep failure out of your self-development plans. Let's carry this a few steps further.

To eliminate self-development failures, you can apply methods of scientific inquiry to address your fears. A scientific pursuit is one of discovery. It's nonjudgmental. You want to discover a slice of reality or perhaps see how something works. A scientist sets up hypotheses, or propositions, to test and takes actions to see what happens. Through this process, you don't fail. Rather, you see what works, what doesn't, and what lies in-between.

As with any useful scientific study, you would start with a question: "What actions do I take to get past this barrier to change?" You could then generate the following cognitive, emotional tolerance, and behavior hypotheses:

Hypothesis 1: *All reasons for intolerance for uncertainty are valid.* Now, examine this hypothesis to see if you can falsify it. Instead of looking to prove that your ideas behind a fear of uncertainty are true, find ways to poke holes in your fearful thinking.

Hypothesis 2: *It's impossible to build emotional tolerance for uncertainty tensions.* Test this hypothesis by acting to substitute emotional tolerance for the intolerance of uncertainty. A test is to allow yourself to feel the feeling but in a different way. Isolate the location of the tension sensations. Mark their locations (for example, stomach, shoulders, neck). Isolating areas of tension is a step in the direction of transforming them into a manageable experience. You can then decide if you can tolerate what you don't like to experience.

Hypothesis 3: *Facing conditions of uncertainty is a formula for unbearable tension.* To test this proposition, enter your region of uncertainty to determine if you can find answers, make discoveries, and develop tolerance.

Accommodation

Accommodation means taking in and adjusting to new ways of thinking, and taking action. In the five-phases-of-change process, accommodation specifically means to reconcile opposing thoughts, say, about intolerance toward uncertainty. On the one hand, for your own self-development, you have a problem to solve and want to chart a course for change. On the other hand, you fear the uncertainty that change will bring.

In this active intellectual-integration phase of change, you put your fear into perspective. This fear is only a part of your circle of experiences. If you think that all there is to life is fear, putting fear into context is part of an accommodation process.

If you enter a region of uncertainty for self-development purposes, you'll often find that what you feared wasn't as bad as you expected it to be. This contrast can show that you need not capitulate to a narrow category of intolerance for uncertainty thinking.

ACCOMMODATION AND COGNITIVE DISSONANCE

Cognitive dissonance is the perception of incompatibility between two cognitions (Festinger 1957; Festinger and Carlsmith 1959). The term may describe what you think and how you feel when faced with contradictory information about yourself, your relationships, your beliefs, or events.

Examining disparities between parasitic anxiety beliefs and contradictory observations can prompt an unpleasant feeling of tension. The tension may be greater if you think you can't stand uncertainty. How much do you prefer certainty? How bad is the feeling of tension? Can you accommodate it? Would you accept $10,000 a day for living with uncertainty?

Cognitive-dissonance conflicts come in different forms. Suppose you think ill of yourself and yet receive positive feedback from others. What are you to think? You can say "They are only telling me good things to make me feel better." Or you can judge the accuracy of the feedback by tying it to your accomplishments. What is the more accurate proposition of truth? How do you resolve the dissonance?

ACCOMMODATION AND INCONGRUITY

Accommodation often involves reconciling differences between dire predictions and legitimate, optimistic, and reasonable alternatives.

Believing that you are helpless to change, yet having evidence that you can make voluntary changes, is an incongruity. Both views can't be 100 percent right. If you have the power to make self-change, you can't be helpless. By making past changes, you have already shown that you can navigate conditions of uncertainty.

Our inner struggles frequently involve conflicts between our negative and positive views. We have conflicts between fears and self-mastery, doubts and self-command, certainty and uncertainty. Through accommodation thinking, you can compare negative thinking to sensible alternatives and see which has the greater validity.

When you take steps forward without recoiling from uncertainties, you are likely to discover that the world doesn't end. Cats and dogs don't fall from the sky. The earth doesn't open and swallow you up. Instead, you learn that you can learn. Accepting that discovery comes through experience and education can be a major antidote to recoiling from uncertainty.

CREATING AN ACCOMMODATING ATTITUDE

You can feel a jump in anxiety when you seriously think about what might happen as you start to address your anxieties and fears. True, there are many uncertainties. You may not be sure of what you are doing. You could feel awkward and self-conscious. But perhaps you can come up with a more accommodating perspective. To do this, you can redirect your thinking toward the benefits of solving fear-related problems and reducing uncertainties. The following short- and long-term benefits analysis chart shows how to put fear of uncertainty into perspective:

Course of Action	Short-Term Benefits	Long-Term Benefits
Maintain anxiety for uncertainty	Avoid immediate discomfort. Experience relief from worry when feared events don't happen.	Avoid immediate discomfort. Experience relief from worry when feared events don't happen. (Note that the short-term relief benefit can become a negative long-term benefit. But in this case, the benefit from relief is specious; it helps reward and fuel avoidance.)
Challenge anxiety for uncertainty	Begin to see that constructive actions lead to clarity and the sort of relief that follows taking charge of your life.	Reduction in anxieties over self-initiated changes. Reductions in fear about uncertainty. Discovering opportunities, acting on them, and benefiting. Decreased frequency, intensity, and duration of anxieties and fears about uncertainty. Fewer fantasy fears. Increased ability to handle inconvenience. Improved problem-solving skills. Less stress on the body. Probably fewer health complaints. Probably increased emotional tolerance. Probably clearer thinking. Probably improvements in following through with positive actions.

By doing a benefits analysis like this, you reveal incongruities between maintaining and challenging fears about uncertainty. These incongruities can evoke cognitive dissonance. Dissonance can evoke a pressure to resolve the conflict. Resolving the conflict by accepting uncertainty helps boost tolerance for uncertainty, which may decrease anxieties over ambiguities and the unknown.

Now do your own benefits analysis.

YOUR BENEFITS ANALYSIS

Write down the benefits for maintaining anxiety for uncertainty and the benefits for challenging this anxiety. Do the benefits of challenging anxiety for uncertainty outweigh the benefits for maintaining it?

Course of Action	Short-Term Benefits	Long-Term Benefits
Maintain anxiety for uncertainty		
Challenge anxiety for uncertainty		

Acceptance

Acceptance is the emotional integration phase of change. Acceptance comes into play when you choose to emphasize reality over your fantasy fears.

The spirit of acceptance is that of resigning yourself to outside realities that are not going to change. Acknowledging that rivers sometimes flood is an acceptance of the reality that rivers flood. Recognizing that you can have different political views from your cousin shows acceptance of that reality. But you don't have to like the fact that rivers flood, especially if a flooding river swept your house away. You may not like your cousin's political perspective. But such things are as they are.

There can be many things that you'd like to control but can't. But you need not distress yourself over such matters. Knowing that you can't control the speed of the sun is unlikely to bother you. In situations where control can make a difference, and that control is in doubt, the picture can change. You want your neighbor to live according to rules you find worthwhile, such as using a pooper-scooper for her dog's messes. But your neighbor doesn't have the same belief as you. Here, acceptance doesn't mean that you are stymied. You could ask your neighbor to keep her dog off your lawn. You could put up a fence.

In an acceptant state of mind, you recognize that you can view many events from different perspectives. That position is radically different from polarized thinking, where an event is one way or another; you either have certainty, or there is none.

Acceptance doesn't mean you are passively bound to a turnstile. Acceptance means seeing events as they are. Acceptance means acknowledging what is going on within and around you. When necessary, you make mental adjustments to tolerate discomfort, disappointment, fear, and frustration. When you can make physical changes, you act to do so.

In an acceptant state of mind, you focus on what you can develop, improve, cope with, change, or accomplish. In short, if you don't like a situation, take action to effect a change. If you can't change a negative situation in process, find a way to adjust. If you miss out on something positive, find an alternative.

Acceptance of uncertainty can be addressed by working to do the following:

1. Accept facts and reality.

2. Accept that you can progressively master methods for overcoming uncertainty fears.

3. Accept that a prime solution involves experiencing uncertainty fears at the time and in the space in which they occur.

4. Accept that preparing for uncertainty may prove uncomfortable but is instrumental to positive change.

5. Accept that overpreparation, such as repeatedly going over every possible scenario, supports a misguided view that perfection is the solution for controlling tension.

Actualization

Actualization means stretching your abilities to develop self-efficacy skills. *Self-efficacy* is your goal-directed ability to organize, regulate, and direct your actions toward achieving meaningful and constructive results (Bandura 1994). These directed efforts involve taking constructive risks to discover the limits of what you can do in areas where you want to improve.

In this actualization phase of change, you no longer struggle with many incongruities. Instead, you experience congruence between awareness, action, accommodation, and acceptance. You feel much more in command of yourself and in charge of your life.

Moving toward resolving uncertainties, you constructively absorb yourself in meaningful, self-development and socially beneficial pursuits.

EXPERIMENTS IN ACTUALIZATION

What have you missed out on because of needless uncertainty fears? You can look back to the past to try again for what you lost, or you can pick a new area that involves dealing with uncertainty to obtain a positive long-term benefit.

Instead of using the five phases of change to challenge negative thinking, low emotional tolerance, and self-defeating behaviors, shoot directly for something positive. You'll still have to face uncertainty barriers. By striking out in a positive direction, you can reach beyond your uncertainties as you move toward gaining clarity and making gains.

A prime actualization object is to decrease negatives by striving for positive results. Try putting yourself through the five phases of change to move yourself forward on an enlightened pathway toward what you'd truly like to accomplish. Use the following space to chart your way toward your constructive goal.

YOUR ACTUALIZATION PLAN

Measurable and attainable goals to pursue	
Motivations for pursuing goals (short- and long-term benefits)	
Barriers to goal accomplishment and talents and capabilities that apply to achieving desired result (awareness phase)	Barriers: Capabilities:
Action planning for goal attainment	
Accommodations, reconcilations, and compromises	Accommodations: Reconciliations: Compromises:
Reality acceptances: what are the insurmountable barriers?	
Areas to stretch capabilities	

Voluntary personal change doesn't have to follow a specific order of steps. Awareness can follow action: you may develop new ideas and insights from the results of your actions. You can start with a radical shift in your views through accommodation. By accepting reality, you have no need to rely on fantasy projections of what reality may be like. By actualizing your resources by stretching them, you can accomplish more and gain confidence in yourself as someone who can make advancements.

KEY IDEAS AND ACTION PLAN

What key ideas from this chapter can you use to rid yourself of your parasitic anxieties and fears? What's your action plan? Write it down. Test it out. Record what happened.

Key Ideas

1.

2.

3.

Action Plan

1.

2.

3.

Results from Actions Taken

1.

2.

3.

POSTSCRIPT

Understandably, having perfect control over events would be a big advantage. But eliminating uncertainty from your life is impossible. Since you can't avoid change, you might as well shape what you can control, which is yourself.

PART II

Intensifying Your Campaign Against Fear

- Learn how to challenge fearful thinking through the use of the ABCDE and PURRRRS methods.

- Develop emotional tolerance for anxiety sensations and reduce their occurrence.

- Use tested techniques to build your frustration tolerance.

- Learn to use behavioral methods to train your brain to tone down needless fears.

- Address phobias by controlling what you fear.

- Learn to use the card-sort method to disable fear.

- Learn multiple techniques to get past procrastination barriers.

- Create a plan for dealing with mixed anxiety and depression.

- Learn how to overcome worry.

- Break a perfectionism-fear connection.

- Develop assertiveness skills to overcome needless inhibitions.

- Build a solid, fact-based self-concept.

- Free yourself from social-evaluation fears through learning and using three levels of intervention.

- Learn how to contain and control panic.

- Use preventive maintenance methods for stopping anxieties and fears from coming back.

CHAPTER 7

Developing the Mind to Stop Anxiety

Frightening visions can be the subject of popular fiction. In the nineteenth century, Mary Shelley wrote her science-fiction story *Frankenstein*, and Bram Stoker wrote *Dracula*. These classics of horror continue to be read today. Movies about the murderous doll *Chucky*, the fiery *Carrie*, and vengeful mummies show the magical power of the human mind to create stories of demons and to entertain others with them.

If you don't like a horror movie, you can always switch the channel. But how are you to escape terrors when the movie is in your own mind and nowhere else? One way is to learn to recognize the magical phases of parasitic thinking, so you can blow the cover on the magic show.

Once you scare yourself with your own fantasy-horror show, you've entered the world of *magical thinking*. This is a nonscientific form of causal reasoning that commonly starts in early childhood. But it can arise anytime thereafter.

Parasitic anxieties and fears grow from imagination and fantasy, sprinkled with some plausibility and partial truths. This chapter describes two major self-observation techniques that you can use to step back from your own fictional fear thinking. They are the ABCDE and PURRRRS methods.

THE ABCDE FACTOR

Albert Ellis (2000) devised the ABCDE method to organize a campaign against mental parasites. This method provides a framework for looking at an adversity or activating event, your beliefs about the event, and your emotional and behavioral consequences, and then disputing erroneous and harmful beliefs, such as parasitic beliefs. Hence the first four letters of the ABCDE acronym stand for *adversity*, *beliefs*, *consequences*, and *disputation*. The *E* stands for new *effects* resulting from the disputation. The story of Fred illustrates how you can use this method to confront persistent parasitic anxieties.

Fred's Background

Fred was a forty-eight-year-old widower with two grown children. Because of his successes as an inventor, he had retired early with ample resources.

Fred had strong social interests. After his retirement he spent several hours weekly in volunteer work. He was also strongly family oriented. Whenever he had the opportunity, he would spend time with his children and his grandchildren.

Fred had an older sister, Ginger, with expensive tastes but without the pocketbook to pay for them. She spent excessively. She lived in an upscale neighborhood. She took out loans to buy exotic cats and to fund other luxury habits. She lived beyond her means and was routinely cash starved. Her daughter's compulsive shopping added to her debt. Ginger helped fund her daughter's habit. Costs to correct her son's cocaine use added to the family's financial troubles. Her husband generally stayed in the background but did offer guidance about getting bailouts from Fred.

To make up for her dollar deficits, Ginger was a regular guest at a casino. Like most gamblers, her losses exceeded her winnings.

When Fred and Ginger were children, Ginger was the dominant sibling. Taking advantage of being older, she micromanaged Fred. When Fred was in high school, if Ginger did not like one of his girlfriends, the girlfriend was history. However, when Ginger did not approve of Fred's fiancée, Fred took a stand and refused to leave the woman he loved.

Ginger's life revolved around financial crises. At one point, she claimed she would lose her home and that she and her family would be left homeless. Fred wrote a check to pay off her second mortgage. Next, her daughter's college tuition was overdue. She claimed Fred's niece would be kicked out of college unless the account was brought up to date. Fred wrote the check. Then her son needed to get a car so that he could deliver pizza. She claimed that without the delivery job, he would go back to using cocaine. Fred bought the car.

Ginger normally acted so desperate that she did not have to directly ask for money. Fred would write the check to avoid continuing to experience pressures from her to bail her out.

Fred tried to play down the extent of his sister's, niece's, and nephew's problems by saying to himself that they'd eventually come to their senses. But this hope was an illusion.

Fred's relationship with his sister was not entirely negative. Fred liked many aspects of his relationship with Ginger and her family. When his wife was alive, the two families had gone on vacations together. He had good memories of his sister's children growing up, and the birthdays and holidays the family had shared together. His children and his sister's children continued to enjoy positive relationships. So he did not want to risk losing the positive aspects of his relationship with his sister. But he also wanted to stop feeling tense over feeling helpless about her financial demands.

Fred hated confrontation of any sort. Predictably he capitulated to his confrontation fears by allowing himself to be manipulated by Ginger. He rationalized this, saying that "We're a loving family and should share."

His anxious feelings about ugly confrontations were complicated by a sense of entrapment, guilt if he didn't bail out his sister, and resentment over his sister's claims on his finances. His own children saw what was happening and were disgusted by their aunt's behavior. But they were unable to assert influence over their father.

Fred entered therapy when his anxieties over confrontation and his resentment began to dominate his psychic life. He wanted freedom from tension.

Gaining Control from Within

Those who can control the events that take place within themselves are normally better able to manage events that take place outside of themselves. Fred was far from taking charge of himself, but he could see the merit to this proposition.

Family difficulties are rarely simple. Fred experienced many connected conflicts. But he also created his own personal suffering by what he thought and believed about himself and the situation. This was an area where he could learn to take charge of himself.

There were many ways to support Fred's goal of taking charge of himself. He could have looked at his past associations with his sister and her tendency to manipulate and control him. But he was already pretty clear on that issue. He also had read extensively about the problem of enabling another's bad habits. Unfortunately, this information only upped his sense of guilt and helplessness.

Fred saw that his sister felt entitled to his help and would do whatever she could to get it. Pointing out what I call the *three Es—excesses, entitlement,* and *exploitation*—in his sister's behavior helped Fred put what she was doing into perspective. Showing him how she would act to *defend, deny,* and *deflect* (the *three Ds*) also helped put her behavior into context. When he raised questions about her excesses, she would act defensively, both denying and deflecting responsibility. With this analysis, he better understood why he could not get through to her with appeasement.

Fred's main problem was with himself. He feared a confrontation with his sister if he denied her money. He feared a loss of his relationship with her and her children. Resentment wove through his other emotions. However, Fred's priority was to get over feeling preoccupied with his anxious and tense thoughts.

Using the ABCDE Technique

Fred's most pressing concern was his own anxiety. He hated feeling tense over his tension. He reported feeling awful about seeing himself as a weak person for not facing up to his sister. He believed he couldn't stop the flow of tension. With these views, he seemed like a prime candidate for the ABCDE method. He would focus initially on his confrontation anxiety with his sister.

Again, the ABCDE method provides a way to break down a parasitic thinking process into an organized framework to eliminate this needlessly negative way of thinking. There are five components:

1. The *A* stands for an *adversity* with the power to activate a reaction, such as health problems, nightmares, a down mood, annoying thoughts, loss, or divorce. Fred recognized that his most obvious adversity was his sister's manipulative style.

2. *B* stands for *beliefs* you have about the adversity. Beliefs can come in different forms, ranging from negative and unrealistic to fact based. In this case, Fred needed to look for the irrational beliefs that supported his parasitic anxiety. Irrational beliefs can be magical interpretations, false explanations, erroneous assumptions, overgeneralizations, and other forms of faulty reasoning. Fred's belief that he couldn't stand his tension and that he would be overwhelmed by his sister grew out of his confrontation anxiety. Fred magnified and dramatized and overgeneralized his fear of Ginger's wrath. In a parasitic world of distorted thought,

anxiety-triggering beliefs represent self-absorbed interest to avoid and escape situations you view as threatening.

3. *C* stands for emotional and behavioral *consequences*. Charged interpretations, explanations, definitions, ascribed meanings, and so on link to what are called *secondary emotions*, or emotions that reflect problems in the use of language or interpretations of reality, such as parasitic anxieties. These secondary emotions are the emotional consequences, such as fear, dread, or panic. There can also be behavioral consequences, or reactions that are inappropriate to the situation, such as aggressive outbursts, retreat, or withdrawal. Fred's confrontation anxiety was an emotional consequence of his negative self-devaluing attitude in his dealings with Ginger. Giving her money all the time, depleting his financial resources, was a behavioral consequence.

4. *D* stands for *disputing* harmful belief systems through examining, questioning, and challenging them. The first part of this disputation process is to locate harmful beliefs in your stream of consciousness so that you can carefully examine them. The ABC phases set the stage. In the disputation phase, you ask yourself the following six questions: (1) Does the belief fit with reality? That is, is the belief confirmable through experiment? Is there evidence to support the belief? Is it or is it not fact based? (2) Does the belief support the achievement of reasonable and constructive interests and goals? (3) Does the belief help foster positive relationships? (4) Does the belief contradict parasitic thinking? (5) Does the belief seem reasonable and logical in the context in which it occurs? (6) Is the belief generally detrimental or generally helpful? These six questions provide a framework for separating realistic from harmful or dysfunctional thinking. They also promote self-observant thinking and behaving.

5. *E* stands for new *effects* that result from recognizing and effectively disputing parasitic thinking. Having identified and clarified emotionally charged magical parasitic beliefs, you can now create a constructive alternative perspective based upon plausibility, reason, and experiment. While this process will not defer normal emotions, such as loss, regret, frustration, and realistic anxieties and fears, it can go far to reduce needless tensions that grow from parasitic views. Thus, a prime effect can be that of feeling more in command of yourself.

FRED'S ABCDE RESOLUTION

The following ABCDE chart describes an organization of information about Fred's confrontation anxiety and how he first worked to overcome it.

ADVERSITY or activating event: Sister engaging in exploitative manipulations to get "entitlement" dollars to cover financial excesses.

Reasonable BELIEFS about the happening(s): "I don't like being put into a corner where I capitulate to my sister's insistence and demand for money to bail her out from the consequences of her own excesses."

Potential emotional and behavioral CONSEQUENCES of the reasoned belief: Regret, disappointment with sister's behavior, and dislike of the situation. Refusal to capitulate to sister's expectations.

Parasitic beliefs about the happening(s): Magical belief that appeasement through acquiescence will solve parasitic anxiety reaction. Self-view of weakness and ineptitude.

Potential emotional and behavioral consequences of the parasitic beliefs: Self-loathing for capitulation. Intolerance for tension and retreat from tension through capitulation.

DISPUTING problem-related parasitic beliefs: Fred started by reminding himself of his basic family values. He recognized that he would want to help his sister if she were ill or if she had no control over adverse events, but not when she was repeating self-destructive habits and had a choice to change. With that in mind, Fred asked and answered five questions:

1. "Does my belief that I cannot stand up to my sister fit with reality?" Answer: "No. There are exceptions. I married my wife despite my sister's strong protests and had a wonderful marriage. I have the power to say no."

2. "Does my belief that I must avoid conflict with my sister over money help me achieve my constructive interests and goals?" Answer: "No. It actually defeats my interest in overcoming anxiety related to her demands."

3. "Does my belief in avoiding conflict by capitulation foster a constructive relationship with my sister?" Answer: "No. My relationship with her is dysfunctional and likely will continue that way as long as she believes she can get what she demands from me."

4. "Do my beliefs that stir a confrontation anxiety contradict parasitic thinking?" Answer: "No. The belief that I'm too weak and will be overwhelmed by her if I defend my position is, itself, parasitic."

5. "Does my belief in capitulation to avoid conflict seem reasonable and make sense in the context in which it occurs?" Answer: "No. My sister's excesses, entitlement beliefs, and exploitive manipulations are unreasonable. To avoid conflict, I allow myself to deflate my own sense of self-worth by labeling myself weak and inept. That conclusion is based upon a magical view that my worth depends upon her approval."

6. "Is my belief in capitulation generally helpful or detrimental?" Answer: "In this case, it is generally detrimental. It costs time, emotional energy, and money, with no beneficial return."

EFFECTS from the values-analysis and disputation: "A better perspective on the issues. A sense of encouragement. A resolve to refuse Ginger's urgent pressures to bail her out of her financial troubles. A recognition that my worth does not depend upon capitulation to another's expectations and demands. I can accept myself fully, with or without her approval. Now I need to work on my tolerance for tension as another means of establishing the sense of inner control that I so strongly want to experience more often."

Following this analysis, Fred saw himself as doing better. He had clarity on the situation and a better sense of direction. He was on his way toward controlling his fears and anxieties, and thus gaining greater command over the form and direction of his thinking. With less sapping of his resources and misdirection of his efforts, he found himself better able to manage critical events that took place around him.

Following this preliminary ABCDE analysis, Fred took a direct behavioral action. He stopped capitulating to Ginger's financial demands. When he told Ginger that he would not help her out financially, he reported feeling uncomfortable. He reported disliking her efforts to get him to change back to the old generous Fred that she loved. But he did not retreat from his new position. He reported feeling less anxious as a result. He also noticed that Ginger started to live within her means and put herself on a budget when she gambled.

Now it is your turn to use the ABCDE technique to build your self observant-skills and personal problem-solving skills to start to resolve a parasitic anxiety problem.

YOUR ABCDE RESOLUTION

Choose an adversity. Then start to resolve your problem using the ABCDE method.

ADVERSITY or activating event:

Reasonable BELIEFS about the happening(s):

Potential emotional and behavioral CONSEQUENCES of the reasoned beliefs:

Parasitic beliefs about the happening(s):

Potential emotional and behavioral consequences of the parasitic beliefs:

DISPUTING problem-related parasitic beliefs:

1. Does the belief fit with reality? Is the belief confirmable through experiment? Is there evidence to support the belief? Is it or is it not fact based?

2. Does the belief support the achievement of reasonable and constructive interests and goals?

3. Does the belief help foster positive relationships?

4. Does the belief contradict parasitic thinking?

5. Does the belief seem reasonable and logical in the context in which it occurs?

6. Is the belief generally detrimental or generally helpful?

EFFECTS from the analysis and disputation:

The ABCDE process has cognitive, emotive, and behavioral components. The first part of the process addresses logic-tight parasitic anxiety thinking. The emotive phase includes building tolerance through taking time to turn what can seem like inner emotional chaos into a logical sequence of situation, thought, emotion, and behavior. The behavioral phase helps you to disable emotive cognitions of fear by planning and engaging in fear-stimulating solutions. This component involves applying problem-solving solutions that you might find uncomfortable, yet taking this step may provide a welcome boost in your tolerance for discomfort. Most importantly, the ABCDE process helps bring magical thinking to light and provides tools to make the feelings of fear less fearsome.

Executing Behavioral Assignments

Ellis (2000) is famous for his *behavioral assignments*. The idea is simple: you take actions to correct recognized problems. But doing them may involve pressing yourself to take responsible steps despite parasitic anxieties and fears. For example, based upon your ABCDE problem analysis, what concrete steps can you take to engage what you parasitically fear? Are you ready to take them?

As an exercise, if you have a confrontation anxiety, you could think out and then express your opinion about a controversial event to ten people you know. You could watch how they react. Do you get agreement from some? Do others partially agree? Do some argue the other side? What could you learn from carrying out this experiment? You may find that you develop norms about people's reactions. As a result of this experiment, you may be less likely to overgeneralize by thinking that "everybody" will respond in an identical way to what you say. Indeed, different people have different personalities, interests, and preferences when it comes to responding to matters of opinion that you present in a reasonable manner.

Responses from others will generally range from indifference to support or to a contrasting view. However, if you express to a biker gang the opinion that motorcycles should be taken off the road, expect disagreement. If you act abrasively and defensively, expect a backlash.

Even when you know what you need to do, your anxieties can continue to get in the way of taking action. The PURRRRS technique can help you put these anxieties into perspective.

PURRRRS PLAN TO BUILD PERSPECTIVE

You can view parasitic thoughts as default stressful thoughts. Default thoughts are conditioned to specific situations. You fear confrontation. In a situation where you may have a disagreement with others, you think, "I'll get overwhelmed and rejected if I say what I think and feel." You feel fearful. You back off. You view yourself as a wimp.

You can view default associations between thoughts, emotions, and actions as being automatic. But they are not like reflexes, where a stimulus directly causes a response. Rather, they work through an associative process. For example, if I said "black," what would you associate with this word? A common association would be "white." If I said "tall," you might think "short." In a similar way, you associate predictable thoughts and responses with certain situations. But since there is some thinking involved, they are not fully automatic.

Anxious default reactions can occur smoothly without appearing to require much forethought. But the ease of making associations also includes choices and decisions. These stealthy choices can hide beneath your conscious awareness. You may experience a startle reaction if you see a vehicle with blue flashing lights trailing your automobile. But if a police officer friend turns on flashing blue lights as you walk by his parked vehicle, you may experience a feeling of friendliness. It's not the light that triggers the response. It's the context. It's what you make of the situation. What you feel and decide to do involves a split-second assessment or appraisal of the situation.

Default fear cognitions have the power to stimulate your brain to trigger adrenaline, increasing your heartbeat and breathing. It takes concentration to go the extra steps to act to break this pattern of response.

The PURRRRS technique gives you a method for replacing default parasitic thinking with a reasoned approach, where you can truly give yourself better choices. The acronym stands for *pause, use, reflect, reason, respond, review,* and *stabilize*. To see how this technique works, I'll continue with the confrontation anxiety theme:

Pause: This means to stop and think about your thinking. Take time to consider what is happening when you feel anxious or fearful. You are then in a better position to separate legitimate concerns from self-terrifying beliefs. So if you fear being challenged, confronted, and overwhelmed for expressing an opinion, take a moment to pause.

Use: You use your cognitive and emotive resources to resist letting parasitic thinking go unchecked. You slow down. You organize your thoughts by writing them out.

Reflect: In the reflective phase, you expand upon the issues by separating out parasitic reactions from realistic thinking. You can use the six questions from the ABCDE analysis to help separate harmful from helpful thinking. For example, you discover that the word "overwhelmed" pops into your mind. You fear you will be overwhelmed whenever you express your true views. Now, you've pinned down an important emotive cognition that can bring about a self-fullfilling prophesy.

Reason: Using your educated power of reason, you can, for example, assess definitions, probabilities, and follow-up responses: (1) Ask yourself, how do you define "overwhelmed"? (2) If you speak up and express your views, what is the probability that you'll be overwhelmed? (3) If you are unable to effectively make your points, for whatever reason, why can't you accept yourself despite this setback, that is, unconditionally? (Note: If you can accept yourself in the face of unpleasant encounters, you are well on your way to establishing an inner command that can boost your chances to command events around you.)

Respond: What active behavioral steps can you take to address your confrontation fears? Rather than continue to worry about theoretical possibilities, you can directly find out what will happen when you express your views. You can talk yourself through the paces of taking concrete steps to approach and address your fear. You can accept tension as part of the process, thus not retreating because of a double-trouble fear of fear.

Revise: Plans rarely go without a hitch. But there are advantages to this. By acting to make a positive change, you can get new ideas. You can make adjustments. You can build skills. Through executing your plan, you may recognize gaps in the process and fill them in. In a nutshell, if your response plan does not produce the results you want, try a different way.

Stabilize: Repeating PURRRRS helps boost and stabilize gains. This process involves a commitment to keep advancing your positive self-interests. Perhaps you can pass on what you have learned to others. (Note: sometimes the best way to learn is to teach.)

By using PURRRRS to address confrontation anxiety, you can do at least three positive things for yourself. You can advance the education of your reason by assessing and then addressing a parasitic fear situation. Through repetition, you can reduce the chance of your fears coming back. Finally, you can set the stage for being clear with others and improving your relationships.

YOUR PERSONAL PURRRRS PLAN

Cite your fear and apply the PURRRRS system to examine and defeat your fear.

What is your target parasitic anxiety or fear? _____

PURRRRS	Actions
Pause: Stop and prepare for action.	
Use: Apply your will and other resources to resist anxious impulses.	
Reflect: Think about what is happening.	
Reason: Think it through.	
Respond: Put yourself through the paces of change.	
Revise: Review the process and make adjustments when results suggest trying another way.	
Stabilize: Persist with the evolving process until parasitic anxiety is under control.	

By shifting from tension thinking to taking the extra step of the PURRRRS awareness-and-action change approach, you can steer yourself away from needless fears and toward positive life choices.

A LIFE JOURNEY

Anthropologist and author Carlos Castaneda (1968) described four enemies of humankind that can be part of life's process. They can be viewed as a possible map for progress:

The first foe is fear. This treacherous and difficult enemy lies in waiting and erupts at its pleasure. Clarity of mind defeats fear. But then clarity can become the next foe in the form of ill-timed responses to what you see evolving.

When seeing new possibilities and opportunities, the challenge of clarity is to take what you know, and time and pace your response. Acting too quickly or deliberately can spoil opportunities. Reflecting over and timing your judgments opens opportunities for wisdom.

Mastering clarity unlocks the gates to knowledge and power. But capriciously and cruelly used, power is another potential enemy. The choice to use power in measured ways to achieve constructive results is a sign of self-mastery and maturity.

Then comes the final enemy: old age. This enemy can be partially but not fully defeated. By pushing off the tiredness of old age, you position yourself to bring together the knowledge of a lifetime. Here you pass on what you know and exit the world as a person of wisdom.

Castaneda's work has been criticized as being based upon a fantasy rather than legitimate anthropology. It is controversial. However, you can sometimes find gems in fiction. The concept of the four enemies provides a framework for organizing ideas about how to approach fear and what lies beyond. For example, when restricted by fictional threats, needless disappointments and lost opportunities are inevitable. Fear can drive you deeply into a shadow world of terrors that clouds clarity. Through seeking clarity and truth, you can take steps to address your parasitic fears. Through clarity, you bring yourself to the gate of personal power, the kind that lies within awaiting an awakening.

Knowing and doing the right thing is a mark of maturity and power. A constructive assertion of personal power relies on a self-observant way of being. That assertion involves a responsible outlook. But the effort expended can feel commanding when matched against a dominant foe of fear.

KEY IDEAS AND ACTION PLAN

What key ideas from this chapter can you use to rid yourself of your parasitic anxieties and fears? What's your action plan? Write it down. Test it out. Record what happened.

Key Ideas

1.

2.

3.

Action Plan

1.

2.

3.

Results from Actions Taken

1.

2.

3.

POSTSCRIPT

Mental karate is the idea that when you feel in command of yourself, you are better able to take charge of the events that take place around you. You can build mental karate skills by honing your clear-thinking skills. But you can also earn a higher-level belt in mental karate by building your emotional tolerance abilities. The next chapter will help you do that.

CHAPTER 8

Building Emotional Tolerance

Facing up to parasitic anxieties and fears includes building emotional tolerance, or the willingness to put up with unpleasant sensations. This chapter takes a look at how to build emotional tolerance for negative sensations, emotions, and frustrations.

SENSATIONS AND INTERPRETATIONS

If you are prone to anxiety, small negative changes in mood or abrupt but slight changes in physical sensations can grab your attention. As you try to figure out why you feel the way that you do, you might scan your environment. Perhaps, you think, it's your ungrateful boss. You start thinking nasty thoughts about your boss.

Psychologists Stanley Schachter and Jerome Singer thought that both changes in sensations and a cognitive label are needed to experience emotion. When you become aroused for no obvious reason, you'll tend to look for clues to explain what is going on. Your explanation defines the emotion (Schachter and Singer 1962).

Furthermore, individuals who are sensitive to tension tend to give negative meaning to unpleasant somatic changes (Wine 1971; Weekes 1979; Knaus 1982). If you are sensitive to anxiety sensations, you may be alert to slight but sudden physical changes that trigger anxious thoughts. These changes can include sweating hands, a slight uptick in your heartbeat, or increases in your breathing pattern (Taylor 1999). Even if an increase in your heartbeat comes about from climbing a flight of stairs or drinking a caffeinated soda, anxious thoughts about the meaning of these sensations can fog the more obvious reasons.

Sensitized to physical signs of anxiety, you may skip over a visible cause for a quickened heartbeat, such as climbing the stairs. This sensitivity for somatic changes increases your risk for various forms of anxiety (Rector, Szacun-Shimizu, and Leybman 2007).

Developing Emotional Tolerance for Unpleasant Sensations

The physical sensations you associate with anxiety often link to *anxiety-triggering cognitions*. These cognitions escalate the tension you feel. An example of a triggering cognition might be "oh no, here it [the anxiety] comes again" or "I'm going to have a heart attack." You can also have *amplifying cognitions* that follow and add to the clamor: "I'm going out of control. Something is wrong with my mind. I'm going crazy." The more you practice defusing these triggering and amplifying cognitions, the less often you'll have these problems to address.

How can you nip this negative-thought process in the bud before your risk for anxiety turns into an anxious episode? First, call on your self-observant talents. Use the principle of *Occam's razor*. This is the idea that the simplest explanation is probably more accurate than a more complex one. A quickened heartbeat from climbing has a simple explanation: exercise heightens your heart rate. A complex explanation might involve telling yourself that your heart is beating out of control, accompanied by such thoughts as, "I am about to feel anxious. I can't think straight. Other people will see that something is wrong with me. This would be awful." With Occam's razor, you cut away complex assumptions, like the above anxious chatter. With fewer assumptions, you have less to drive your anxiety.

It also helps to use *realistic labeling*, which means naming what happened in realistic terms. You climbed stairs. That is probably why you had a faster heartbeat. So you can label your heartbeat "exercise reaction." You explain to yourself that faster heartbeats come about through moderate exercise. Exercise is normally a good thing. You can add to this realistic labeling by using *affective relabeling*, employing more accurate but blander emotional words to describe the experience. Words like "unpleasant" or "uncomfortable" convey a different message from "awful" or "I can't stand it." Blander affective labels may trickle down from the prefrontal cortex to the amygdala to help tone down negative emotional images (Lieberman et al. 2007).

If you have anxiety sensitivity and want to stop overreacting, test out a three-step anxiety-sensitivity countermeasure approach. This approach uses the principle of Occam's razor, realistic labeling, and the practice of challenging anxiety triggering and amplifying cognitions. Here is an example of how it works:

ANXIETY-SENSITIVITY COUNTERMEASURE APPROACH

Links in the Sensation-Sensitivity Process	Psychological Countermeasures
Sensation sensitivity leading to anxiety-triggering cognitions: A jump in heart rate	**Emotional tolerance-building measures:** 1. Occam's razor: What is the simplest explanation to explain a jump in heart rate? To start, count your heartbeats. Chances favor that they will be within exercise limits. (If the rate is sustained at over 200 beats per minute, call 911. You probably won't be making many, if any, calls.) It's the change in your heartbeat that triggers your anxiety, not the rate. Remind yourself that over any given week, some fluctuations in breathing, heart rate, or blood pressure are normal. 2. Realistic labeling: Tell yourself, "The sensations feel unpleasant." No more, no less.
Triggering cognitions: "I don't know what is happening. I don't know what to do."	**Responses to triggering cognitions:** Remind yourself that viewing yourself in a state of uncertainty and confusion can lead to feeling overwhelmed by the unknown. Labeling this "uncertainty thinking" or "powerlessness thinking" or "fear of the unknown" gives you target cognitions to address. Addressing the target, you can ask "what" questions. For example, what do you know about what's happening that links to your fears? What was the trigger? What options are open? By raising such questions with yourself, you've started a process of taking charge of the problem.

| Amplifying cognitions: Jumping to conclusions and magnifying the threat theme: "I'm going to spin out of control. I'm going to lose my mind. This will not stop. I can't stand this." | Responses to amplifying cognitions: Ask yourself, what does it take to be out of control? Does it take a belief that you are out of control? If so, then what other beliefs are equally plausible? Ask yourself, if you feel uncertain and tense, how does that mean you are going to lose your mind? If you did lose your mind, what do you believe that would be like? How could you find your mind if you lost it? Ask yourself, where is the proof that the tension will go on forever? Even if you remain tense for the rest of your life, why can't you eliminate the double-trouble part? If you believe you can't stand feeling tense, then what does "can't stand" mean? Could it mean that you don't like feeling tense? Who does? To end this review, consider this: tension means you are alive and are surviving. |

Now it's your turn to challenge your anxiety sensitivity with this countermeasure.

YOUR ANXIETY-SENSITIVITY COUNTERMEASURE APPROACH

Use this three-step technique to address anxiety or sensation sensitivity.

Links in the Sensation-Sensitivity Process	Psychological Countermeasures
Sensation sensitivity leading to anxiety-triggering cognitions:	**Emotional-tolerance building measures:** 1. Occam's razor: 2. Realistic labeling:
Triggering cognitions: 1. 2.	**Responses to triggering cognitions:** 1. 2.
Amplifying cognitions: 1. 2. 3. 4.	**Responses to amplifying cognitions:** 1. 2. 3. 4.

By solving an anxiety-sensitivity problem, you're less likely to play a version of "The Boy Who Cried Wolf" with yourself. You can reduce your risk of going into alarm mode over every quick somatic change. Instead of going into alarm mode, you can develop norms about your sensations, so you know what is typical for you or what merits a closer look.

A No-Nonsense Plan to Get Tough on a Sensation-Sensitivity Problem

Tension sensations are not the problem. The problem lies in the meaning that you give to them. Tension sensations are cues and stimuli. You can interpret them in different ways. You may not be able to control physical sensations, but you can choose how to view them.

When responding to anxiety sensitivity, you can take the following five no-nonsense steps:

1. Remind yourself to unconditionally accept yourself as a fallible human with sensitive anxiety sensors.

2. Take a no-blame position. The idea is to help yourself solve the problem and not to find fault with yourself.

3. Work to uncouple fear cognitions from the sensations. For example, can you find evidence for catastrophizing? If so, how can you tone down your descriptive language and make it more realistic?

4. Practice emotional tolerance by working to accept the tension that you don't like. This means agreeing to live through the tension.

5. Accept reality. Even if you learn to uncouple fear-escalating thoughts from changes in sensations, under unusual stress, an anxiety-sensitivity reaction can recur. By redoing exercises that have worked before, you'll likely find it easier to break the connection than the first time around.

YOUR EMOTIONS

Sensations can exist without visible reason or object. Emotions, on the other hand, normally link to something visible, such as to a person you know, to events, to memories, to images, and so forth.

Emotions are spontaneous feelings with different hues, such as love, hate, fear, sadness, happiness, frustration, and jealousy. A poet can scribe them with a pen. An artist can stroke them with a brush. A composer can capture them with a song that tells a story. But you are the only one to feel your own emotions.

Throughout the ages, philosophers, poets, and psychologists have contemplated the meaning and origins of emotions. The ancient Greek philosopher Aristotle said that people think themselves into superiority, anger, and shame. Around 100 AD, the Stoic philosopher Epictetus added that it is not so much events that cause us to feel as we do, as what we make of them. William Shakespeare said, "For there is nothing either good or bad but thinking makes it so" (*Hamlet*, Act II, Scene II). According to Richard Lazarus (1991), emotion centers on how an individual evaluates the impact of an event. Lazarus thought that emotions arise from hot cognition in situations where we take our well-being into account.

Emotions and Cognitions

Your emotions are always right. Your thinking may be wrong, but your emotions accurately reflect what you think.

Your emotions are reflective of what you perceive or think, and they are typically attached to events. You feel anger because you can't find your keys. You blame your mate and cause an emotional stir. Then you discover the keys in the ignition of your car. Your emotions change. A colleague bad-mouths a coworker to you, saying she lies. When you get to know the person, you discover she is truthful to a fault. You simultaneously learn that the same colleague is telling others that you lie. Your emotions may change when the information changes.

Las Vegas psychologist Jon Geis (personal communication) tells a story of identical twin boys on the beach. One jumps up and down with glee. He speeds toward the water yelling "whoopee!" The other clings to his mother. She holds his hand and tries to bring him to the water. His eyes welling with tears, he digs his heels into the sand. What's the difference? One boy sees the water as fun. The other sees it as a threat. Each boy's emotion—one of joy and the other of fear—accurately describes what he thinks. The primary difference between the boys, in this instance, is a difference in perception. So your feelings are always right, but your perceptions may be off. Beliefs, thoughts, images, memories, or other cognitive processes that can call forth emotions are *emotive cognitions*. Perhaps most of your emotions come about from how you think.

If perception and beliefs influence what you think, and they can be distorted, can you ever trust your emotions? Your emotions include your natural fears and anxieties, and they are clear enough so that you don't need to question them. You feel saddened over the loss of a close friend. You feel anger toward someone who visibly acts to harm you. These emotions need no review or close analysis. So how can you tell a parasitic anxiety from a legitimate one? There are two basic ways:

1. Develop standards for parasitic thoughts, that allow you to separate parasitically anxious from fact-based or plausible thoughts. Review chapter 2 for a discussion on how to separate rational (plausible) from irrational thinking.

2. Link patterns of parasitic beliefs and their emotional spin-offs to their self-defeating results. For example, if you believe that you can't stand feeling tense and create a prison in your mind, you've walled yourself in by anxious thoughts about the feeling of fear and your inability to tolerate fear sensations. That belief can validate itself through the emotions it creates and the avoidance behaviors that normally accompany the belief and the emotions. When you free yourself from harmful cognitive distortions, such as "I can't stand feeling tense," you'll find it easier to trust your feelings.

A main self-development task is to clear away parasitic anxiety-and-fear thinking, the intellectual clutter that interferes with your experience of life.

Derailing Cognitive Fears

As you attempt to develop greater emotional tolerance for parasitic anxiety-and-fear sensations, it's helpful to take a look at how your parasitic thoughts may be triggered and amplified. Uncoupling parasitic beliefs from emotions can lead to less stress, and tolerating less needless stress is ordinarily easier than tolerating more needless stress.

When you actively address parasitic anxieties and fears without retreating, you are allowing yourself to experience tension while working on a problem. You can decrease your tension along the way by taking designed actions to counter default parasitic thinking.

Most people are generally poor at riding herd on their thoughts, connecting their interpretations to their feelings and reactions, then examining their thinking. Monitoring, recognizing, examining, and defusing parasitic thinking boosts your self-observant and self-supervising skills.

THE FIVE-STEP METACOGNITIVE APPROACH

You can use a five-step metacognitive approach to build emotional tolerance as you defuse anxiety-and-fear thinking. First you identify what originally stimulates the fear, such as a physical change or being in a situation you associate with fear. The second step is to pause, reflect, and recognize cognitive triggers and amplifiers that can add to your miseries. Step three involves developing a coping perspective. Step four is to devise coping actions to confront the parasitic anxiety or fear. Step five is to design specific emotional-tolerance tactics that fit the situation.

Two examples of this approach follow. The first describes an exaggerated fear. The second example describes anxiety over loss. An exercise follows where you can take these five steps to boost emotional tolerance as you face your own parasitic experience.

FIVE METACOGNITIVE STEPS TO BOOST EMOTIONAL TOLERANCE FOR AN EXAGGERATED FEAR

Fear activator: You hear bushes rustling outside your bedroom window.

Cognitive triggers and amplifiers: You wonder if a burglar brushed the bushes. In a moment, this possibility escalates to certainty. This overfocusing on a possible catastrophe feeds on itself.

Coping perspective: Apply Occam's razor. What is the simplest explanation that is likely to be correct? An animal rustled the bushes? A breeze rustled the bushes? From a metacognitive perspective, which parts of this thinking are factual? Which are exaggerated?

Coping actions: How can you test the Occam's razor hypothesis, keeping in mind the improbable but still possible view that a burglar lurks outside who was foolish enough to give you an early warning signal?

Emotional-tolerance tactics: Live with the feeling of tension as you actively work out the problem. Reward yourself for sticking with the issue by doing something pleasant for yourself after the mystery is solved. Read your favorite newspaper. Have a glass of warm milk. Phone an upbeat friend. By following coping efforts with a designed reward, you increase the odds that you'll be inclined to cope rather than retreat.

FIVE METACOGNITIVE STEPS TO BOOST EMOTIONAL TOLERANCE FOR AN ANXIETY OVER LOSS

Fear activator: Your steady date broke up with you to go out with someone else.

Cognitive triggers and amplifiers: You engage in nervous thinking about the loss of the relationship. You worry about how you will manage without that person. You experience fear that you will never find anyone else.

Coping perspective: From a metacognitive perspective, which parts of this thinking are factual and which are blown up? Is it possible to accept the sadness of the loss and to live beyond it?

Coping actions: Pick an hour each day for five days in a row when you allow yourself to feel the loss. You are likely to feel less anxious when you choose to grapple with the loss without avoiding sadness.

Emotional-tolerance tactics: Live with the feeling of tension as you actively work out the problem. Recognize that emotions from loss soon become emotions from distant memories. Each new memory varies slightly from the one before it. With each new memory, implant a new realistic, moderate, affective label to describe the experience. That doesn't diminish the sadness of loss. This affect relabeling can help put the loss into perspective.

Now it's your turn.

FIVE METACOGNITIVE STEPS TO BOOST EMOTIONAL TOLERANCE

Try the five-step metacognitive approach to boost your emotional tolerance by solving a parasitic problem.

1. What is your fear activator?
2. What are your cognitive triggers and amplifiers?
3. What coping perspective can you take?
4. What coping actions can you devise?
5. What emotional-tolerance tactics can you use in this situation?

By showing yourself that you can cope with an adversity and live through the accompanying tension, what else is there to fear?

THE SELF-DOUBT SENSATION-SENSITIVITY CYCLE

If you both doubt yourself and fear tension, you are likely to be overly sensitized to your visceral feelings, and thus overfocus on these sensations, magnify them, and then impulsively act to dodge them. This discomfort dodging feeds self-doubt and vice versa.

The self-doubt downing process can feel extraordinarily distressing. Faced with a threat and in a self-doubt mode of thought, you are likely to second-guess yourself and hesitate. You will often put yourself down. Perhaps you'll view yourself as unique or different from others, whom you see as better able to handle their problems.

The two vicious circles of self-doubt and sensation sensitivity interact and reinforce each other (see figure 1). When active, this reciprocal relationship supports the continuance of unwanted parasitic anxieties and fears.

Figure 1

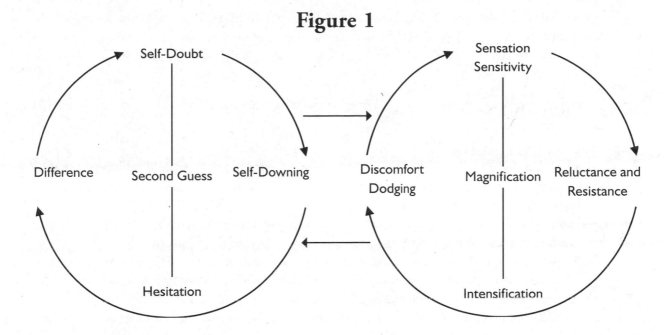

RESISTANCE AND RELUCTANCE

People will often find ways to avoid personal change when these changes don't come with an airtight guarantee of success. So, when you get to the point of contemplating action, you may have another barrier to face. It's called resistance. Resistance is a special case of avoidance.

When you resist taking on the problem of fear, you may tell yourself that the situation could get worse and that you are not up to the task. If you fear change because you expect to feel discomfort or fear, you might view yourself as vulnerable and unable to act. Telling yourself this creates an artificial problem that distracts from facing the real problem. This is why defusing discomfort anxieties is so important as you work on extinguishing your parasitic fears.

You can resist change out of a fear that, like Humpty Dumpty, you'll fall and shatter. However, what if your situation improves through the actions you take? What adjustments in thinking and living would help make your life better?

In the area of self-development, change normally occurs slowly but progressively with positive break-throughs occurring from time to time. You normally have ample time to develop motivation, coping, and problem-solving skills. When on this path, it is useful to ask yourself questions to promote insight into what happens when you feel resistance to dealing with your parasitic anxieties and fears. You can ask yourself (1) "What purpose does my resistance serve?" and (2) "What am I avoiding? What can I do to face the fear?"

Reluctance is a milder form of resistance. In this case, you don't have an overwhelming fear of fear. You don't experience any major anxiety. You've never had any major panic attached to the experience. But you do have a dull feeling of discomfort when you anticipate engaging in an activity you don't like. You don't want to expose yourself to something you find unpleasant. But you know you can do it. When you feel under the gun, you will do what you find unpleasant. Nevertheless, you put it off as long as you can.

You can deal with reluctance in a straightforward way. Forcefully refuse to avoid the feeling of discomfort associated with the activity. Keep focused on the long-term positive benefits of overcoming avoidance thinking and behaviors. Practice overcoming reluctance until acting promptly becomes habitual.

FRUSTRATION-TOLERANCE TRAINING

Even when life seems good, you don't have to wait long to have something unpleasant happen. The roast gets overcooked. You have an electrical outage while you are giving a party. Your child spills paint on your rare Oriental carpet. Your employer downsizes and you're out looking for a new job. Even when you accept the normally disruptive events of life as manageable inconveniences, you are likely to feel frustration. If you keep these disruptive events in perspective, however, you probably won't rehash your difficulties, load your mind with grievances, and subject yourself to anxieties and other forms of distress.

Nobody goes through life without facing frustrations thousands of times. Frustration is a primary emotion that comes about when you feel hindered or blocked from achieving what you set out to do. This emotion is present from the start of life and needs no verbal direction to surface fast.

You start life with many frustrations and discomforts. Your discomfort reactions signal your parents to take away the source of the frustration. You're hungry. You cry to be fed. You wet your diaper. You cry to have it changed. You have cramps. You cry for relief. At one month old, you're not thinking out what you want to achieve. You are not consciously aware of the cause-and-effect relationship between signaling discomfort and getting results. You're reacting. But you can also appear charming. You smile. You coo. You laugh. You get good strokes for that.

As you develop, it's how you handle your frustrations that partially determines the quality of many of your life experiences. Along the pathways of life, you learn to suppress many types of urges that can get you into trouble. You learn to delay gratification when this can benefit you. But you also learn when to trust feelings of frustration and respond without wavering.

Frustration can be a motivational trigger where you hop right onto a problem to resolve it and put it behind you. You receive a notice for nonpayment of a bill you paid weeks earlier. You feel frustrated and are motivated to take corrective action. You don't hesitate. You get on the phone to get the problem corrected. A customer-service person denies accountability. That's another source of frustration. Fortunately, you have the canceled check in hand.

At other times, the barrier may be too high, but you may remain motivated enough to try a different way or to put your attention onto something else where you can have an impact. Feeling frustrated by a problem that is of value to you to solve, you might work for years to find a solution. You want better fuel economy. You work to invent a cost-effective way to turn grass into liquid fuel.

From time to time, frustration may mix with irritation or anxiety. You are busy working on a complex problem. Your mate interrupts you to take out the newspapers now. You feel frustrated and irritated. Your employer pressures you to stop doing what you are doing and shift to another project. The interruption frustrates your need to bring closure to the project you are on. In that context, feeling frustration raises your risk for anxiety.

Erroneous beliefs can provide a source for many lingering frustrations. You hold to impossibly high standards. You feel driven by your expectations. The gap between reality and some of your expectations results in frustration. You may escalate the tension. You interpret the gap as something that you absolutely have to fill.

From an outside perspective, others may look at you as highly productive. You urgently drive yourself to achieve according to your expectations. You put in more time than most. Now operating like a driven achiever, you often worry about your performances.

Expectations can lead to frustration and exasperation in other ways. Having a secret mental book of rules you expect others to follow, you often feel frustrated when people don't act according to this secret script. These and other self-induced frustrations raise your stress level. This too can increase your risk for anxiety.

Low Frustration Tolerance and Frustration Disturbances

If you suffer from parasitic anxieties or fears, you are likely to also have an inappropiately *low frustration tolerance* (LFT). LFT is an impulsive tendency to throw off tension without much foresight. This hair-trigger urge to discharge tension can yield momentary relief. From a self-development perspective, however, there is rarely any meaningful long-term benefit. When combined with parasitic anxieties and fears, LFT typically substitutes impulse for reflective efforts to alter emotionally distressing patterns. The higher your level of LFT, the higher your level of stress may be (Mahon et al. 2007).

LFT is typically event oriented. Someone cuts in front of you in traffic. You turn beet red with anger. That reaction can partially or even wholly start with LFT thinking.

Frustration disturbances are extensions of LFT. A *frustration disturbance* is a lifestyle tendency to overreact to frustrating circumstances. It can attach to almost any inconvenient situation. If there is no readily available event, and you have a frustration disturbance, you can invent one.

Low frustration tolerance and frustration disturbances filter through every form of needless human distress. As with anxiety sensitivity, LFT and frustration disturbances are risk factors for anxiety-and-fear thinking. A sensitivity to unpleasant sensations raises the risk that you will magnify and intensify uncomfortable sensations. Here is where Occam's razor may come in handy. Rather than try to unravel everything, what is your basic assumption? Is it that frustration is intolerable?

Building Frustration Tolerance

Learning to build frustration tolerance is normally a direct route to reducing much needless suffering. A direct route does not necessarily mean quick or complete results, however. If you choose to go this route, here's a look at what you can do.

If you set as one of your goals the development of higher frustration (emotional) tolerance, any LFT event becomes an opportunity to work toward this goal. But don't expect perfection. Don't expect to eliminate all harmful LFT reactions. But if you work to meet this challenge, you'll likely notice a positive difference in how you generally manage tension. A 10 percent change is a noteworthy improvement.

MINDFULNESS-BASED COGNITIVE THERAPY FOR EASING TENSION

Mindfulness-based cognitive therapy (MBCT) is a nonjudgmental method where you view present-moment thoughts and feelings as transitory. They are not you. You can engage this mindfulness view any time parasitic thoughts race through your mind, as well as when in a state of meditation or during other forms of relaxation.

MBCT differs from classical cognitive behavioral methods, where you actively work to identify and dispute distorted thoughts and false beliefs. MBCT combines Buddhist and cognitive therapy methods. Instead of questioning irrational belief systems, you accept them as passing thoughts.

The MBCT philosophy is similar to Gestalt therapist Fritz Perls's in-the-present-moment form of therapy. You don't disown parts of your thinking and feelings. Research support for the Gestalt method is marginal (Smith and Glass 1977).

MBCT shows slight promise as a means of reducing tension (Bishop 2007) and general anxiety (Evans et al. 2008). The method's supporters provide data to show that this approach can help reduce relapse among people with repeat depressions (Teasdale et al. 2000; Ma and Teasdale 2004). But controlled studies show no pronounced effect (Toneatto and Nguyen 2007). When effective, the reasons are clouded (Coelho, Canter, and Ernst 2007).

MBCT may be helpful. I've included it here, for it has features that support frustration-tolerance and emotional-tolerance development. You may find it a way to reduce needless suffering, leaving you with less stress to tolerate.

MBCT may be useful for taking away reasons for double troubles, assuming a nonjudgmental perspective takes away needless self-blame. Here are some ways to take a nonjudgmental approach:

1. Define parasitic thoughts as mental events that do not define your global self.

2. Recognize that parasitic thoughts and feelings are passing thoughts.

3. Rather than actively avoiding or attempting to push them aside, accept them as coming and going experiences.

4. Recognize that parasitic thoughts and emotions that exist in the present moment are separate experiences from what has happened before and what will happen next.

5. Recognize that life includes unpleasant events and suffering that occur like passing breezes.

MBCT is not an exclusive system. You can use it in combination with techniques for challenging erroneous thoughts and beliefs. Accepting that parasitic anxiety-and-fear thoughts are as vaporous as clouds allows you to take them seriously but not personally. With less clamorous self-talk, you can examine and dispute them. (If you are interested in learning more about MBCT, see *The Mindfulness and Acceptance Workbook for Anxiety* under Suggested Reading.)

NEUTRALIZING LFT THINKING

LFT thinking comes in different but often overlapping forms. The first step to neutralize this thinking is to recognize it. Here are three common forms:

1. *Distress view:* "I can't cope. I'm having a nervous breakdown." This is taking an uncomfortable feeling and twisting it into a major upset or emotional disaster.

2. *Urgency view:* "I can't stand feeling stressed. I must have immediate relief." This view turns a preference into a necessity.

3. *Intolerance view:* "I can't endure this any longer." This perspective can promote a needless sense of resignation.

When reconstructed under tension, LFT thinking reflects impulsive thought habits where words exaggerate the experience. This thinking is a form of double trouble: stress plus exaggerated meanings. Defanging LFT thinking decreases tension.

From an MBCT approach, you can view the thoughts as you might watch clouds float by. You can't control the direction of the clouds. Why worry and upset yourself over what you can't control? The phrase "let it be" captures the spirit of this design.

LFT self-talk is impulsive self-talk that adds to stressful feelings that can trigger a sense of urgency to escape them. You can follow a PURRRRS plan to slow down your LFT tempo by shooting for a realistic perspective. Here is a skeletal PURRRRS plan:

Pause: Stop to recognize the connection between LFT-thought and LFT-feeling sensations.

Use: Take advantage of your coping capabilities to redirect your thinking toward addressing and correcting this impulsive process.

Reflect: Think about what is going on. Connect the dots between LFT urges, LFT self-talk, and an escalation of tension.

Reason it out: What are you telling yourself or believing that you connect to LFT urges? What plausible alternative but mildly emotive words can you use to describe the frustration you experience? "Unpleasant"? "Bothersome"? "Troublesome"? What is going on to stimulate an LFT response? What problem do you attach to the reaction? How might it be solved?

Respond: This might be a good time to attempt to uncouple dramatic LFT phrases from who you are by reminding yourself that the words and feelings are transitory. Intentionally use affective labeling, such as the word "unpleasant," to balance the more dramatic phrases. Guide yourself through steps to resolve the problem.

Review: What seemed effective? What didn't work? What can be improved?

Stabilize: Keep practicing. Repeating the exercise can slow the impulsive flow of thought. You show yourself how to put reason between impulse and reaction. You act to tolerate what you don't like.

You can reduce your level of tension by engaging the sources of that tension. One source to address is distressful, urgent, and intolerant thinking. By addressing and defusing this intolerance thinking, you are less likely to cave in to tension.

KEY IDEAS AND ACTION PLAN

What key ideas from this chapter can you use to rid yourself of your parasitic anxieties and fears? What's your action plan? Write it down. Test it out. Record what happened.

Key Ideas

1.

2.

3.

Action Plan

1.

2.

3.

Results from Actions Taken

1.

2.

3.

POSTSCRIPT

There is no lifelong relief from uncomfortable situations. A discomfort-free state is probably impossible. But you do have a wide range of emotions to experience including happiness, joy, love, affection, ecstasy, and contentment. You have successes, accomplishments, and delightful surprises to look back on and to look forward to. Life need not be like the Russian dirge, *Song of the Volga Boatmen*, with a dismal musical tone that strikes the mood of a barge hauler. But moving toward that often-vague sense of emotional freedom involves accepting natural sensations, emotions, and frustrations. It involves a disciplined effort to contest the parasitic kind. This leaves you free to experience the results of a healthy perspective, a wider range of positive emotions, and more experiences that you can cherish.

CHAPTER 9

Behavioral Methods to Quell Fear

This chapter will take a look at exposure methods to train the brain to suppress parasitic fears. It will illustrate how to use a graduated exposure technique through the story of a young woman suffering from debilitating fears. You can use a similar approach to address your own parasitic fears. This chapter also covers a basic card-sort technique to help you organize information about your fears as you prepare to take action. And it covers relaxation techniques that you can use alone or in combination with exposure.

THE BRAIN AND FEAR

The amygdala carries instructions for sparking fear in situations that early humans found dangerous. In a robot-like way, it powerfully responds to a predator, a coiled snake, a sudden movement, or being pushed to the edge of a cliff. Shadowing your senses, the amygdala alerts you to danger. It doesn't wait for a complete picture to develop before it excites emotions and stress hormones. You freeze or retreat.

The amygdala acts fast. This can save your life. It can also make you vulnerable. You cross a street. A speeding automobile heads toward you. In this instance freezing is the wrong thing to do. Jumping out of the way can save your life. Still, you hesitate. In prehistoric times, freezing was the best survival tactic. Predators pay attention to movement. They may not notice motionless prey.

The amygdala doesn't know the difference between primitive and modern times. It has a simple mission that spans the millennium: to avoid harm, freeze or flee from a visible danger. When it comes to danger, the amygdala represents your lizard mentality.

The amygdala can do more than respond to darting shadows, however. Through conditioning, it can learn new things to fear. If you lose control of your car on an icy road, understandably you may later feel tense when driving on icy roads. That is, you can learn to fear situations that stir a sense of danger and where you lack a sense of control. But some of your learned or conditioned fears may be parasitic, such as fear of the dark, fear of conflict, or fear of rejection.

Whatever the amygdala learns to fear is indelibly etched into memory. As far as we know, that etching doesn't go away, but it can be suppressed.

The amygdala contributes to negative feelings by increasing your perceptual sensitivity for negative stimuli (Barrett et al. 2007). If you have a sensitive amygdala, you may receive a lot of false alarms. You are likely to be on high alert when low alert is just fine. You are more likely to react to things that are not where you expect them to be, strange sounds, or quick movements.

The good news is that with practice you can overcome practically any fear. You can even overcome fears that preserve your life. For example, high-wire circus performers overcome their fear of falling. The fear is replaced by a sense of controllability. This sense of controllability is partially a higher mental process activity from the prefrontal cortex signaling other parts of the brain that the situation is under control. But other brain regions can also signal the amygdala that things are under control.

The *anterior cingulate cortex* (ACS) can regulate both emotional and cognitive centers of the brain, resolve conflicts between competing areas, and correct errors. It can signal the amygdala to stop freezing or bolting. A gradual mastery of walking a high wire, for example, can signal the ACS to tone down the amygdala. But what is an asset can also be a problem.

The ACS responds to mild emotional rewards. Most people want to avoid discomfort or fear, but successful avoidance can send the wrong message to the ACS. Relief through retreat can cause the ACS to favor retreat.

A prime way the ACS resolves conflict is through corrective experience (Posner and Rothbart 2007). The theory is that having comparative experiences, the ACS can switch on and block the amygdala before it causes a visceral storm of fear.

Overcoming a parasitic fear partially involves training the ACS to tone down the amygdala. And the toning-down process probably comes about through corrective experiences: if the ACS doesn't experience an error, there is no error to correct. Under these circumstances, telling yourself not to be afraid can prove insufficient.

Facing your fear, on the other hand, can help correct errors in perception that fire the amygdala. *Behavioral exposure therapy* is a prime part of this corrective process.

Neuroimaging studies illustrate that exposure influences the prefrontal cortex, anterior cingulate, and medial orbitofrontal cortex. These regions are involved in the evaluation of situations that evoke emotions (Schienle and Schäfer 2006). When exposure leads to relief from a specific fear, neural imaging of the amygdala and ACS shows decreased amygdala activity and increased cingulate activity (Goossens et al. 2007; Felmingham et al. 2007).

The ACS does not have prime authority over regulating fear impulses. The brain has many regulatory systems, including cognitive and emotional restraints in the prefrontal cortex (Lewis and Todd 2007). Nevertheless, the message is clear enough: it is probably insufficient to educate your reason without also taking behavioral actions to educate the brain to shut off a needless fear. And even if the prefrontal cortex can't reevaluate emotive situations, and the cingulate suppression theory is completely wrong, behavioral exposure therapy is a proven way to overcome phobias and other intense forms of parasitic fears. Boston University professor David Barlow (2000) provides ample evidence to support exposure as the best method to manage fear.

A COGNITIVE AND BEHAVIORAL WAY TO ADDRESS A FEAR OF DARKNESS

The following story is about a young woman named Judy who overcame an oppressive fear of darkness by taking graduated corrective action.

Judy's Background

Ever since she was a child, Judy had a morbid fear of darkness. She thought it started from a story her uncle told her about "the bogeys." These were haunting apparitions who flew invisibly through darkness to steal the souls of little children who misbehaved. After hearing that story, she recalled feeling petrified of the dark. She knew she wasn't perfect and figured the bogeys would come to get her. Thereafter, as dusk covered the sky, she would run to her parents for protection.

To help quell her fears, her father suggested that she keep a light on in her room. Her mother said, "The bogeys can't get you in the light." This magical belief calmed her. But she continued to have a morbid fear of being cloaked in darkness and of having her soul torn away by invisible bogeys.

Judy worried about what would happen if the lights went out and she had no safe place to hide. She solved this problem by having backup systems. She kept candles and a battery-operated lantern in her bedroom. Her parents thought this was excessive. They also believed she would grow out of her fears.

Judy's fear of darkness continued through her adolescence and into her adulthood. Of course, the bogey story was silly. Judy figured this out around the same time she stopped believing in the tooth fairy. Yet her fear of the darkness continued. A fear of losing her "self" in darkness substituted for her fear of invisible bogeys.

Her fear affected her social life. As a young teen, Judy refused to go to summer camp. She knew that there would come a time when the lights would go out. She wanted to avoid panicking and being ridiculed by her peers. She refused to go to sleepovers. As a young adult, she missed going to her best friend's wedding reception. It was held at night.

Her fear generalized to other conditions of darkness, such as driving at night or through dimly lit tunnels. In these cases, she magically believed she'd be safe with the dome light on in her car. When asked out on dates, she automatically refused. She could not control the time of the proposed dates. She feared that she'd expose her fear of darkness to her date. She believed she'd be seen as nuts.

Judy was down on herself for her fear of darkness. But this was only one of many double troubles she experienced. Another was fear of exposure. Others were fear of the feeling of fear, fear of loss of control, and fear of losing herself by going crazy.

Judy likened her fear of darkness to an alien force that overcame her at night. She said she dreaded the dark. Now into the twenty-sixth year of her life, Judy continued to sleep with a lamp on.

A Time and Proximity Plan for Defeating Fear

To the outside world, Judy looked as though she lived a normal life. If you didn't know about her fear of the dark, you'd think she was a lovely upbeat young woman without a care in the world. She had attended college during the day and received a degree in journalism. She did freelance editing for a major publication house. Meanwhile, Judy continued to live with her parents, who encouraged her to get help for dealing with her dread of darkness. She decided to see if she could find a way to break free from her fears.

Judy was motivated to get past her fear of darkness. She felt bound to her fear, overwhelmed, and not in control of her life. She believed that a combined cognitive, emotional tolerance, and behavioral exposure approach held promise. She decided to give it a try.

Logically, Judy knew that darkness was not harmful. Sure, her ancient ancestors may have gathered around a fire at night to gain safety from predatory animals. But most of humanity sleeps in the dark. They don't go crazy. They don't get devoured by predators.

Judy knew she was not alone with this type of fear. Knowing that millions of others feared darkness was somewhat comforting. But more than anything, she wanted the chance to lead a reasonably normal life.

Judy organized her campaign around time and proximity dimensions. Within each dimension, she used cognitive, tolerance, and behavioral approaches to help quell tension. She addressed her double troubles with a cognitive approach. To develop emotional tolerance, she planned to live through the tension of fear to avoid feeling relief for retreating. She would take a behavioral exposure approach to train her brain to stop signaling danger in darkness. By taking three major actions, she believed she could cover her bets.

JUDY'S TIME AND PROXIMITY PLAN

Fear of Darkness	Cognitive	Tolerance	Behavioral
Time dimension	Counteract double troubles and parasitic-fear thinking.	Refuse to accept parasitic-fear thought that you can't stand tension.	Design an exposure plan to progressively master a fear of darkness by taking graduated steps to bring about that result.
Proximity dimension	Tackle parasitic-fear thoughts that can start a cascading feeling of fear and evoke impulses to retreat.	Use intelligence, ingenuity, and will to live though tension for purpose of defeating fear.	Directly face fear by taking successive steps to experience fear but under conditions where you are in charge of what you do and where fear plays second fiddle.

Employing Cognitive and Emotional Tolerance

After recognizing that she was double-troubling herself, Judy felt relief that she could do something concrete to contest this parasitic thinking. Accepting that double troubles were a habit of mind, Judy began to see that other perspectives were not only possible but also more realistic. Adopting the slogan "tolerance tames fear," she saw that she could give herself the right to have a problem fear habit. With that perspective in mind, she addressed her double troubles.

Judy harbored several double troubles:

1. She saw herself as a weak person for having a fear of darkness.

2. She feared her fear of darkness, because she thought that fear could cause her to lose her sense of self and she would go crazy.

3. She blamed herself for losing opportunities because of her fear.

Judy used the following cognitive interventions to defuse her double troubles:

■   Reading a passage from *Hamlet* reinforced Judy's idea that she could think about her thinking. In Act II, Scene II, Hamlet says to Rosencrantz: "Why, then, 'tis none to you; for there is nothing either good or bad, but thinking makes it so: to me it is a prison." This passage reinforced Judy's newfound belief that by changing her thinking, she could exit her prison.

■   Judy feared going crazy with fear. When she learned that a fear of going crazy was a common phobia and even had a name, phrenophobia, this fear quickly vanished. Instead, she came to view panic as highly unpleasant. This description better fit with reality.

■   Judy interpreted her fear of darkness as a sign of weakness. This was, in her mind, a character flaw. In time, she came to accept that experiencing parasitic fear was more a matter of having a bad-thinking habit than a character flaw. She realized that she had called herself weak to explain why she felt afraid. By redefining her fear of darkness as a learned habit, she developed confidence that she could learn to break the habit. Judy concluded that calling herself weak for having a fear was an unreasonable interpretation of her whole self.

■   Judy blamed herself for lost opportunities. Living with damning herself about lost opportunities was like living life in reverse gear. Blaming herself for not having acted to overcome her fears earlier was also unproductive. The past won't change. The only thing that can change about the past is the view we take about prior events. Judy thought about this idea that though the past was gone, she could reexamine and reinterpret events. Although she couldn't go back to do things differently, she could start today to live her life differently. She could start by breaking from her prison of fictional fears.

Working to diminish her double troubles, Judy learned that she felt more tolerant of herself and less worried about feeling fearful. The time was ripe to apply her new beliefs and motivation directly to the challenge of addressing her fear of darkness.

Using a Graduated Exposure Technique

Judy's solution for overcoming her fear of darkness involved experiencing the fear. She expected to show herself that darkness wouldn't kill her; nor would panic about being in the dark do her in. She saw exposure as a way to train her brain and boost her tolerance for discomfort. Now she was ready to deal with the proximity issue where the darker it got, the greater her sense of dread.

Judy enjoyed reading horror stories about things that go bump in the night. When reading scary stories, she always knew she could choose to close the book. And because she knew she had this control, she didn't need to exercise it. Thus, the idea that she could control aspects of darkness appealed to her.

A big part of an ongoing parasitic fear involves a sense of being out of control and powerless. But what happens when you have a way to assert some control? Will that change a perception of a situation? Will a change in perception send a different message to fear-suppressing centers in the brain? Judy decided to try a graduated exposure to darkness, in which she would learn to tolerate feelings of tension in manageable doses. The plan enabled her to gradually increase her own exposure to her fear. This would put her in control of the experiment.

Judy agreed to try using a dimmer switch at night in her bedroom. The dimmer switch gave her a way to regulate the level of illumination. This way she could control how dark it was in her bedroom.

She started with the light fully bright. By design, she gradually dialed down the intensity of the light. When she felt tense, she did not increase the level of the light but stayed with the feeling of tension until it lifted. In the process, she discovered that her tension didn't last. She found this emotional tolerance phase easier than she had first expected.

With the dimmer switch in hand, Judy felt largely in control of the light and her fear. But there was an exception. On one occasion, Judy retreated from facing her fear of darkness. Realizing that this setback did not prove that she was defeated, she returned to her bedroom an hour later. This time she kept the light on a bit brighter until she felt comfortable at that level. Then she turned the switch down another notch. She found that she no longer felt a need to retreat.

After ten days of progressively dimming the light, Judy could turn out the light and stay in darkness for a minute before she started to feel tense. She increased the amount of time she stayed in darkness in three-minute increments.

When Judy achieved the milestone of remaining six minutes in darkness, she began using a dim night-light in her bedroom at night. This substituted for the higher intensity lamp that she was accustomed to using. At the three-week mark, Judy shut off the night-light and fell asleep in darkness. Thereafter, she could have the night-light on or keep it off. It didn't seem to matter. She also discovered that her newly gained freedom from fear of darkness in her bedroom had generalized. She could go into a dark basement without panicking.

Through this graduated exposure method, Judy showed herself that her fear sensations were time limited and tolerable. She knew she could stand experiencing fear sensations that she did not like. She felt a sense of accomplishment.

Did Judy's experience in boosting her sense of control over her fear of darkness lead the anterior cingulate cortex to signal the amygdala to calm down? That's a matter of conjecture. But clearly, graduated exposure was a basic solution for her fear.

One criticism of behavioral exposure methods is that what you learn in one situation normally won't automatically transfer to another. But there does seem to be a time-and-effort savings. You can take what you learn to quell a fear in one situation and apply it to a related condition.

Judy next addressed her fear of driving at night. She used opaque plastic sheets to control the light level of the dome light on her car to where she could drive at night without the dome light on. She repeated the process when driving through tunnels. Within a week, she was driving at night without the dome light and could drive through tunnels.

Judy's Plan

The following summarizes Judy's cognitive, emotive, behavioral plan:

- Attack double troubles whenever this form of thinking arises.

- Design an exposure sequence into manageable phases.

- Start with the least intense phase and stick with it until mastered. Then move on to the next.

- Pace yourself. There is no need to rush. It takes time for the brain to integrate new information from experience.

- If you have a setback, try again, perhaps with a modified plan.

Through executing this plan, Judy increased her sense of control over her fear of darkness. To make this happen, she shifted from a self-view of powerlessness to one of self-efficacy through organizing, regulating, and directing her efforts to achieve a highly meaningful goal. As a consequence of her actions, Judy shed several oppressive parasitic fears.

It is normally not enough to shed fears. What do you then do with your time and your life after you are no longer limited because of your fears? Judy dated. She attended night courses in journalism. She obtained a master's degree. She went on vacations, something she had not done before. Still, her life was not idyllic. She had her share of setbacks and losses. Nevertheless, she experienced her life as far more exciting and meaningful. She looked toward the future with optimism.

THE BEHAVIORAL CARD-SORT TECHNIQUE

Using graduated (also known as *graded*) exposure methods like Judy's is a standard practice for addressing serious fears, such as dental phobias, injection phobias, elevator phobias, snake phobias, stage fright, and others. As you've seen, the method involves first analyzing a fear by breaking it down into situations ranging from mild to severe. Using this method, you then confront your fear at your own pace, engaging in a set of activities designed to extinguish your parasitic fear as you gradually expose yourself to it.

If your fear of harmless snakes interferes with the quality of your life, you might start this graded exposure process by first looking at a snake in a glass case at a thirty-foot distance. You would stay at that distance until you developed emotional tolerance. You would then move to the next level, say, a few steps closer to the case. You repeat the process until you reach the highest level, such as standing close to a harmless snake without being afraid.

Such exposure methods can dramatically reduce extreme phobias, though they can also seem unappealing (Choy, Fyer, and Lipsitz 2007). But consider the alternative: living with the fear.

Graduated exposure techniques can seem boring, as well, but they tend to be highly effective. If you fear snakes, the idea of standing near a snake may cause you to shutter and retreat. However, when the steps toward change are gradual, you can take tension in measured doses.

The key to this approach is that you start with what you can manage. When you get to the point where you are at your highest-level fear situation, you've already built up significant emotional tolerance. The level of discomfort between the top level and the one below it is probably no different from the same mild emotional intensity you experience as you move from step one to step two. The idea is to put your attention onto the next step so that eventually reaching the highest level is just another small step away.

Unless you work with a trained professional who helps rank exposure experiences, however, creating a graded ranking system can prove challenging. The behavioral cluster card-sort method can simplify this process (Knaus 1982). This technique involves using three-by-five-inch index cards to organize your exposure experience according to location and other critical factors, such as proximity. Each card represents a different feared situation; by organizing the cards in order of least feared to most feared situation, you can use them to guide your exposure process.

The first set of cards refers to *location conditions*. You rank these conditions according to their intensity. Say you fear crowds and want to overcome this handicap. Your most feared location might be a mall during peak holiday hours; you would then write down this location on an index card. Another feared location might be a town-hall meeting; this location goes on another card. These are the locations upon which you would focus your attention.

The second set of cards refers to *proximity conditions*. For example, you might experience the most discomfort when you are in the middle of a crowd. You might experience the least discomfort when you are near the location but outside of the crowd.

Once you've written down your different conditions on index cards, you can sort the cards to develop a list of ranked items. The card-sort method simplifies the process of developing a list of ranked items. But it does require a shift from a self-absorbed to a self-observant perspective. The next story, about how Del faced his phobia, shows how the card-sort method can work.

Del's Background

Del was a thirty-five-year-old undergraduate biology major. He enjoyed biology but not where he was taught. He panicked if he went into a classroom where he did not have the seat closest to the classroom door. He wanted to be close to the classroom door so that he could quickly exit the building should he suffer a panic reaction during the class. His primary fear was that of not being able to escape if he panicked. The farther he was from the exit, the worse his fear,

To avoid panicking over not getting "his seat," Del habitually arrived twenty minutes early for class. Proximity to the door was critical to him.

Being close to a classroom exit was only the tip of the iceberg, however. His fears grew worse at higher stories. Thus, he selected his college based on the height of the buildings and proximity to his home. At the small liberal arts college that he'd picked, most of the academic buildings were only one story high. One building had three stories. That was the science building, where his major subjects were taught. When the classes he needed to take were scheduled on the first floor, he'd take them. Otherwise, he'd wait.

With a small family inheritance, Del originally had no need to work. But his inheritance would eventually run out. That reality, along with being fed up with accommodating his fears, prompted a decision to act to stop feeling afraid.

Del tried medication for his anxieties and panic. It was ineffective. He did a paper on CBT and anxiety for a psychology class. Based on this research, he prepared himself to face what he feared.

Using the Card-Sort Technique

Del wanted to use graduated exposure, but he needed a plan. First, he needed to rank his fears. To do this, he turned to the card-sort technique.

Del's card-sort ranking involved three locations and five proximity conditions. The locations were the first, second, and third floors of the science building. Del defined the proximity conditions based on distance from the classroom door. His lowest-level proximity condition was attending a class on the first floor and sitting two seats away from the door in the row closest to the door. The highest-level proximity condition was sitting in the middle of the middle row in a third-floor classroom. The number of students in the class was a factor, but not a significant one, he said, since enrollments were typically small. Del devised a graduated exposure plan with the following location and proximity conditions:

Location Conditions

1. First floor

2. Second floor

3. Third floor

Proximity Conditions

1. Two seats away from door in the row closest to door

2. Two rows from door in seat closest to the door

3. Five rows from door in seat closest to door

4. Five rows from door, middle seat

5. Middle row (row farthest from the door), middle seat

Del started his behavioral card-sort exposure sessions in the spring semester. That spring, he took four courses on the first floor of the same building. This provided plenty of learning opportunity: He could repeat the card-sort plan daily. He started with the first location and proximity condition and mastered it at his own pace. When he felt reasonably comfortable with step 1, he took the second proximity step, which was to sit two rows from the door in the seat closest to the door. By the end of the semester, Del could comfortably sit anywhere in the classroom. He was pleased with the results of his exposure program.

For the summer semester, Del enrolled in courses taught on the second and third floors. He decided to use the break between semesters to address his fears of being in the classrooms on these higher floors. The first challenge was to get up the stairs to the second and third floors. For this purpose, a different tactic seemed more efficient.

Del hired a psychology graduate student to be his helper. The student first walked with him up the stairs. This provided a sense of security if Del panicked. Next, the student followed thirty seconds behind Del, then one minute behind him, then two minutes, then not at all. Del repeated the same *lag-time* program going from the second to the third floors. Within a week, Del found he could walk on his own up to the third floor.

As an experiment, Del entered the second- and third-floor classrooms when they were empty. Starting with the second-floor room, he switched seats according to the card-sort plan. Then, he sat in every seat in the room (about thirty) for about a minute. He repeated this exercise on the third floor. He reported feeling bored with the redundancy. He also reported an absence of fear.

When he began his classes, he did so with trepidation. The presence of a professor and students in the classroom had a greater impact than he'd expected.

Del faced this issue by thinking through his fears of what others might think if they saw him panicking. He faced an incongruity: if different people can view the same situation in different ways, why would the members of his class see him only as he thought they would? Accepting that many of his classmates would likely not notice him even if he did panic and that, if the worst happened (if he panicked in the class and was unable to exit), he could still unconditionally accept his fallible self, he began to develop a different perspective.

A week after classes started, he reported that he could comfortably sit anywhere in either class. He got past a significant hurdle to finishing his degree.

Del's progress did not automatically generalize to other locations. In addition to his classroom entrapment fears, he continued to feel fearful about restaurants and concerts where he could not control his seating location. Additionally, he realized that crowd size at those locations was an important condition. The more people present, the greater his level of distress.

Del's second graded exposure experiment involved eating at restaurants. Whether the restaurant was formal or was a fast-food establishment didn't seem to matter to him. The real issues were how close his seat was to the door and how crowded the restaurant was.

Del picked fast-food restaurants to start graded exposure. He used the following card-sort ranking system:

Location Conditions	People Conditions	Proximity Conditions
1. Fast-food restaurant	1. Almost empty	1. Close to door
	2. Moderately crowded	2. Middle location
	3. Crowded	3. Farthest location

The least-worrisome condition was sitting close to the door when the restaurant was nearly empty. The most-worrisome condition was sitting in the farthest seat from the door when the restaurant was crowded. Interestingly, Del expressed no fear of going to the counter to order food. The counter was far from the door, but he believed that being on his feet made a difference. He could more easily escape. Otherwise, he had no explanation. But the fact of his easiness at the counter caused him to rethink his need to be close to the door.

Within three weeks of following graded exposure, Del stopped worrying about where he sat at the fast-food restaurant. He did feel greater apprehension when eating for the first time at a more formal restaurant. But he found the apprehension manageable and probably more related to eating in an unfamiliar place than to being unable to escape easily.

Use the following space to create your own card-sort ranking system for a parasitic fear:

YOUR CARD-SORT PROGRAM

Choose a fear that you want to address. Using Del's card-sort system as a model, list the location and proximity conditions that affect your fear. List these conditions in order of their intensity to create a graded ranking system.

Location Conditions	**Proximity Conditions**

LEARNING TO RELAX

You can use relaxation techniques to help you confront your fears. You might find that it helps to use a relaxation technique before you attempt exposure. Edmund Jacobson's muscular relaxation method involves tightening and loosening individual muscle groups until your entire body feels relaxed (Jacobson 1938). It takes about two weeks to master this method. For some types of anxiety, such as generalized anxiety, relaxation methods seem effective (Siev and Chambless 2007).

Here's how Jacobson's method works. First, you find a comfortable location to sit. When seated, you gradually tighten a muscle group for five seconds, hold the tension for five seconds, and then slowly release the tension over the next five seconds. You do this to produce some tension, but not to tighten your muscles as you would a drum. Most people have no physical difficulties with this form of relaxation, but if you have physical problems with stretching and straining muscle groups, you might want to try a different way to relax, such as deep-breathing exercises or visualizing pleasant and relaxing images.

A Relaxation Exercise

As a muscle relaxation exercise, try tightening your various muscle groups in the following order:

1. Hands: Tense by making fists. Relax by letting fists go loose.

2. Fingers: Tense by extending. Relax by letting your fingers go loose.

3. Biceps: Tense by making a muscle without making a fist. Relax by dropping your arm to the chair.

4. Triceps: Tense straightening your arms. Relax by letting your arms go loose and limp.

5. Shoulders: Tense by pulling shoulders back. Relax by letting them go back to normal. Repeat sequence by hunching the shoulders forward. Relax by letting them go loose and limp.

6. Neck: Tense by moving your head slowly to the right until you feel tension. Relax by returning neck to normal position. Repeat sequence by turning neck to the left. Repeat sequence again by dropping head slowly down toward your chest until you feel some tension.

7. Mouth: Tense by opening your mouth as far as possible. Relax by letting your mouth close.

8. Lips: Tense by pursing your lips as tightly as possible. Relax by letting them go loose and limp.

9. Tongue: Tense by extending your tongue as far as possible. Relax by letting it lie loose at the bottom of your mouth. Repeat the sequence by pulling your tongue back toward your throat. Repeat the sequence again by pressing your tongue to the roof of your mouth. Repeat the sequence again by pressing your tongue to the bottom of your mouth.

10. Eyes: Tense your eyes by opening them as wide as possible so that your brow furrows. Relax them. Repeat sequence by closing your eyes tight and then relaxing.

11. Back: Tense by pushing your body forward so that your back is arched. Relax.

12. Butt: Tense tightly. Relax.

13. Thighs: Tense by raising and extending your thighs without tensing your stomach. Relax by letting your thighs go loose and limp.

14. Lower legs: Tense your calves by pressing the balls of your feet into the floor or by pointing your toes. Relax by letting your feet go loose and limp. Then flex your feet back toward your shins. Relax.

15. Stomach: Tense by pulling in the stomach. Relax by letting it go loose and limp. Repeat by pushing the stomach out to make a "pot belly." Relax by letting it go loose and limp.

16. With all your muscle groups now limp and loose, breathe in for four seconds while thinking the word "calm." Hold your breath for five seconds while thinking the word "calm." Breathe out for five seconds while thinking the word "calm." Repeat this sequence three times.

By practicing this muscle relaxation sequence, your body and mind should feel relaxed. Eventually, you may find that just thinking the word "calm" can bring about a similar relaxing effect, for you will have begun to associate this word with relaxation.

Pairing Relaxation with Uncomfortable Imagery

As part of a graduated exposure, you can look at various images of feared objects. Say you are afraid of snakes. Before encountering a live snake, you might look at images of harmless snakes. You could adapt your card-sort method to include images of feared objects on index cards. As with any graduated exposure, you would start with viewing the least-fear-provoking images and work your way up to viewing the most-feared images.

To lower your anxiety, you can pair a relaxation technique with viewing images of feared objects. If you use the Jacobson relaxation method, first assure yourself that you can deeply relax yourself before visualizing situations presented through the card-sort method. Partial relaxation can void the exposure plan.

As an extension to the pairing of muscle relaxation with fear images, you can add this action step. Here is the process:

1. Put yourself into a state of deep relaxation.

2. Pair relaxation with the image on the card you are working on from your card-sort list. When you feel relaxed with this pair, add a third step.

3. Relax yourself and then expose yourself to the condition described on the card.

4. Following a successful relaxation-exposure experience, move to the next step in this relaxation-imagery-action process.

Admittedly, graduated exposure can be a tedious. That's because graduated exposure involves taking many small steps for progressive mastery over a specific fear. However, when you consider that overcoming a phobia involves calming the amygdala, and the amygdala is a primitive force, it's no wonder that training that part of the brain generally takes time.

Watch Your Breathing

In the foreword, psychologist Jon Carlson describes an aboriginal belly-breathing technique that seems to send calming signals to the brain. It's worth reviewing: The technique involves breathing so that your belly expands as you breathe in and contracts when you breathe out. The theory is that you can't be both anxious and calm at the same time. The belly-breathing method can produce calm.

As an experiment, you can pair belly breathing (or diaphragmatic breathing) with viewing images of feared objects. Do two minutes of belly breathing. In the first minute, you attend to your breathing by breathing in and out for about a minute. Then, over the next minute, as you breathe from your belly, you attend to both the feared image and to your belly breathing. See what results. Hopefully, this process will help defuse tension that can be evoked by fear images. If so, you can use it as an aid in training your brain to respond differently to feared images and situations.

As an alternate breathing method, you can consciously regulate your breathing through your belly by taking in a full breath in a two-second interval. Hold your breath for two seconds. Exhale all your breath in the next two seconds. Don't breathe in for another two seconds. Repeat the sequence eight times within a minute. Again, this method can be used in combination with viewing feared images. Follow this breathing sequence for the next minute while viewing a feared image. When you feel relaxed with the image in mind, take a five-minute break and move on to the next image in your card-sort sequence.

As a rule of thumb, limit your exposure to two images per sitting. Take a two-day break between exposure sessions. This gives you time to digest the change. However, you can also use your response to the breathing and imagery experiment to determine appropriate timing and pacing for this exercise.

Some fear situations don't require a comprehensive card-sort plan. You can use the above muscle relaxation or breathing exercises immediately before entering a situation where you'd normally feel mildly to moderately tense. By first using a muscle relaxation or breathing method, you may recalibrate your body so that you feel less apprehensive. Feeling less apprehensive, you may be emotionally prepared to face your fear and start rendering it moot.

MAKING PROGRESS WITH DESENSITIZATION

As you begin to confront your fears through exposure, you will have questions about how long the process will take, how fast to pace yourself, and what to do when you're done.

Desensitization takes as long as it takes. It may be surprisingly quick. But even if the process seems tedious and takes longer than you'd like, the key is to stick with it. Exposure works. How fast can you pace yourself? If you are making progress, keep to one or two levels per session. Go two days between sessions. Expect some setbacks. When they occur, drop down a level. Repeat the process. Then return to the next level in the sequence.

What do you do after you've completed your desensitization program? Test its effectiveness by shifting from imagery to behavior. Without application, the desensitization process can seem like an academic exercise.

KEY IDEAS AND ACTION PLAN

What key ideas from this chapter can you use to rid yourself of your parasitic anxieties and fears? What's your action plan? Write it down. Test it out. Record what happened.

Key Ideas

1.

2.

3.

Action Plan

1.

2.

3.

Results from Actions Taken

1.

2.

3.

POSTSCRIPT

Like hundreds of millions of others, you may be inclined to put off facing unwanted tension until another day or time. Welcome to the world of procrastination. This complex process can bedevil your best intentions.

If you find yourself in a procrastination trap, chapter 10 can help you get on with resolving your challenging and emotionally charged parasitic problems.

Breaking the Procrastination-Fear Connection

Do you feel walled in by your anxieties and fears? Do you play it safe and duck risks because you fear failing? Do you miss out on close relationships because you are afraid to express your feelings? If you are like most people, you have at least one personal area in your life—probably more—where you procrastinate and then miss out on valuable life experiences. This is a form of *lifestyle procrastination*, or a habit of putting off a beneficial behavior.

When most people think of procrastination, they think of putting off certain obligations or filing tax forms at the eleventh hour. Procrastination is also commonly seen in academic settings among students who wait until the last minute to study for a test. But these delays are the tip of the procrastination iceberg. Putting off personally relevant activities is often the more serious form of procrastination. For example, practically everyone has put off at least one important life goal, such as quitting smoking or overcoming a parasitic fear.

Like parasitic anxieties and fears, procrastination is a redundant process. It is probably the most common human foible and fault. And this brings us to the timeless question: why do normally intelligent people often repeat patterns that can cause them harm? Can they not see what is happening?

Procrastination explains why so many continue to follow patterns that they swear they want to change. You have a solution for addressing your anxieties and fears. You put off the solution. You continue to experience fear as a lifestyle habit. That's a sad situation. But it is one that you can learn to change through education and action.

In this chapter, you'll learn how to recognize and act against a procrastination-anxiety-fear connection. There is a bonus for this learning. You can apply this procrastination technology to other areas of your life where fear is not a factor and where procrastination is a hindrance. If you want extra help reducing procrastination in this and other areas of your life, you can also refer to *The Procrastination Workbook* (see Suggested Reading).

THE DOUBLE-WHAMMY EFFECT

When procrastination coexists with anxiety, you have a double-whammy effect: the anticipated fearful situation and a habit of putting off facing what you fear. Here is some information about the procrastination phase of the process:

What is procrastination? Procrastination is an automatic habit leading to a needless delay of a timely, relevant activity until another day or time. In brief, you procrastinate when you (1) habitually put off a priority with a fixed deadline or (2) needlessly delay a self-development action that can affect your health, happiness, effectiveness, relationships, sense of worth, or other important personal state. This complex, cognitive, emotive, and behavioral habit process always involves substituting something less timely or important for the delayed activity. So you read a magazine rather than go to a party where you anticipate feeling socially uncomfortable. Procrastination practically always includes some form of procrastination thinking, such as "I don't want to," "not right now," or "I'll get to it later."

What can kick procrastination into gear and keep it going? Procrastination starts with an anticipation. You face a priority activity that you initially perceive as uncomfortable. (You may associate a new activity with one that you have put off before and delay the new activity because of memories you associate with the prior task.) You *evaluate* (judge, interpret, define) this timely activity as uncomfortable, inconvenient, threatening, tedious, boring, or parasitically frightening. When you avoid discomfort or fear, you feel relief from this retreat. You are likely to repeat what you did to obtain relief.

What is the connection between procrastination and parasitic anxieties and fears? Parasitic anxieties and fears and procrastination share a common feature: an impulsive reaction to avoid discomfort. Fear involves unpleasant sensations that trigger escape impulses. You are uncomfortable "making small talk." You find a way to excuse yourself when an acquaintance approaches you. Rather than learn the art of conversation, you procrastinate on practicing conversation skills.

Why might this connection persist? When a fearsome situation looms, you may not think about your thinking. You have a report to write that is due in five days. You feel awkward about the writing task. You believe you'll botch the job and get criticized. Instead of examining your fearful thinking, you associate the activity with discomfort. You retreat. You are likely to miss a significant self-observant step in the process: what you tell yourself about the situation you're avoiding and about the emotion that you feel. By taking a metacognitive approach—thinking about your thinking—you can identify your procrastination thinking, debunk it, and refocus your attention on what you want to accomplish. This refocusing increases your chances for following through on what is constructive to do.

SIMPLE AND COMPLEX PROCRASTINATION

Procrastination falls into simple and complex categories with many degrees in between. *Simple procrastination* means putting off relevant and timely short-term tasks when you don't want to experience inconvenience or discomfort. You have a warranty form to complete for your new lawn mower. You decide you don't want to waste your time doing it now. You tell yourself you'll sit down and fill it out later.

As an alternative, you then pull weeds from your garden. You keep finding reasons to repeat the delay. Could you quickly finish the form? Sure. But you don't like to fill out forms. You brush the task aside by distracting yourself through excuses and diversionary activities. You continue to engage yourself in less pressing activities.

Complex procrastination involves a combination of procrastination and coexisting conditions such as perfectionism, depression, anxiety, and self-doubt. Perfectionism, for example, can tie to a need for certainty, along with self-doubts, indecision, hesitation, and fears of failure, all of which gives rise to procrastination.

If your procrastination is of the complex variety, it's getting in the way of your taking corrective actions against your major parasitic anxieties or fears. You need to cut through this barrier to begin applying solutions to both basic parasitic fears and coexisting conditions. Recognizing how your procrastination habit is organized will put you in a better position to confront your fears.

A PROCRASTINATION HABIT PROCESS

Procrastination involves a pattern of thoughts, emotions, and behaviors where you turn a proximity issue into a time-avoidance matter. As when you face a parasitic fear and retreat out of fear, with procrastination you face discomfort and retreat. However, a procrastination form of retreat is typically more complex.

What follows is an example of procrastination in reaction to a parasitic fear of an upcoming test:

1. You feel apprehensive about studying for a test, for you expect the process to prove difficult.

2. You escalate your apprehension by telling yourself that you could fail and failure can ruin your future. As these thoughts stampede through your mind, your tension intensifies.

3. You ease the tension by telling yourself that you'll study tomorrow when you feel rested and can think clearly. Then, when tomorrow comes, you make up another excuse to delay.

4. You seamlessly shift your attention to a substitute activity, such as daydreaming, reading, nibbling starchy foods, watching TV, playing video games, communicating through computer chat rooms—anything but working at the uncomfortable task.

5. You rationalize that you work better under pressure.

6. As time runs out, you start studying and do enough to pass the test.

7. You swear you won't put yourself through this trauma again.

8. When the next time comes, you repeat the habit of delay.

When you veer from the task you want to avoid, you may experience relief in the short run. It is typically costly in the long run, however. When you focus on gaining relief, you can take hours avoiding what may take several minutes to do. You can repeat this hesitation waltz and continue to stress yourself. That's the procrastination paradox: the benefits of avoiding mild discomfort are often offset by long-term stress and fewer achievements.

PROCRASTINATION DIVERSIONS

You may not procrastinate in the same way when it comes to addressing different anxieties and fears. But whatever form your procrastination takes, you'll engage in diversionary processes. Diversions include sidetracking yourself with behavioral, mental, and emotional distractions.

What is a behavioral diversion? When you procrastinate, you always substitute something less timely and relevant for what you put off. These substitutions are behavioral diversions, such as bickering with your mate, watching television, or visiting friends. It's amazing how many people don't realize that they are procrastinating when, in lieu of addressing a problem, they shop. A special form of a behavioral diversion is the *rotating procrastination pattern*. You start by dealing with one fear. Then you shift to another one before the first is resolved. Then you go on to a third before the second is resolved. And so on. This pattern can lead to feeling defeated.

What is a mental diversion? A mental diversion is something you tell yourself to justify sidetracking yourself. For example, when you think that tomorrow is a better time to face the fear, you've engaged the *mañana ploy*. You may feel good for a moment: you made a decision to finish at a future time. But when later comes, you repeat the pattern. We humans can be quite creative in what we tell ourselves to justify needless delays: you tell yourself that you'll face a fear that you know is parasitic, but only after you've researched the scientific literature to find the best way to address your fear. Then you put off doing the research. This is the *contingency mañana ploy*. You make dealing with your fear dependent upon doing something else first; then you put off the conditional task. The contingency mañana ploy may appear in many guises: you avoid facing, say, a social fear, until you look thinner, have plastic surgery, or lose twenty pounds. Then you procrastinate on completing the contingencies.

What is an emotional diversion? Emotional diversions are a special form of a contingency mañana ploy, but they have an emotional twist. It goes something like this: you must feel inspired or emotionally ready before acting to do something unpleasant. But there is a fallacy in this thinking: why would anyone want to use moments of inspiration to do uninspiring things? Waiting for inspiration typically leads to delays and frenzied actions to catch up as time runs out.

This diversionary process suggests that you construct procrastination thinking and avoidance in a more or less automatic way. It's a stealthlike process you can trigger as easily as you can tie your shoes. This is not a thoughtless process, however. Excuse-making and diversionary behaviors are constructed. What is automatic is the tendency to construct excuses and divert attention.

RECOGNIZING AND COUNTERING DIVERSIONS

If you can construct procrastination thoughts and behaviors, you can also construct ways to change the pattern. Using fear of failure as an example, the following diversion recognition and action chart shows how to start curbing a parasitic fear:

A DIVERSION RECOGNITION AND ACTION CHART

Situation: Fear of failing an upcoming test and thereby delaying studying

Dimensions	Procrastination Diversions	Alternative Goal	Action Plan	Results
Behavioral	Attend party.	Use party time to study.	Announce to your friends that you intend to study.	Friends support your decision.
Mental	Tell yourself that you'll feel more relaxed and ready to study after attending party.	Focus on the benefits of having time to study.	Accept that studying can feel frustrating and that frustration is a normal part of formalized education.	Greater tolerance for frustration. Progress with studying.
Emotional	Tell yourself that you have to be in the right mood to study.	Consider the idea that motivation can follow action.	Accept that you don't need to feel inspired to do what you consider uninspiring but is still instrumental to achieving the goal of passing a test.	Proceed to study as you would approach other work tasks that involve time and concentration.

Now, it is your turn to take action.

YOUR DIVERSION RECOGNITION
AND ACTION CHART

Describe a situation in which you procrastinate. Write down your behavioral, mental, and emotional diversions. Then come up with alternative goals and action plans. After taking action, describe the results.

Situation: _____

Dimensions	Procrastination Diversions	Alternative Goal	Action Plan	Results
Behavioral				
Mental				
Emotional				

MEETING SCHEDULES

We live by the calendar and the clock. In an organized society, we have due dates for social responsibilities. We file taxes on or before April 15. Libraries have due dates for returning books.

When you live by the calendar and the clock, you have a concrete way to measure punctuality and delays. You have a choice as to whether you'll follow the schedule or not. But when it comes to socially legislated or contract deadlines, lateness carries penalties. The penalties are relative to the importance of the subject and the deadline.

When you consider tackling a self-development activity such as overcoming a parasitic fear, you can set objectives and deadlines for yourself. Sure, you have a choice as to whether you will commit to make a change. Taking action is a choice. But choosing not to take action carries penalties as well.

Suppose you experience agoraphobia and fear leaving your residence. You panic when you anticipate going outside to get the newspaper. You center your life around avoiding going outside. You also procrastinate on executing solutions to your agoraphobia because of the discomfort you associate with those solutions.

Avoidance and delays in personal development will normally carry unintended consequences, such as repeating the pain of living with agoraphobia and the secondary distresses of feeling helpless and discouraged. But delaying personal development can also have social implications. If you fear to exit your abode unless accompanied by your mate, you may control your mate's activities in a way that can cause a disruption in a valued relationship. Here, responsibly addressing procrastination can prove both personally and socially beneficial.

CHANGE INVOLVES MORE THAN A DECISION

There are many ways to overcome procrastination. The most obvious is to "just do it." This is the advice that you or anyone else can give. But that advice rarely helps when you face something that you don't feel like doing or that you fear.

Here's one way to visualize this process. Pretend you are on a horse. The horse is like the powerful primitive brain that goes for pleasure and avoids pain. The horse's normal inclination is to follow the path of least resistance. When the horse is in control, it goes where it wants.

What happens when you take the reins and direct the horse in the direction of facing a fear? At first you may experience a strong resistance. The horse tries to bolt. But you grip the reins. You channel the horse's energy and strength into going the direction you've decided is best.

When you take charge of your more primitive impulse, you guide your own destiny. This takes mental effort. But by using your higher mental powers to guide your destiny, you are less likely to be carried off by a frightened horse.

There are many ways to grab the reins. For example, psychologist John Dollard (1942) suggested that "those who know how to think and plan use fear as a constructive force. When fear comes, they stop (don't run) and think" (1).

What's going on when the horse takes charge? Your higher mental processes usually justify the horse's reactions.

To start grabbing hold of the reins, examine the horse's perspective. By listening to your self-talk, you can gain knowledge about the words you use to describe an experience that you fear. Some self-talk can invite clarifying questions: "I will look like a fool" or "this proves I'm a nothing." "Why?" you may ask yourself.

"Because" clarifications—asking yourself why you tell yourself these things—can help expose flaws in your thinking and open opportunities for decreasing tension when fearful exaggerations characterize your main flow of thought. The following chart illustrates how to use "because" clarifications to help bring about a change in perspective from fearful thinking to more realistic and acceptant thinking.

Frightening Phrases	"Because" Clarification	Alternative Perspective
"I will look like a fool."	"Because I think I will. Because I think I know what others will think before they think. Because I overestimate my ability to predict."	Suspend judgment until there is a reason to render one.
"This proves I'm a nothing."	"Because I think that an anticipation of looking foolish is the same as being a fool. Because I'm certain that I can do no better than err. Because I place too much confidence in a negative overgeneralization."	Avoid being swamped by negative overgeneralized thinking.

Now it's your turn to apply the "because" clarification to your own frightening self-talk, seek an alternative perspective, and guide the horse to a better pasture.

Frightening Phrases	"Because" Clarification	Alternative Perspective

A FALSE LOSS OF FREEDOM

When a valued freedom or privilege is threatened or interrupted, most people will act to preserve the privilege. In social psychology, this is called *reactance*.

A social psychology theory of reactance is that people who have privileges and freedoms will resent attempts by others to place limits on such freedoms. If your employer eliminated your coffee break, you would likely resist the change. You may not own a firearm, but if the government threatened to repeal the Second Amendment, you might be up in arms against the loss of this right. You are in the middle of solving a complex problem, and your mate insists that you help move a piece of furniture right now. You are likely to experience both reactance and frustration over the interruption.

Reactance is an understandable response to an arbitrary threat to a privilege. But what happens when the privilege you currently embrace is dysfunctional? Because you enjoy certain fattening foods, you might resent a physician's recommendation to lose weight by cutting down on what you find tasty to eat. Or you drink too much but resent losing the use of a beverage you claim relaxes you. Besides that, your social life is at the local bar. Or you don't want to be hassled by solutions to overcome a fear of flying; you tell yourself this effort will waste the time you could spend golfing.

One way to decide if procrastination includes reactance is by comparing the benefits of staying with the familiar pattern of not facing a fear with the benefits of addressing the fear. Here you match the short- and long-term benefits of following through on dealing with a fear against the short- and long-term benefits of delaying follow-through. Doing so serves a second purpose. This type of reflective exercise can slow a reactance impulse. More importantly, through this process, you can more clearly see the tradeoffs: the privileges you gain through making a change may exceed the privileges you lose.

The following cost-benefit chart gives a framework for comparing the short- and long-term advantages and disadvantages of reactance procrastination with the short- and long-term advantages and disadvantages of leaving a comfort zone to make a change. The example is the fear of going to the dentist:

A REACTANCE-PROCRASTINATION COST-BENEFIT CHART

Situation: Reactance about disrupting a comfortable routine to address a dental fear associated with fear of needles, suction sounds, the whirring sound of a drill, pain, and a sense of lack of control over the procedures

Action	Short-Term Advantages	Short-Term Disadvantages	Long-Term Advantages	Long-Term Disadvantages
Avoid fear	Put off discomfort and inconvenience.	Reinforces avoidance through specious rewards. Expends time avoiding discomfort that could be used to address the fear.	Maintenance of the short-term benefits associated with specious rewards.	Risking dental diseases that may have been prevented. Increased dental care costs. Continuation of the fear.
Face fear	Begin process of overcoming fear. This starts a process in motion for developing fear-prevention skills.	Experience discomfort and urges to procrastinate.	Get necessary dental work done. Experience probable increase in self-efficacy that comes from translating intention to action.	Unless experiencing discomfort in the service of overcoming a fear and promoting health is a disadvantage, there are no meaningful disadvantages.

Now, it is your turn to do a cost-benefit analysis of continuing with a procrastination-fear connection, in which you compare a short-term specious gain with a longer term health-and-happiness advantage.

YOUR REACTANCE-PROCRASTINATION
COST-BENEFIT CHART

Describe your situation and then compare the advantages and disadvantages of avoiding what you fear with the advantages and disadvantages of facing it.

Situation: _____

Action	Short-Term Advantages	Short-Term Disadvantages	Long-Term Advantages	Long-Term Disadvantages
Avoid fear				
Face fear				

REWARDS THAT REINFORCE PROCRASTINATION

Why does procrastination persist despite poor long-term results? There are many reasons. Procrastination involves inertia. This is the tendency to do nothing or to remain unchanged. You also can get a temporary payoff for procrastinating.

In *The Expression of Emotions in Man and Animals*, Charles Darwin's first principle of expressive actions is that behaviors (expressions) followed by relief or gratification are repeated and become automatic and habitual (Darwin 1965). A decision to delay doing something you view as uncomfortable typically brings a feeling of relief. In short, you can condition yourself to procrastinate by seeking short-term relief.

If going for immediate gratification means that it is more likely that you'll procrastinate, and you want to stop doing this to yourself, what are your choices? You can act now to change the results of procrastination and reshape that part of your future that links to the procrastination-fear connection. The choice is yours.

If you like the relief that comes from making procrastination decisions, but don't like the future results of the decision, you can apply the *Premack principle*. The principle is simple. You can make a less desirable action more attractive if taking that action leads to something you want. You follow up your anti-procrastination actions with what you'd normally do to divert from your priority. For example, you play a video game to avoid certain actions and tensions. The game gives you relief from tension. But what if you made playing the video game a reward for taking steps to face your fear? Instead of using the game as a diversion, you'd use it as a reward for taking a purposeful action. The following action plan describes this process:

NEW REWARD APPROACH

Parasitic fear situation: Fear of going to the dentist

Avoidance Activity	New Goal	Steps to Achieve Goal
Decide not to think about the situation now and instead play video games.	Address the fear of going to the dentist and complete the task of decreasing your fear's frequency, intensity, and durability.	1. Compare the immediate advantages of playing video games with the potential future hassles of procrastinating in addressing fear. 2. Think beyond the task to future benefits of feeling free from the fear and having a healthier set of teeth. 3. Look for practical ways to dispense with the fear, such as having an initial consultation with a dentist to get information about your dental health and to desensitize yourself to the surroundings. 4. Take action steps to address the fear: learn about dentists that specialize in dental fears; call and make an appointment. 5. Follow the above tasks with playing a video game for a set amount of time, such as an hour.

Now, it is your turn to fill in the blanks and follow through on what is useful and important to do.

YOUR NEW REWARD APPROACH

Describe your situation and define your action plan by setting a goal and detailing the steps you need to take to achieve it.

Parasitic fear situation: _____

Avoidance Activity	New Goal	Steps to Achieve Goal

HOW TO BREAK A PROCRASTINATION-FEAR HABIT

What can you do about a procrastination-fear habit? By working to recognize procrastination urges, tolerating the urge to divert yourself, and redirecting your efforts toward addressing what you fear to do, you can make visible progress.

The following ten-point program suggests a direction:

1. When you feel tempted to procrastinate, use the temptation as a signal to evoke your self-observant skills.

2. Rather than retreat from discomfort, accept the reality that a prime solution for both procrastination and fear includes facing and tolerating discomfort.

3. Keep a procrastination log to gather information that you can use for self-observant purposes. In the log, describe your parasitic anxiety situation, procrastination thinking, and how you are feeling. (By evaluating the contents of your procrastination log, you can uncover the procrastination-avoidance connection.)

4. Do a short- and long-term cost-benefit analysis to assure yourself that a personal change to address the parasitic impediment is truly meaningful to do.

5. Avoid diversionary actions. (If you didn't divert your attention away from a timely and relevant activity, you would not be procrastinating.)

6. Design a metacognitive system for positive change. (Remember, this involves several steps: Think about your thinking, set a mission, establish goals, make a plan, organize your resources, execute the plan, review the results, and make revisions.)

7. Make a written contract with yourself. The contract establishes what you'll do, when you'll do it, the rewards for following through, and a penalty for not following through. Set a time. Fix a reward that is equal to the task.

8. Use self-instructions to guide your actions. Spell out the steps for how you are going to arrive at the desired result. Walk yourself through the paces in executing the plan.

9. Take a bits-and-pieces approach. Most challenges can be broken down into bits and pieces. Even the most complex challenges have a simple beginning. What is the most basic action that you can take first? Second?

10. Follow a five-minute drill. Once you've decided on the first step, commit five minutes to taking it. At the end of that five minutes, decide if you'll commit five minutes more, and so on until you've progressed through living through the discomfort associated with taking that step. Then move on to the next step, using the same five-minute plan.

By directly facing the parasitic procrastination-fear connection, you will help yourself build tolerance for discomfort. This tolerance boosts your chances of simultaneously decreasing procrastination and fear.

You can change parasitic procrastination anxiety-and-fear thinking by examining and questioning both the process and its results. As a by-product of changing the process, you can change the results.

THE PROCRASTINATION ENDGAME

The procrastination endgame involves grinding it out to produce new results by using your intelligence, ingenuity, and will to overcome a complex procrastination combination.

Acceptance of this grind-it-out reality can enable you to do the following:

1. Strengthen both a value and capability for executing your responsibilities efficiently and effectively.

2. Develop maturity of thought through competent action.

3. Avoid needless stress and behavioral consequences that can come from excessive delay.

4. Create more free time for pleasurable pursuits.

5. Gain advantages that come from developing a reputation as an effective person.

6. Experience self-confidence that comes from directing your actions to achieve purposeful and positive results.

7. Boost your tolerance for frustration as a buffer against needless distresses.

By resigning yourself to the fact that uncomfortable priorities require effort, you are less likely to delude yourself with "later is better" procrastination thinking. You can discover that unpleasant avoidance feelings ebb as you live through them. You can teach yourself to create a positive momentum toward achieving reduced stress, more accomplishments, and greater joy in living. Remember: doing gets it done!

KEY IDEAS AND ACTION PLAN

What key ideas from this chapter can you use to rid yourself of your parasitic anxieties and fears? What's your action plan? Write it down. Test it out. Record what happened.

Key Ideas

1.

2.

3.

Action Plan

1.

2.

3.

Results from Actions Taken

1.

2.

3.

POSTSCRIPT

Using your intelligence, ingenuity, and will, you can reshape that part of your future that would otherwise be clouded with parasitic fears. Severing the connection between procrastination and fear can begin with a look at how future results depend on your present actions: starting corrective actions now means that you won't have to start them later. When you don't procrastinate on executing solutions for overcoming procrastination about addressing your fears, you've taken an important step to liberate yourself from fear.

CHAPTER 11

Overcoming Mixed Anxiety and Depression

Anxiety and depression often overlap (Barlow and Campbell 2000). High levels of these combined sources of distress are more than painful. They are fatiguing. But depression seems the more serious of the two in its contribution to an overall sense of distress (Mayszczak et al. 2006).

When anxiety and depression play off each other, they make for a roller-coaster ride with ups and downs and little in between. With mixed anxiety and depression, you will go from feeling normal to feeling frazzled to feeling down. You sometimes feel overwhelmed with worries and troubles. At the extreme, you can feel immobilized by anxious and depressed moods that twist together.

You can act to overcome parasitic anxiety and depression, and reduce the risk of continuing to experience these problems. This chapter will begin with a brief history of depression. It will then look into the pits of depression and explore ways to address a core thought present in both anxiety and depression: powerlessness thinking. To help lift a mixed burden of anxiety and depression, a PURRRRS plan follows that describes how to disable powerlessness thinking.

A BRIEF HISTORY OF DEPRESSION

The history of depression reaches back to ancient times. The ancient Egyptians saw that depression was serious. Their solution was dance, diet, and travel. The early Greek physician Hippocrates prescribed diet and exercise as the first line of defense against depression. If this didn't work, he tried "bleeding." In the Middle Ages, the Eastern Orthodox Church used rational methods to fix wrong thinking, which they saw as the root of depression. In the seventeenth century, Robert Burton wrote a 1,500-page book about depression and its cures (Burton 2001). Many with depression reportedly read and reread the work. Burton's book describes many techniques to cope with depression that we use today, including exercise.

Depression is still with us. By the year 2020, depression may be the second most frequent disability behind coronary heart disease (Murray and Lopez 1996). But at present, anxiety is the most common form of needless human misery.

THE PITS OF DEPRESSION

You may say you feel "depressed" if you are having a bad day, but this expression is probably more descriptive of the moment. Depression is more than a down mood, sadness, or feeling let down. Depression is a process.

What makes for a serious depression? The signature of a serious depression is an ongoing melancholic or depressed mood. But there is more to serious depression than feeling down. Depression feels immobilizing. Living with persistent downheartedness can feel as if you are viewing life from behind the bars of a dark dungeon. But even milder forms of depressions are painful.

What triggers depression? Depression can come out of the blue. It can follow insomnia. But depression more commonly starts with a traumatic happening. Traumas come in different forms. A major setback, such as an uninvited divorce, death, betrayal, or job loss, can start the cascade. You can overextend yourself for a number of years, and depression slows you down. But depression can also follow patterns of negative thinking, frustrations from unrealistic expectations, and anxiety. Those with histories of sexual, physical, or psychological abuse are at heightened risk for depression. Vulnerability plus situation plus perception are a potent depression-risk threesome.

What are the physical signs of depression? Some depressions have distinct biological features, such as sleep and appetite problems, fatigue, headaches, gastrointestinal discomfort, losses of concentration, and loss of pleasure. When only physical symptoms of depression are present, these are uncomplicated depressions. But uncomplicated depressions are relatively rare. More often, depression coexists with anxiety, panic, anger, perfectionism, and other unpleasant emotional states.

What are some psychological signs of depression? Depression practically always includes depressive thinking (Knaus 2006). Aaron Beck, the founder of cognitive therapy, describes what he views as a triad of depressing beliefs: distorted negative beliefs about the self, experience, and the future (Beck 1976). If you believe you are helpless and inept, you'll filter your experience through this belief system. You may view yourself as "stupid" or as a "loser." When you expect negativity in your experiences, you are likely to feel what you expect. You'll search for what is wrong. You are prone to create crises by magnifying minutiae. In looking toward the future, you are apt to think pessimistically, "My god, will this never end?" Your future looks gloomy. Beck's theory of depression has its share of gaps and holes. However, Beck's practice of educating people about depression and teaching them how to change distorted depressive thinking helps reduce depression and prevent it from coming back.

Do cognitive techniques for addressing depression help reduce depression? Yes. By developing educated reasoning skills, you can begin to defuse depressive thinking. The relief that comes from debunking depressive thinking can be measured through brain-imaging techniques. Depression is less likely to come back after you've developed educated reasoning skills directed toward challenging depressive thinking.

POWERLESSNESS THINKING

Sadness, grief, and anxiety come with normal living. When losing a cherished friend brings sadness and you also have anxiety over financial troubles, this double effect of sadness and concern is understandable. Add powerlessness thinking to the mix, and your misery index rises.

Powerlessness thinking is the belief that you have no control over yourself or the events around you. If you believe this is so, you'll feel vulnerable. If you think you can't act, you won't act. But there's a difference between can't and won't. It's not that you can't do it but that you won't do it, because you think you can't. There is an old Chinese proverb that captures this distinction: "You can't prevent the birds of sorrow from flying over your head, but you can prevent them from building nests in your hair."

Powerlessness thinking in anxiety and depression can twist together. With anxiety, you see yourself in a powerless position without control. In a depressed state of mind, you may think there is nothing you can do to change your fate. The opportunity in both cases is to uncover parasitic forms of powerlessness thinking and challenge them.

When depressed, powerlessness thinking can translate into hopelessness. In this state of mind, bad situations become worse. Your future looks gloomy. You fear you'll stay miserable forever. You have no appealing solution. You are also likely to feel fatigued and sluggish, and these sensations can give greater credibility to powerlessness thoughts.

With parasitic anxieties and fears, powerlessness thinking seems to have both the opposite and a similar effect to that experienced with depression. Powerlessness thinking in anxiety links to excitability and inhibition. You feel threatened. You see yourself as incapable of defending yourself. You feel tense or agitated. You may think, "I've got to avoid this situation, but I can't."

Examining Powerlessness Thinking

If joint parasitic anxieties and depression keep coming back, you might believe that you can't change. And if you feel powerless, you can fall into the trap that the founder of individual psychology Alfred Adler (1927) observed: "A person does not change his behavior pattern but turns, and twists, and distorts his experiences until they fit it" (11). But a ride on the anxiety and depression roller coaster may not be the way you are, but rather the way you think and feel at that moment.

Does being in a powerless position automatically trigger powerlessness thinking? Powerlessness thinking is an attitude of mind that reflects the meaning you give to a situation. Think you can't cope, and you've entered the realm of powerlessness thinking. Being in a powerless position does not necessarily lead to powerlessness thinking. Say you're a great basketball fan. You'd like to be a professional basketball player. Unfortunately, your five-foot-two-inch height and low level of athletic ability puts you in a noncompetitive position. You don't have to brood over that. Rather, you can undertake challenges that fall within your talents. Similarly, you can't stop a volcanic eruption. If you upset yourself thinking that you should be able to stop a river of lava, that's magical thinking. Similarly, you are powerless to change what has already happened in your life. You can't travel back in time and change your past. But you can shape your present to promote a brighter future. A cancer victim is powerless to will away cancer but can still take steps to get the best treatment possible. You can't change the fact that you sometimes think powerlessness thoughts. But you can educate your reason to challenge those thoughts.

When is powerlessness thinking legitimate in depression? Normal human suffering exists. The loss of a child, job, or relationship is as it is. You're powerless to change what is. A regretful sense of acceptance may be the best that you can do to offset double troubles of distress. In time, you can turn the jolt of a loss into a sad remembrance. But view yourself as overwhelmed and powerless to stop feeling depressed, and this double trouble can boost your chances for feeling psychologically depressed. Fortunately, you can change both powerlessness thinking and depressive thinking.

Why do many put off dealing with their joint anxiety and depression? Having solutions available and using them can be two different matters. You may define some profitable solutions as too difficult because they involve experiencing discomfort. When anxious, you may procrastinate on testing promising solutions that involve partially engaging in what you dread. When depressed, you may succumb to the inertial pressures of the mood. Even if you had an ironclad guarantee that you could set yourself free, you still might not act. When powerlessness thinking dominates, you may not want to try. But thinking you are powerless doesn't make it so.

Can casting blame activate powerlessness thinking in anxiety and depression? You can feel powerless over your emotions when you believe you are under the thumb of outside forces that you can't control: "Jack made me mad." "Office politics disturb me." If Jack makes you mad and you can't control Jack, what can you do? If you disturb yourself over office politics, and you can't wipe out the politics, what are your other choices? You can also blame yourself: "If I were a better wife, my husband wouldn't be an abusive drunk." Unless you have a large military to enforce your will, you probably cannot make others unfailingly act as you wish. But you are not powerless over these thoughts. You can put yourself into the driver's seat by owning responsibility for your part of the problem. What do you tell yourself about Jack's behavior that evokes anger? What do you believe about office politics that feels disturbing?

You can neutralize groundless powerlessness beliefs by accepting reality and developing emotional tolerance for that reality. If you can accept what you don't like, you won't make something bad seem worse.

Because it represents a choice, acceptance is a form of control. If you can choose acceptance, you can't be powerless! By tolerating—but continuing to dislike—the sensations of anxiety and depression, the chances are you can avoid succumbing to powerlessness thinking. This can feel delightful compared to the alternative.

The following PURRRRS plan puts the spotlight on powerlessness thinking.

PURRRRS FOR POWERLESSNESS THINKING

Target: Powerlessness thinking with mixed anxiety and depression

PURRRRS	Actions
Pause: Stop and prepare for action.	If you feel powerless to change, take time out. Gear up to problem solve. Get out a pad of paper and pencil. Pick up your tape recorder. Load your word processor. Take whatever preliminary steps you can to prepare to meet the powerlessness-thinking challenge.
Use: Apply your will and other resources to resist impulses to get self-absorbed and sidetrack yourself.	Put yourself into a self-observant problem-solving mindset. The problem, in this case, is powerlessness thinking. Write out your thoughts. If you prefer a tape recorder, record your thoughts. In short, create a thought record that you can evaluate.
Reflect: Think about what is happening.	If you find yourself worrying, in a down mood, and distressed, look at your recorded thoughts. Listen to your inner response. Think about your thinking. What parts are assumptions? What parts are overgeneralizations? Do you tell yourself that you are trapped and can do nothing? If so, what does this mean? Does this translate into a core belief that you are powerless to change? If so, then move on to reasoning it out.
Reason: Think it through.	Once you've identified powerlessness thinking as a core factor in your mixed anxiety and depression, look for exceptions to this form of thinking. Have you ever thought of yourself as powerless and then found something you could do to make a difference? Is it possible to accept reality, even though you may not like it? Choosing acceptance is an assertion of power. Powerlessness thinking can surface in any parasitic threat situation. In situations when powerlessness thinking is your default response, you may believe that this thinking is realistic. But if reality is created by thoughts, what if you have *conflicting cognitions*? These are two contradictory thoughts about the same situation. For example, you may think that you are powerless and also think that you have opportunities for change. The fact that you can change your thinking suggests that you are not powerless over your thoughts. For example, what is the weakest point in your powerlessness argument? Can you change that? If so, how can you be powerless?
Respond: Put yourself through the paces of change.	What steps can you take now to deal with powerlessness thinking? For example, can you act to change your thinking through doing an ABCDE analysis? What step do you take first? Second?

Revise: Review your process and make adjustments when results suggest trying another way.	What if you devise a good plan, then you behaviorally procrastinate? In *behavioral procrastination*, you plan, organize, and may even begin to take steps. Then you stop. This is the equivalent of a long-distance runner who prepares to run a marathon event. The runner starts the race but when within visual distance of the finish line, the runner sits on the side of the track while others run past.
	A revision, under these conditions, is to look at how you can be powerful enough to start and move forward but not powerful enough to finish? Why do you stop yourself? Does powerlessness thinking resurface and get in the way? Is it that you don't expect yourself to finish (powerlessness thinking) and then do what you expect? If so, go back to reflect on powerlessness thinking. Now armed with this new information, reconsider what is happening. Use this information. Try again.
Stabilize: Persist with evolving process until powerlessness thinking is under control.	Routinely reassert your self-observant and self-directed efforts to challenge powerlessness thinking in all its forms. Simulate conditions to keep in practice. Review what you've already worked out. Through this process, you help strengthen your reason as a buffer against parasitic powerlessness-thinking intrusions.

Now it is your turn to target your form of powerlessness thinking and apply the PURRRS system.

YOUR PERSONAL PURRRRS PLAN

What form does powerlessness thinking take for you? Describe it in the space provided. Then adapt the PURRRRS plan to examine and defeat it.

Powerlessness thinking: _____

PURRRRS	Actions
Pause: Stop and prepare for action.	
Use: Apply your will and other resources to resist impulses to get self-absorbed and sidetrack yourself.	
Reflect: Think about what is happening.	
Reason: Think it through.	
Respond: Put yourself through the paces of change.	
Revise: Review your process and make adjustments when results suggest trying another way.	
Stabilize: Persist with evolving process until powerlessness thinking is under control.	

KEY IDEAS AND ACTION PLAN

What key ideas from this chapter can you use to rid yourself of your parasite anxieties and fears? What's your action plan? Write it down. Test it out. Record what happened.

Key Ideas

1.

2.

3.

Action Plan

1.

2.

3.

Results from Actions Taken

1.

2.

3.

POSTSCRIPT

A depressed cat watches a mouse scurry across a room but does not chase it. At another time, the mouse would be in peril. Meanwhile, the cat doesn't think it's a bad cat or that it is powerless to catch the mouse. It lives in the moment without judging itself and thinking powerlessness thoughts.

Unlike the cat, you can think in words. You can define your state as a powerless one. You can pessimistically predict what is to come. But like the cat, you experience yourself in the present moment. In this present moment, you can honestly tell yourself that you are thinking powerlessness thoughts but that those are thoughts of the moment. You can accept them without judging yourself. You can question them. But whatever you do, they remain only thoughts.

CHAPTER 12

Defusing Worry

Do you worry about too many minor matters? Have you felt tense thinking that you had a fatal disease and then found out that you were okay? Have you ever believed that a delayed friend got into an accident? Welcome to the world of worry.

Worry is a form of mental uneasiness about negative possibilities that rarely happen. This state of mind probably originated with the development of language, when we first thought about what might have happened to members of the tribe who had not yet returned from a hunt. Our ability to fret and sweat about frightening possibilities has truly been around for a long time.

The Old English word *wyrgan* meant to choke or strangle. In the seventeenth century, "worry" meant to stress, trouble, or prosecute. In the nineteenth century, the word took on its current meaning: a feeling of apprehension, trouble, and unease about a possible event. This chapter looks at worry as an uncomfortable parasitic state of mind. In the following pages, you'll learn some self-observant ways to recognize, manage, and overcome worrisome thoughts.

WORRY RECOGNITION

Uncertainty is part of life. From time to time, practically everyone can show concern about new situations, such as how a new political leader might govern. But as is also well known, worry goes beyond a feeling of concern. This form of thought involves getting wrapped up in contemplating frightening possibilities.

Worry is thinking about negative possibilities associated with uncertainties. Milder worries can fly in and out of your thoughts like occasional gnats at a picnic. At the other extreme, your mind can be swamped with recurring worries about getting lost, forgetting to turn off a stove, being criticized, or contracting cancer. This generalized worrying can feel normal, especially if you can't think of a time when you didn't worry.

WHAT'S THE WORRY?

The following inventory describes some common worries. You can complete the inventory by checking "true" if the item applies to you or "false" if it does not.

Worry Inventory	True	False
1. "I often think of bad things that can happen."	_____	_____
2. "When a friend is late, I worry that my friend has been harmed."	_____	_____
3. "I often think that people are rejecting me."	_____	_____
4. "When I hear the phone ring, I think I will get bad news."	_____	_____
5. "I think the world is becoming a more dangerous place."	_____	_____
6. "I fret that people are dishonest with me."	_____	_____
7. "I worry about getting into accidents."	_____	_____
8. "I often think about not having adequate retirement funds or health care insurance."	_____	_____
9. "I sometimes think I have a fatal disease."	_____	_____
10. "I worry about paying bills and taxes."	_____	_____
11. "I feel tense when I think about my weight and appearance."	_____	_____
12. "The idea of global warming troubles me."	_____	_____
13. "I feel uneasy at the thought of dying in a crash."	_____	_____
14. "I worry about being cheated or exploited."	_____	_____
15. "I sometimes worry about having a brain tumor."	_____	_____
16. "I think about getting caught in an undertow when swimming."	_____	_____
17. "I worry about losing my job."	_____	_____
18. "I worry that someone will abduct my children."	_____	_____
19. "I worry about death and dying."	_____	_____
20. "I worry about choking in social situations."	_____	_____
21. "I worry about contaminants in my water and food."	_____	_____

The worry inventory is a small sample of worrisome possibilities. You may worry about your place in the universe, what other people think of you, money, health, world peace, genetic engineering, corruption, sexual attractiveness, failing a test, making a wrong decision, the possibility of a shark attack, the afterlife, germs, AIDS, the ozone layer, alien abduction, water fluoridation, or a mass attack by rabid bats. The list of what people worry about could fill a book.

If you checked "false" to every item in the preceding inventory, you likely have a low incidence of worry. This suggests that you also have a low incidence of parasitic anxieties. If you checked "true" to most items, you likely experience a high degree of worry. But even if you checked many items, the numbers are less important than what you can do to take corrective actions.

Most people who worry suffer from common worries as well as unique worries. A *common worry* would be to fear the worst if someone is tardy. A *unique worry* would be to fear a surprise encounter with a great mole rat (zemmiphobia) or with an angry Bigfoot, even when you suspect that such creatures are probably myths.

You may identify yourself with worry: "I'm a worrier." "I'm a worrywart." "It's my personality." However, most worries reflect false beliefs about uncertainties and possibilities. False beliefs can be recognized, clarified, and defused.

Unlike your temperament, thinking can be changed. Your ideas about a scary possibility can change with new information. You receive a letter from an unknown lawyer. Before you open it, your stomach sinks as your mind churns out words of dread. Then you discover you inherited money. You feel relief. Where did the terror go?

When thinking about worry, it is helpful to keep a fair perspective. Even if you worry a lot, there are probably many more instances where you do not make hurricanes out of passing breezes.

IS IT WORRY OR ANXIETY THAT YOU FEEL?

Is there a difference between worry and anxiety? The terms *worry* and *anxiety* may have different scientific meanings but, like *anxiety* and *fear*, are often used interchangeably. Nevertheless, if you think you worry too much, the following discussion can help you distinguish worry from anxiety.

Is there a difference between anxiety and worry? Worry normally involves "could have" and "what if" thinking. ("My friend could have died in an accident." "What if the world comes to an end?") Worry represents an attempt to explain an unknown or uncertain situation where you decide there is a scary possibility. When worried, you will likely feel uneasy but otherwise experience no other significant sense of arousal. A parasitic anxiety typically involves dramatizing a threat and a notable feeling of physical arousal. Anxiety is on a time dimension. There is a probable danger coming up that you dread happening. You still have time to avoid the danger or to cope.

Do worry and anxiety reside in different parts of the brain? Worry and anxiety seem to reside in different places in the brain (Engels et al. 2007). Anxious apprehension (worry, rumination) tends to be more verbal and shows more left-brain activity. Anxious arousal (anxiety) shows more right-brain activity. Although both worry and anxiety have their unique features, under real-world conditions, worry and anxiety often overlap.

Is there a difference in intensity between anxiety and worry? Although the physical and psychological signs of anxiety may differ from person to person, anxiety involves a notably high arousal coupled with physical signs, such as a quickened heartbeat, a change in breathing, and tightened muscles. Worry is more of a negative-fantasy-thinking condition of mind that feels uneasy.

Is there a crossover between worry and anxiety? The brain has many cross connections. Worry can change to anxiety when "what if" thinking about dreaded possibilities escalates into catastrophic thinking. In a catastrophizing state of mind, you can experience an increased heart rate, sweating, and feelings of unreality. Worry can also escalate into anxiety through double-trouble beliefs, which can include believing that you can't control your tension and you will lose control. This threatening idea can stimulate the brain to experience danger. As you worry about feeling anxious and losing control, you may stir up the anxious arousal that you fear.

ADDRESSING YOUR WORRIES

Worry is more cognitive than anxiety and fear are. As a practical matter, many of the cognitive techniques for quelling fear and anxiety can be adapted for coping with worry thinking. But there are some special ways to address worry to prevent it from spilling over into anxiety.

WHAT ARE YOUR MAJOR WORRIES?

You may have some worries that you particularly want to stop. What are the major worries or situations that you worry about?

1. _____

2. _____

3. _____

4. _____

5. _____

The remainder of this chapter covers techniques that you can effectively use to address your worries.

CREATE A WORRY LOG

A worry log is a practical place to begin to address worry. To make a worry log, get a small pocket-sized notebook. Write down your worries as they occur. Then question them and write down your answers.

Suppose you worry that you'll lose your job; you've had the same worry for the past ten years and have daily worried about losing your job during that period. Like a kindly and supportive friend, log your counterarguments to your worry thinking. For example, where is the evidence that the possibility of losing your job is a certainty today? The answer is clear. A possibility is never a certainty. Besides, if you've been worrying for ten years about something that has not happened, the odds highly favor that your worry prediction is wrong.

Use the following space to write down examples of your worry talk and rebuttals.

Worry Talk	Worry-Talk Rebuttals

SEPARATE THE POSSIBLE FROM THE PROBABLE

Worry involves making a magical leap from possibilities to probabilities. It's an odd paradox that some who fear uncertainty create uncertainties that masquerade as reality.

We do a Chicken Little number on ourselves when we make inferences about possibilities and then fret over what probably won't happen. (Chicken Little is the fabled barnyard chicken who, upon feeling a stick hit its wing, panicked itself and the other animals into thinking that the sky was falling down.)

People who routinely worry sometimes make a case to justify their worries: Your boss appears indifferent. You think you could lose your job. Now the torrents of worry start. You remember that your rival seems friendlier with the boss. There was some scuttlebutt last week about the economy slowing. You assume that your company will have to cut back on its workforce. You recall that you were a day late with an important report. It's all very clear. You conclude that you will be fired at the end of the day. The following day, you repeat this cycle. You do so for the next ten years.

Having made the leap from speculation to certainty, you create other worries for yourself. How will you explain your job loss to your family? What will you do if you can't get another job? How will you explain the job loss to a prospective employer? While all this goes on in the echo chambers of your mind, you scarcely realize you have created an alarming illusion based on a speculative assumption.

Use the following space to evaluate worry logic.

Possibility Worries	Probability Rebuttals

BREAK THE "COULD BE" TRAP

Suppose you conclude that something bad could have happened: A drunken driver could be on the road and could have run over your child.

When "could be" translates into worry feelings, you've created a certainty out of a fiction. This "could be" logic has an especially strong magnetic pull when you are facing an irregularity in what you ordinarily expect. A situation such as your young teen's failure to arrive home from school on time could be a fertile field for tension if you are prone to worry. In this case, you have an expectation. The expectation is that your teenage son will arrive home on schedule. You're alert to the disparity between expectation and reality. How is this to be explained?

You fill in the gaps to support the worry. You saw a strange automobile in the neighborhood. The driver wore a dark hat. The car swerved slightly without a visible cause. You try to reassure yourself that one thing has nothing to do with the other, but you can't stop thinking that the driver was drunk and drunk drivers do kill people.

In rebutting such "could be" thinking, you might ask yourself, "How often has my son been late in the past?" The answer: "My son is normally home on time, but not always." What is the most common explanation? "My son is probably hanging out with a friend or had an after-school project."

Next you compare this explanation with what you've been speculating. Which is more likely, that you son has been hanging out with a friend or has been killed by a drunken driver? The probable answer is "hanging out with a friend."

Of course, if your son is unreasonably late, as a responsible parent, you may also actively try to locate him. This would be acting out of concern for your son, which is different from needless worrying.

Bad things do happen to people. You can read about them every day. But these are very low-probability events. It's the frequency of media exposure to deadly events that can lead to a conclusion that death by drunken drivers is an epidemic in your neighborhood.

By walking yourself through this exercise, you can teach yourself to switch off worry in favor of probability thinking. By repositioning your perspective on "could be" logic, you open opportunities to shift from needless worry to appropriate levels of concern.

Use the following space to evaluate "could be" worry thinking.

"Could Be" Worry Talk	"Could Be" Rebuttals

ESCAPE THE FREQUENCY TRAP

Despite evidence that repeatedly disconfirms the probability of dire predictions, people continue to worry because they recall episodes that did occur and forget the vastly greater number of times when the dreaded event did not happen. This is the *frequency trap*.

You get into this trap when you think of a possible calamity that could happen. You hear a report of a thunderstorm heading toward your area. The thought crosses your mind that you could get hit by lightning. You think of examples of people who were struck by lightning. You reason that because such things have happened, they will reoccur in the present. This time it is your turn to be the victim. But this is a form of needless worry. By exercising prudent caution (not standing at a high point with an iron rod in your hand), the odds strongly favor that you are not going to get struck by lightning.

Twisted logic also entices gamblers to bet on the lottery. You hear of many winners and believe that because so many others have won multimillion-dollar lotteries, you can also win. There's truth in that. But what are the odds of that happening?

When you move from the realm of possibility to the realm of probability, you know that getting struck by lightning is actually more probable than winning a big lottery. The odds of coming up with a winning ticket are as likely as putting on a blindfold, reaching into a dump truck full of beach sand, and picking out the one green-painted grain of sand. Getting struck by lightning may be more likely than winning the lottery, but it is nevertheless highly improbable.

Discriminating between legitimate concerns and conjecture-filled worries can make all the difference. Use the following space to evaluate a frequency-thinking worry trap.

Frequency-Thinking Worry Talk	Frequency-Thinking Rebuttals

CONTEND WITH THE "IF THEN" TRAP

Some of us have "if then" worries. For example, "If John doesn't call in the next five minutes, then he has gotten into an accident." This thinking is magical. There is nothing sacred about five minutes. Time has nothing to do with whether an accident will occur or not. Perhaps John's phone went dead.

"If then" logic is unreasonable when the connection is more magical than actual. Assumptions are not the same as facts. A misguided major premise (if John doesn't call), followed by an erroneous secondary premise (five minutes is the standard), can become the foundation for a speculative conclusion (John got in an accident).

You can neutralize this sequence by adding the question, "If not, then what?" Five minutes passes, and you don't hear from John, so you think, "If it's not an accident, then what?" You might consider that the phone went dead or John's taking out the garbage. Of course, asking yourself this question, you could always think of something worse, but the spirit of the exercise is to refocus your attention to neutral or positive outcomes.

Classifying worries into two groups (what you can do something about and what you can't) can also help spring the "if then" trap. If you can't do anything about an "if then" outcome, why worry? If you can, then devise a coping strategy. However, you may soon discover that you spend a lot of time planning solutions for disasters that never arrive.

Use the following space to evaluate an "if then" worry trap.

"If Then" Worry Talk	"If Then" Rebuttals

AVOID THE RELIEF TRAP

We are a suggestible and conditionable species that is normally responsive to short-term specious rewards. You can get a short-term reward for worrying. The reward is in the form of relief. You worry that something bad has happened or could happen. When the dire prediction proves false, you are likely to feel relief. This positive experience of relief increases your chances of having needless worries in the future.

When you daily worry about getting fired and don't get fired, what's up? Doesn't experience teach that the worry is foolish? Extended worries over the same event can have a superstitious feature. Just like avoiding walking away from a black cat's path to avoid "bad luck," worry can be part of a magical process. If worry precedes keeping your job, the myth-making part of your brain may paradoxically act as if worry makes for job stability. (But you may also work harder because you worry about losing your job.)

If you decide that this reward for worry is specious, then how can you break this pattern? You can look at alternative possibilities that are more positive. Instead of assuming that a delayed friend is cooking in a fiery crash, consider that the person got caught in traffic or forgot about meeting with you. If your boss is scowling, maybe he or she has something other than you in mind.

Coming up with alternative explanations can feel immediately rewarding. But when you generate positive possibilities, you are also stimulating an area of your brain that is next door to your worry center. This adjacent region of the brain is involved in positive assessments.

Use the following space to evaluate a worry-talk relief trap.

Worry-Talk Relief Trap	Positive Alternatives for Relief

DODGE THE THEORY TRAP

Worries are like theories: you can make them sound reasonable and then think they must be true. But theories are general propositions. The goal of science in testing a theory is to disconfirm it. Meanwhile, you accept theories that are supported by evidence until you are able to find a new theory that explains more.

A theory is not the same as a fact. For centuries, we operated under the geocentric theory that the earth was at the center of the universe. At that time, the theory was functional enough. During the first thousand years AD, most thought that the world was flat. Before the days of using compasses to stay on course, "the world is flat" theory was a functional theory.

Operating on a flat-world theory, sailing ships tended to go along known sea paths or within the sight of shore. A common fear was that of traveling out of sight of land and falling off the face of the earth. There was a practical value to this fallacy. By sticking to known shipping channels, you were less likely to get lost at sea. But suppose you still believed the world was flat. That belief doesn't change the reality that the earth is spherical.

To break from a worry-theory trap, look for ways to support the opposite theory. If you theorize that a rogue asteroid will hit the earth in six months, what facts support a conclusion that an asteroid will not hit the earth within the next six months? For example, it has not shown up on anyone's telescope.

Use the following space to evaluate a worry-theory trap.

Worry Theory	Worry-Theory Rebuttals

MAKE YOURSELF LAUGH

By putting your worry talk into a ridiculous but humorous extreme, you can help yourself, as you laugh at the fantasy, not at yourself. For example, you worry about using the wrong word in a conversation. Blow that up. Envision yourself mangling phrases by misusing words. Then picture yourself on the cover of *Time* with the caption, "Can't say anything right." Can anything be any more ridiculous?

By injecting a humorous exaggeration into worrisome thoughts, you've taken an extra step. You've shifted your perspective. It is hard to blow up a worry idea and laugh at the thought and still worry over the possibility.

Use the following space to evaluate a worry-theory trap.

Worry Thinking	Exaggerating the Thinking

WORST-CASE SCENARIO EXERCISE

Suppose that you were to misuse a word (or actually get fired from your job). Could you imagine anything worse? Your automobile could simultaneously be stolen. Your pet could run away. You could develop gangrene. Now could anything be worse? In addition to the above, your house could burn down. You could lose a leg. Could anything be worse or more awful? You bet!

Your situation cannot be 100 percent bad unless you think it is. And if you think that way, someone can likely show you ways that your situation could be worse. For example, would it be worse if you were slowly boiling in oil with gleeful cannibals sharpening their knives for the feast?

Use the following space to defuse a worry by exaggerating it.

Worry Thinking	Exaggerating the Thinking

Is the above worst-case scenario technique a variation on counting your blessings? Yes and no. The worst-case scenario technique can induce you to look at the broader scope of your life that also includes positive experiences. You might view being alive as a blessing.

GENERAL TECHNIQUES FOR DEFEATING WORRY

You can add the following practical techniques to your quiver of ideas to address worry thinking:

1. Label the worry process for what it is: *verbal rumination* that kicks up emotional dust. Labeling worry this way helps give you a more accurate perspective on your worry talk.

2. When in a cycle of worry, your mood is likely to become progressively negative. A simple question can sometimes help disrupt the cycle: "Do I feel like continuing?" This question implies that if worry thinking is no longer enjoyable or profitable, you can terminate it (Davey et al. 2007). The answer to the question may be less important than the awareness that you are engaging in worry thinking, which can galvanize you to devise a legitimate nonworry perspective.

3. Perhaps a first step away from worry is to separate concern from worry. When you have concern for yourself, someone else, or a situation, you care about what is happening. You act responsibly because you care. Next time you worry, ask yourself, "How can I care? How

can I act responsibly? How can I show respect to myself and others?" Perhaps the answers to such questions will get you onto a different path.

4. Put yourself into someone else's shoes. If a friend is late and you start to worry, what you're thinking is that you don't know what's happening and can't control what you don't know. Flip this perspective about. If you were late, would you not know what you were doing? Would you want someone else to worry about you? Would you see yourself in greater control than you see your friend?

5. Schedule a ten-minute time to worry. Pick the same time every day. During that time, think about what you have to worry about. Write down the worries. After a while, you may discover that your mind starts to drift from the worries. This approach is paradoxical in the sense that you are doing what you want to avoid. But there are a few principles: (1) you control the time for worry; (2) by intentionally practicing worry talk, you may uncouple the ideas from emotions, so they lose their credibility by losing their emotional connection; (3) you can bore yourself with worry.

6. Watch out for the verb "to be." Using it can lead to overgeneralizations and a false sense of certainty. If you act as if you think that something bad *is* going to happen, you've taken a possibility and translated it into a certainty. Affixing a probability estimate to the event can help shrink the impact of a false certainty.

7. Wear an elastic band on your wrist. When you start to worry, snap the elastic band so that it is uncomfortable but won't break the skin. So, instead of getting a reward for worry, you experience an immediate mild punishment. You could also use a thought-stopping technique. When you hear yourself start to worry, silently shout "stop, stop, stop" within your mind.

By attacking worry thinking, you can stimulate that part of your brain adjacent to your worry center that's involved in a positive construction of reality. Of equal or perhaps greater value is that you act to build your reasoning skills. An educated reason can seem like paradise compared to the maelstrom of parasitic anxieties and worries that bombard consciousness and perpetuate themselves by strengthening their own connections.

KEY IDEAS AND ACTION PLAN

What key ideas from this chapter can you use to rid yourself of your parasitic anxieties and fears? What's your action plan? Write it down. Test it out. Record what happened.

Key Ideas

1.

2.

3.

Action Plan

1.

2.

3.

Results from Actions Taken

1.

2.

3.

POSTSCRIPT

Now that you have multiple techniques to apply to worry, you may be prepared to do the following: suspend judgment until the facts are known.

Reason doesn't sterilize creative fantasies. If you enjoy myths and magic, you can still enjoy stories and, perhaps, write and publish fiction to entertain yourself and others. But you don't have to despair over worry demons that crawl from fantasy regions of the mind and drag darkness and torment to the forefront of your thoughts. By vanquishing these demons, you will have a bigger world to enjoy.

CHAPTER 13

Stopping Perfectionist Thinking

In a world of imperfect people, we lead imperfect lives. Behavior is variable. Our information is often less complete than we would wish. False information can muddle our thinking. Mistakes are common. Someday someone will write a book about these and other normal human foibles and faults. Many readers will think the book is about them.

Technically, perfectionism means a tendency to be displeased by anything imperfect or that doesn't meet high standards. In the world of the extreme perfectionist, it is not enough to do well. You or others have to do perfectly well. Like most other human tendencies, perfectionism is on a scale. Some are more affected by perfectionism than others.

Perfectionism is common among people living in achievement-oriented societies where some believe that they must achieve according to their potential or they are failures. But perfectionist ideals don't jibe with human nature or the way things ordinarily work.

Perfectionism and striving for excellence come from different motivations. Striving for excellence is normally motivated by a commitment to responsibly persist, prudently risk, and stretch capabilities to achieve desired but attainable results. Perfectionism is often connected to parasitic conditions of mind, such as a fear of failure, fear of exposing faults, and fear of losing control.

Perfectionists striving to achieve may accomplish much when they invest their time and energy. Driven by a sense of urgency, many sacrifice their health to satisfy their demons of duty. But perfectionist thinking is often accompanied by anxiety and procrastination. Such perfectionism involves setting lofty goals and measuring what you do against standards you can rarely meet. Under the circumstances, you are likely to judge yourself harshly for foibles and failings and flunk yourself when you don't do exactly what you expect from yourself. Understandably, a perfectionist philosophy is an incubation chamber for parasitic anxieties.

Perfectionism weaves through different forms of anxiety and many of its coexisting states. When you have a gap between what you expect from yourself and what you can accomplish, anxiety commonly follows (Flett et al. 1998; Lee 2005). Depression and perfectionism can coexist (Clara, Cox, and Enns 2007). Anger and perfectionism can coexist (Saboonchi and Lundh 2003), and substance abuse and perfectionism can coexist (Holle and Ingram 2008).

Perfectionism is an approachable problem, however. If you find yourself in a perfectionist bind, you can reduce the results of this thinking and experience less anxiety. People with perfectionism seem quite able to change through cognitive behavioral methods (Glover et al. 2007; Ashbaugh et al. 2007; Riley et al. 2007).

This chapter looks at perfectionism from several different angles. By knowing about perfectionism and by challenging perfectionist thinking, you can release yourself from many forms of parasitic stresses, anxieties, and fears.

DICHOTOMOUS THINKING

Anxiety can spin from dichotomous thinking, or seeing things only in black-and-white terms. Taking a dichotomous view, you either are right or wrong, strong or weak, and so on. So the solution is to be perfect. Then you are right and strong.

Make your security and worth contingent on being right, and you've entered the world of dichotomous thinking. If your security and acceptability depend on being right and strong, what does it mean if sometimes you are more wrong than right on an issue. What if you are completely wrong? These polarities smudge the window through which you view reality. They are formulas for distress (Egan et al. 2007).

When preferences for being right convert to needs, and needs to demands, and demands to coercion, feelings of anxiety and worthlessness are logical extensions of this process (Knaus 1979, 1994). However, these contingencies for security are discretionary and debatable. You can defeat them and feel better for the effort.

DEFEATING PERFECTIONIST EXTREMES

In a perfectionist state of mind, you put yourself on a seesaw. You are up when you do well. You are down when you don't. So, let's look at how to clear this perfectionist tarnish from your window on life. Perfectionist thinking is vulnerable to incongruity interventions. Here's a look at four perfectionist contingencies for security (happiness) from an incongruity perspective.

Contingency 1: "I have to be winner." But is it true that you're a loser if you're not winning all the time? It is helpful to think that you are the same person whether or not you find yourself successful in all the big and small things that you undertake. On the one hand, winning can yield advantages. But losing doesn't make you a loser, no more than misspelling a word makes you incompetent. If you come in second in a race, you are not the first loser. One other person was faster. Does coming in last in a race make you a colossal loser or a person who came in last in a particular race at a particular time?

Contingency 2: "I have to be in control or else I feel helpless." Have you thought that to feel secure, you must have control over your thoughts, emotions, and behaviors? With this contingency in place, you can make yourself feel extra anxious over the idea that without perfect self-control, you are powerless. But if being in perfect control is the only solution for overcoming a feeling of powerlessness, and you believe that you are powerless to change, then how can you ever be in control? There has to be a better thinking solution than one where you box yourself in like this. One way out of the box is to conclude that perfect control is a myth, that partial control is better than no control, and acceptance of an inability to control a situation is a form of control in that you've chosen acceptance over despair. This type of incongruity exploration exposes the flaws in this control-bound thinking.

Contingency 3: "I must be comfortable to feel secure." If you think that to feel secure, you have to be comfortable, what happens when you start to feel uncomfortable? Will telling yourself that you must be comfortable help? Facing conditions of uncertainty can include experiencing feelings of discomfort. Conflicts are inevitable. They can feel uncomfortable. So if your security depends upon consistently feeling comfortable, and some discomfort is part of living, then you can't win.

Contingency 4: "I must have universal approval to feel worthwhile." As social animals, it is usually a good idea to try to get along with others. Approval is beneficial. But what if you can't get it from everyone? Partnerships end because of disagreements. Marriages break up because of incompatibilities. People with a special political view normally prefer to hang out with people who agree with them. If you make your security, happiness, comfort, or worth depend on being a universally pleasing person, this is a formula for anxiety. What if someone is not pleased with you? What if you do everything perfectly well, and the person you communicate with dislikes you because you look like someone they disliked in the past? If you think you need to be loved by all, then what happens when another person applies for the job that you want?

Perfectionist thinking teems with other incongruities. If you agree that it is important to maintain a sense of human dignity, but you cling to a perfectionist view, then how do you justify imposing tough standards that can interfere with your sense of dignity? If you believe that you have to express yourself flawlessly and always have witty and brilliant things to say, and at the same time, you view yourself as an average person, how can you be both average and flawless?

If you fall into a perfectionist-thinking trap and label yourself as worthless if you are imperfect, broaden your self-definition. By describing yourself as an imperfect person with a generally gentle temperament, you add a refreshing new dimension to a dichotomous-thinking outlook. Now add a few more dimensions. Tell yourself that you're an imperfect person with a gentle temperament who strives to do the right thing. Adding clarifying conditions to black-and-white definitions takes thought, time, and effort. But this shows that there is much to think about that lies between the extremes.

PERFECT-PERSON TRAPS

The novelist Thomas Hardy (1971) made a compelling observation that when the mighty fall, they have farther to go. The crash of their descent makes a thunderous roar. Similarly, in the world of the perfectionist, the loftier the expectations, the farther the fall, and the louder the crash. But education, reason, and knowledge can help you avoid the crash.

Perfectionism is an enigma. Recognizing this opens opportunities to unravel its many entanglements. As part of this experiment in self-awareness, let's look at some common perfectionism traps and how to get out of them.

1. *Self-perfectionism* is a philosophy that says, "I must behave in a certain way, or I am unworthy. I must not make mistakes. I must have approval to feel worthy. I must maintain my

image and appearance at all costs." To question these ideas, focus on what you can do rather than who you should be and what you must do.

2. *Social perfectionism* is the view that others should comply with your rules. This usually backfires. Other people typically have their own notions. Some notions may fit with your views, but not always. To build emotional tolerance, concentrate on what you can tolerate about people in your life. Balance each negative with one positive.

3. *Learning perfectionism* is when you are your own worst critic when it comes to learning a skill. The fact is that anyone can experience awkwardness when building a new skill. Some failure is instructive. This shows where you can redirect your efforts. If you experience fears of failure when learning something on your own, why fear failure? There are no witnesses to observe you. You have no teachers to correct you. Other than yourself, there is no one present to blame you.

4. *Product perfectionism* is when anything less than perfection in what you do represents a threat that evokes anxiety. All-or-nothing perfectionist thinking often stirs anxiety over imperfections. A writer keeps revising a book until it is perfected. The work never gets done because it is never perfect. The inventor leaves a promising idea because it takes work to develop. By taking an alternate view, recognizing that development is a process, you can contradict one-trial perfectionist thinking. A book is a work in progress. After it is published, you can revise it and print a revision. An invention gets perfected but rarely starts out perfect.

5. The *comparative trap* is when you ceaselessly compare your accomplishments to other people's accomplishments. Picking people with exemplary skills that you must match puts you at risk of downgrading yourself. This view increases your risk of feeling anxious in the presence of others you define as superior. Rather then glue yourself to this view, concentrate on what you can do.

6. *Performance anxiety* may trap you when, sloughing aside reality, you believe that you must succeed in whatever you undertake. There can be no mistakes. A solution for performance anxiety is to perform positive actions to the best of your abilities. Then let the chips fall where they may. How else can you learn?

The various perfectionism traps stir up a tempest in a teapot. By escaping these thinking traps, you can get away from much needless anxiety and other forms of worthless tension.

ESCAPING THE PERFECTIONISM TRAP

In the following chart, list the forms your perfectionism takes. Outline what you can do to challenge the beliefs behind your perfectionism traps.

Form of Perfectionism	Contradiction to Perfectionist Thinking

PERFECTIONIST ANXIETIES FOR SOCIAL SITUATIONS

If you count yourself among the millions who have an uncomfortable degree of social anxieties and fears, you are likely to find that these social tensions are partially or largely grounded in the belief that perfection is attainable. Here are a few social-perfectionism myths and some quick ways to reframe them.

1. The *myth of the perfect opening gambit* is a perfectionist solution that you can be a social success if you make a great first impression. The fact is that although first impressions are often important, feeling natural and showing interest in others is more important than worrying about the perfect opening statement. Dwelling on how to make a perfect first impression can actually get in the way of making a good impression. As an alternative, consider that you will probably not find a universally appealing approach. But you can find many acceptable ways to begin.

2. The *myth of the perfectly articulate person* is a belief that you must refrain from expressing yourself unless you can do so in an infallible manner. Instead of a blind dedication to this ideal, consider that although you normally do not want to stumble over your words, ordinary conversations do not translate into perfectly written text.

3. The *myth of perfect preparation* is the idea that you cannot speak up in groups until you have totally digested the most popular novels, can insightfully analyze the most current news, or are thoroughly knowledgeable about a topic. Who knows when someone might ask you a question about such matters, and you'd better be prepared, right? Instead, try to find out

what others know about topics that interest them. The best conversationalists are often the ones who ask questions that allow others to speak.

4. The *complete comfort myth* is the idea that you have to be completely comfortable to socialize. Instead, consider that a certain amount of discomfort is natural when you meet people for the first time. Initial awkwardness is, perhaps, more the norm than is a sense of total social comfort.

5. The *myth of perpetual cheeriness* is a common perfectionist solution for social success: all you have to do is always act upbeat, outgoing, concerned, happy, and fun loving. These attributes can be advantages. However, in serious settings, such qualities distract. In work settings that require concentration, few kibbitz. At funerals, being continually cheerful would be inappropriate. In whatever situation you are in, try focusing on what is happening rather than on how you must present yourself.

CHALLENGING PERFECTIONISM IN PUBLIC

In the following space, list the forms your social perfectionism takes and outline what you can do to address these myths using information from this chapter and other appropriate sources.

Social Perfectionism Myth	Contradiction to Perfectionist Thinking

ASPIRING VERSUS REQUIRING PHILOSOPHIES

From an *absolute perfectionist*'s perspective, there is only one right way, the perfectionist's way. The absolute perfectionist is primed to turn his or her marriage into a reform school, friendships into contests of will, and jobs into control factories.

A *relative perfectionist* may seem a bit more flexible. The student with weak math skills decides that an A- grade is acceptable. So he stays up studying past midnight for a week, fatigues himself, and receives a B+ grade. He feels like a failure. The B+ was not good enough.

Both of these perfectionists operate with a *requiring philosophy*. Here is the principle: "I must do what I expect of myself, or I am unacceptable." If you are a perfectionist-thinking person, you are likely to feel threatened and anxious if you don't match these contingencies. Now you face the task of attempting to be what you are not.

The requiring philosophy is a formula for anxiety where the threat comes from within. Believing that you can't meet your own standards can cause you to think you're vulnerable. The requiring philosophy has its own language. It consists of demand terms such as "should," "ought," and "must." To imagine the potency of this language, think of a person pointing a finger at you and saying, "You ought!"

Some demands are legitimate, such as insisting that a child not run between parked cars into the road. Others are not, such as insisting that your friend purchase the type of automobile that you would like to drive. Likewise, using words like "should" doesn't automatically translate into a demand. If I say I should buy a new computer, it's a conditional phrase that shows a direction, not a demand (Knaus 1982). It's the semantics, not the syntax, that conveys the message.

Retraining Yourself to Aspire

An *aspiring philosophy* is a more flexible way of viewing life. When you view yourself and the world through an aspiring point of view, you think and express yourself in terms of anticipations, wants, desires, preferences, or wishes. You assert your positive interests and desires by going after what you want.

The meaning behind the words we use can make a difference. Merely using the word "prefer" when you mean "should" probably won't change a demanding tone. Using phrases such as "you'd preferably do this" or "you had better do that" can convey a demand message as surely as saying "you should do this" or "shouldn't do that." If you mean to project flexibility, both the words and the tone you use will carry that message.

AN ASPIRING AND REQUIRING PHILOSOPHY COMPARISON

By comparing requiring and aspiring philosophies, you can sense that each has its own feel. Notice how the words associated with these two philosophies differ.

Requiring Philosophy	Aspiring Philosophy
expect	desire
demand	prefer
have to	would like to
must	wish
ought	favor
should	want

In the space below, identify perfectionist demand words that you tend to use. Then identify words that convey tolerance and flexibility that you can use in place of these demand words. Practice substituting aspiring language for your demand terms. Through this exercise, is it possible to become easier on yourself and others?

Your Demand Terms	Your Preference-Term Substitutions

Both aspiring and requiring ways of viewing reality are discretionary. They also represent value choices. There is no universal law that says you must choose an aspiring over a requiring philosophy. Even if you do choose to develop an aspiring philosophy, you ordinarily cannot snap your fingers and make this happen. However, when you intentionally substitute preference words for demand terms, this shows that your self-observant skills are on the rise.

Here's another angle on cutting back on absolutes where they really don't apply. In communicating with others, the eighteenth century American diplomat and scientist Benjamin Franklin (1986) advised using phrases such as "it appears to me" or "it seems that way." He suggested the use of this flexible language to avoid sounding autocratic and smug and to avoid triggering opposition. By building flexibility into his words, Franklin avoided backing himself into a corner.

A MATTER OF CHOICE

To further help detach from perfectionist demands, consider the difference between expectations and expectancies. *Expectations* are a usual part of perfectionist thinking. You expect reality to bend to your wishes. *Expectancies* are probability statements. Thinking in terms of expectancies can help balance absolutistic demands. If life is filled with probability and only a few absolutes (the sun rises in the morning), then it only makes sense to think in probability terms. This approach can help reduce the number of times you fall into a dichotomous thinking trap. You'll likely feel less anxious when you have fewer demands and absolutes to contend with.

When you evaluate expectancies, you open your mind to a range of outcomes that you may aspire to realize. But it is unlikely that anyone will achieve a purely aspiring state of mind. After all, we're all fallible. Perfect consistency is unlikely. But progress is highly probable.

Most people in westernized societies have been exposed to a heavy dose of "requiring" programming. We're overly conditioned to think based on the structure of our language and its usage. Nevertheless, you can work to improve your batting average. As little as a 10 to 15 percent improvement in aspiration over expectation can make a noticeable difference.

BEHAVIORAL METHODS FOR ADDRESSING PERFECTIONISM

Dealing with perfectionist thinking would primarily seem like a cognitive undertaking. But most perfectionism-based anxieties and fears involve behavioral as well as mental events. By engaging in corrective behavioral experiences, prudently exposing yourself to what you fear, you can desensitize yourself to perfectionist demands. Here are some methods to try:

1. If you believe that you must look flawless to be acceptable, dress down for a day. Wear something casual with a small soup stain. Learn to live with the discomfort of not looking perfect.

2. You may be afraid of making mistakes and compensate by trying to avoid making them. But since making mistakes is part of learning, it's unavoidable. Plan to make some inconsequential mistakes. When you give your phone number, intentionally err by switching two numbers. Then correct yourself without apologizing. The odds are that the other person won't care.

3. If you think that you must be utterly charming for others to like you, practice acting natural without pretense. You may not always be charming, but you can normally be cordial, direct, or whatever else a situation calls for. You may find that others relate to you more comfortably when you are not forcing yourself to act according to a script.

4. If you dread inviting people to a party at your home because someone might disapprove of your decorating tastes, give a party. Observe what happens. You may find that your guests are more interested in socializing than in whether or not you have a smudge on your Tiffany lamp.

5. If you think that you can't start writing until you have researched every book on your topic and have digested every morsel of information, start writing. Do your research as you go. You can always edit what you do.

6. If you think that every statement you make must be unassailable, plan to make some minor mistakes in conversation. Get a date wrong. Quote the wrong newspaper. At worst, someone will correct you. Would that be the end of the world?

GETTING IT WRONG, INTENTIONALLY

Carry out doing something less than perfectly that you ordinarily view as a condition for perfection. For example, alter your appearance slightly or express yourself imperfectly. Use the results of this exercise to determine if you have incongruities to resolve and to desensitize yourself to real or imagined criticism, especially self-criticism.

The following space provides a means of recording the process and results for future reference. An example appears in the first row.

Perfectionist Problem	Test Activity	What You Learned
Example: Fear of making a mistake in public	Mispronounce a famous politician's name	An occasional correction; meanwhile, the Earth keeps rotating on its axis

---

KEY IDEAS AND ACTION PLAN

What key ideas from this chapter can you use to rid yourself of your parasitic anxieties and fears? What's your action plan? Write it down. Test it out. Record what happened.

Key Ideas

1.

2.

3.

Action Plan

1.

2.

3.

Results from Actions Taken

1.

2.

3.

POSTSCRIPT

People who strive for excellence without perfectionist distractions tend to feel more relaxed, reflective, resilient, and in command of themselves. They realistically gauge the likelihood of achieving their dreams and realize that each dream has a start and goals to meet along the way.

Striving for excellence is attainable at any time and echoes this belief: Do the best you can with the time, information, and resources you have available. Gather additional information as necessary. Persist until you come to an insurmountable barrier. Then try a different way, or change course.

CHAPTER 14

Defeating Inhibition

In *The Glass Menagerie* by Tennessee Williams (1974), shy Laura Wingfield lives a quiet isolated life with her collection of glass animals. Having a slight limp, she magnifies its significance, identifies herself with it, and limits herself because she views herself as an unwanted invalid. Desiring love and companionship, she also fears exposing her inadequacies and getting rejected. In the end, her fears win out.

All too often, people fritter away opportunities for happiness by holding back their creativity and desires. The true peril of parasitic anxieties and fears is not so much your experience of dread as it is a lifetime of tragic results that come from maintaining these fears.

This chapter examines parasitic inhibitions that limit normal and desirable experiences. It then offers several exercises to help you overcome these inhibitions.

PERILS OF INHIBITION

Inhibition means restraint or suppression. Sometimes inhibitions can be healthy. When, say, you hold back on actions that could cost you dearly, restraint helps. Because you want to keep your job, you avoid telling off your boss. Despite a disappointing grade in a course, you suppress your urge to quit. You take action to end a substance-abuse habit when the harm far exceeds the benefits.

In addition to having healthy inhibitions, practically all of us have unhealthy inhibitions that work to our detriment. Shyness, acting overly polite when wronged, and not expressing warm feelings are the tips of this iceberg. Parasitic inhibitions can lead to a life filled with regrets about unfulfilled wishes.

Unhealthy inhibitions are known by many names; you might feel uptight, anxious, restricted, held back, withdrawn, overcautious, intense, contained, controlled, passive, habit bound, self-limited, wary, too differential, unassertive, constricted. When one or more of these words describes a pattern of inhibited behavior, it merits a close look. Part of this look involves examining what motivates inhibited behavior.

What lies beneath the surface of unhealthy inhibitions? You often find parasitic fears, anxieties, and core inadequacy beliefs.

When can you first experience inhibitions? You could be born with a tendency toward wariness, shyness, and sensitivity for tension (Kagan 2000; Schmidt et al. 1997). If one identical twin is excessively wary, then the odds are that the other will show the same tendencies (Robinson et al. 1992). These temperamental tendencies can translate into self-consciousness and faulty beliefs, leading to parasitic anxieties and fears and needlessly inhibited behaviors.

How do temperamental inhibitions extend into parasitic anxieties? Because they naturally experience an elevated sense of threat, some inhibited children develop negative insights early in life. They come to believe that others don't like them. They avoid contact. This avoidance promotes a vicious circle.

How common are inhibitions such as shyness? From mild to disabling awkwardness, as much as 50 percent of the U.S. population reports feeling shy (Henderson and Zimbardo 1998). Degrees of shyness and inhibition also depend on context.

Can you feel inhibited or shy and still achieve? Shyness and inhibition are addressable. You can learn to decrease or overcome such tendencies. World-famous psychologist Abraham Maslow exhibited shyness, as did Abraham Lincoln, Lucille Ball, Albert Einstein, and Thomas Edison. Both Julia Roberts and David Letterman have confessed to being shy. The bottom line: dreams, desires, and hard work counter shyness and inhibitions.

Who is responsible for overcoming a parasitic inhibition? If you are a member of the shyness or inhibition club, finding fault or casting blame is useless. Perhaps it would have been nice if some wise adult had helped you when you were a child, by recognizing that early inhibition is a risk factor for later parasitic inhibitions. But if that didn't happen, it didn't happen. You now have the responsibility to get yourself out of this noxious ditch. You were born with the ability to reflect and reason. You can hone this ability into a refined critical-thinking skill. You can teach yourself to withstand emotional tension through directing your actions along positive pathways. These actions are more than a match for a parasitic inhibition.

THE PARASITIC-ANXIETY TRIANGLE

It may help to visualize how inhibition interacts with and supports parasitic anxiety. Imagine a triangle, in which inhibition and insecurity form the base, and anxiety surfaces at the top. Self-doubts and discomfort fears often exist in the center of this experiential triangle (see figure 2).

In a state of doubt with discomfort fears, insecurity and inhibition animate anxiety. This can lead back to self-doubts and discomfort fears. When the elements of this vicious circle are strong, misery certainly results.

Trapped in the parasitic-anxiety triangle, you are likely to feel held back. Living in this state is like living in a hornets' nest. Each hornet buzzes with a different negative message. Labeled "fear of scrutiny," one swoops by. Another trails a banner reading "mistakes from the past." A group buzzes by murmuring, "Watch out. You're vulnerable." Each wasp reminds you of something you want to forget or better not do, or of something you feel needlessly constricted from doing.

During this swarming din, you think about one crisis after another until you feel overwhelmed, powerless, and hopeless. You gasp for breath. Your heart races. Your mind frantically seeks a way to escape. Alas, you find no refuge.

Fortunately, there is a way out. You decide to ditch the triangle. Following this decision, you read about some exercises that can help you decrease your inhibition. "Hey," you think, "this is a better solution. I now have hornet spray."

Figure 2

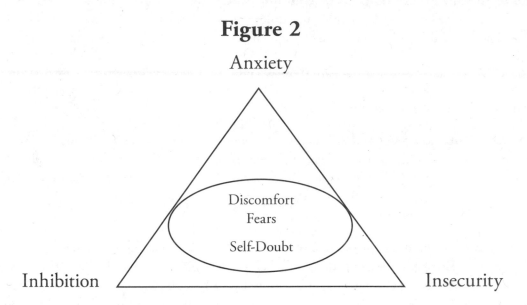

TECHNIQUES TO DEFEAT INHIBITION

An inhibition is not an all-or-nothing event. It comes in different strengths at different times and in different places. Both extremely inhibited and shy individuals have times in their lives when they are outgoing, outspoken, and the life of the party. They might be with good friends, before a classroom as a teacher, standing up for the rights of people who are not able to defend themselves, or efficiently managing a sales territory through a highly organized and efficient approach. However, in a parasitically inhibited state of mind, the same people typically mute themselves and pay a price.

You have choices. You can do nothing and stay stuck in patterns you want to escape but are afraid to abandon. Social thawing can come slowly with age. But do you really want to wait until later in life?

How do you break from a parasitic-anxiety triangle filled with harmful inhibitions? You have many ways to disable inhibitory thinking and behavior. Top among these are exercising restraint against inhibition and stepping out of character.

Exercising Restraint

Inhibition implies exercising excessive restraint based on partially or largely false beliefs. Inhibition is mostly a reaction rather than an action that you consciously decide to take. On the other hand, you can choose to exercise restraint in certain circumstances. Doing so is selective and reflective. You choose what you'll do. You decide to act based on the choice.

Exercising an appropriate degree of restraint is a solution for overcoming both excitable impulsiveness and parasitic inhibitions. In this case, exercising restraint becomes conscious and intentional. Choosing when and how to restrict yourself is a form of emotional freedom.

A parasitic inhibition is a one-choice system. You feel socially uncomfortable. You avoid social situations that you associate with stress. This avoidance is an unhealthy restraint. But you can act to restrain impulsively acting out parasitic inhibitions as you would any undesirable urge. For example, you want to lose weight. You restrain yourself from eating cake or having second helpings. You are in a hurry. You restrain yourself from driving at excessive speeds to avoid an accident. You feel uncomfortable about resisting an unhealthy pattern. You talk yourself into living through the discomfort.

When you act with self-restraint, you do so knowing you could have behaved differently. Acts of self-restraint are acts of free will. You made a choice when you knew you could have made another. Self-restraint by conscious decision shows self-observant control over your actions.

To build healthy restraint skills against harmful inhibition, you can execute the PURRRRS system. Use this self-observant approach to boost your reflective skills and reduce inhibitory impulsiveness.

The following example addresses core feelings of inadequacy where you experience wariness and anxiety about an upcoming event, such as meeting strangers at a party.

Pause: When you suspect that you are unhelpfully inhibiting yourself, pause to consider what is happening. Your cues may be that you are feeling tense, tight, and restricted. It can be a surging feeling of inadequacy. Feelings of inadequacy reflect your inner impressions. When you view yourself as inadequate, you'll tend to hold back on the basis of false assumptions, such as the following: (1) whatever you do socially is likely to lead to discomfort, (2) you are not worthy of experiencing a happier existence, and (3) you should be grateful for any crumbs that fall your way. By purposefully pausing when these thoughts become visible, you've started to put the brakes on a harmful impulsive inhibition.

Use: Once you've recognized a harmful inhibition, what resources can you use to resist falling farther down the slippery slope of inadequacy thinking and behavioral inhibition? At this point, you can show some self-restraint: you agree with yourself to suspend judgment about your inadequacies until you've thought through the situation.

Reflect: What can you do to meaningfully reflect on your impressions of inadequacy? Most people with feelings of inadequacy are highly skilled at finding examples to support this self-view. Dealing with core beliefs about your inadequacy can be challenging. But first things first: is it possible for you to separate self-absorbed views from self-observant views? A self-absorbed view is that you are inadequate and people will dislike you, so you might as well avoid others. A self-observant view is that you can identify and question restricting beliefs that lurk behind your anxious impulses.

Reason: How do you take an educated reason approach to defuse the cognitive parts of a parasitic inhibition? Inhibition normally grows from inadequacy thinking, and therefore, an incongruous relationship exists between your beliefs and what you can actually do. Using your educated power of reason, you can use a modified Socratic technique to identify the inconsistencies between your beliefs and the facts: (1) Start by defining inadequacy as you experience it. For example, the statement "I'm inadequate" suggests you suffer from deficiencies and that can only be characterized on the basis of these deficiencies. (2) Present examples in support of your global-deficiency hypothesis. (3) Identify examples of skills showing that you possess competency (you can think; you can reason; you have accomplishments and achievements). (4) Contrast examples of inadequacy thinking with these examples of competency. You now have an incongruity. You can't be both inadequate and competent. (5) What behavioral steps can you take to build upon your capabilities and decrease your inefficiencies? This is your action plan.

Respond: What response steps can you take to restrain yourself from impulsive inhibitory thinking and behavior? The response phase has a strong behavioral dimension. Now armed with a reasoned way to stop generalizing inferiority thoughts, you put yourself through the paces. If you fear rejection by nameless and faceless strangers at a future party, first work on separating assumption and speculation from fact. This can help you suspend judgment about the unknown. Then at the party, make a point to introduce yourself and get the names of others. Try to find a characteristic in each person you meet that reminds you of someone you know and like. That radical shift can start a benign circle where your acceptance of others can lead to reciprocation.

Revise: What types of revision can follow your cognitive and behavioral plan? Reflecting and reasoning are the cognitive parts of the plan. Your behavioral actions are an extension. Taking this awareness-and-action approach, you've acquired some new information. You are now in a position to decide: (1) What bears repeating? (2) What seems promising that you can modify? (3) What merits ditching? However, you may want to repeat your experiment more than once before coming to any conclusions about revisions.

Stabilize: How do you stabilize improvement? Every new situation has its own unique features. Your perceptions and your level of confidence can vary from context to context and group to group. One person can change the dynamic of a group. Your mood can change for natural reasons, such as a lack of sleep. Your mental, physical, and emotional capabilities can be at a triple peak. So, by intentionally creating experiences to defuse inhibitions, you gain practice and gather norms to show how both consistent and variable your life can be, with many steps in between.

Now it is your turn to cite your inhibition and apply the PURRRRS system.

YOUR PERSONAL PURRRRS PLAN

Write down the inhibition that you want to target. Then develop a PURRRRS plan to boost your self-reflective skills and defeat your inhibition.

Target parasitic inhibition: _____

PURRRRS	Actions
Pause: Stop and prepare for action.	
Use: Apply your will and other resources to resist anxious impulses.	
Reflect: Think about what is happening.	
Reason: Think it through.	
Respond: Put yourself through the paces of change.	
Revise: Review process and make adjustments when results suggest trying another way.	
Stabilize: Persist with evolving process until parasitic anxiety is under control.	

Stepping-out-of-Character Experiments

You may feel inhibited at the thought of receiving an award, giving someone a compliment, or receiving positive feedback. You may feel uncomfortable if someone reaches out to help you. This form of self-consciousness can relate to feeling uncomfortable about being in the spotlight.

A big part of defeating inhibition involves building emotional tolerance. Try making yourself the center of attention and get comfortable in that role.

To help yourself build emotional tolerance, you can do stepping-out-of-character exercises. The plan is to act in socially acceptable ways that draw attention to yourself. Thus, you simulate what you fear in order to decrease needless inhibitions. Here are some suggestions:

- At a restaurant for breakfast, you'll likely see listed on the menu "two eggs, any style." Order one scrambled and one fried egg. See what happens.

- At lunch, you could order a grilled cheese sandwich with one slice of wheat and one slice of white bread.

- Wear one white and one black sock for a day.

- In the summer, wear a winter coat at a local mall.

- Ask three people a day for directions.

- Visit a town where you've never been before. See if anyone stares at you.

- Without making a purchase, ask for change at a store. What response do you get?

- If you normally express yourself with a subdued voice, raise the volume.

- If you haven't done so before, go to a museum by yourself and ask others for their opinions about the exhibits.

By practicing this form of disinhibition, you may find that you aren't bothered by being conspicuous.

OTHER EXERCISES TO DEFEAT INHIBITION

Besides exercising restraint and stepping out of character, several other exercises can help you defeat inhibition.

Use Positive Language

Our language has a leading role in how we read situations and how we conjure up sensations and emotions. Think of a lemon drop on your tongue. Do you start to salivate? Think the words "awful," "repulsive," "horrifying," and "rude." Do those words stir negative emotions?

Insecurity, anxiety, and inhibition involve negative thinking and negative words. And if you are not in the habit, expressing yourself using positive emotional words can at first feel both uncomfortable and unnatural. But what's wrong with using positive expressions? Getting over feeling uncomfortable about positive expressions may help build an adaptable and uninhibited outlook.

Try reciting a list of upbeat sensory words to yourself three times a day. Think them before entering social situations. Use one or two daily in conversation. Here is a sampling of positive descriptive words: "serendipitous," "soft," "pleasant," "warm," "kindly," "joyful," "happy," "mellifluous," "velvety," "sweet."

Defuse Inhibition with Humor

If you tend to look at the dour, the downside of life, spend time intentionally doing the opposite. Humor is a promising antidote for inhibition. What can you do to tickle your funny bone? Here are some options:

- Read books by your favorite humorist.

- Watch movies that you find funny.

- Spend time with people who make you laugh.

- Use your imagination to turn something fearful into something hilarious.

It's hard to laugh and feel inhibited at the same time.

A Sensory Awareness Experiment

The Russian physiologist and Nobel Prize winner Ivan Pavlov lectured that as humans we are first connected to our environment through sensory experience. But with the evolution of language (the secondary signaling system), we depart from our roots. Words increasingly substitute for sensory awareness. This separation becomes the basis for many forms of human distress (Pavlov 1941).

The gestalt therapist Fritz Perls developed a view that was partially compatible with Pavlov's. He thought people waste too much effort intellectualizing and engaging in polarity conflicts, such as between good and bad. Such cognitive states split them off from other aspects of their personalities. His focus was to help people confront their opposites (such as demands and retreats), accept their experiences, and develop a healthy gestalt, or sense of wholeness.

Perls described a sensory awareness exercise that is compatible with stepping-out-of-character exercises (Perls, Goodman, and Hefferline 1951). Here you make a shift from an inhibitory focus to an awareness of your surroundings.

Over the next week, take fifteen minutes a day to move about your outside environment. Observe through your senses. What do you smell, hear, feel, see, and taste? Look for sensory experiences you have not been aware of before.

Preface each new sensory experience with the phrase, "Now I'm aware of. ..." For example, you may see a brown pot with plants on a windowsill that you have not noticed before ("Now I am aware of a brown pot with red flowers"). As you pass a pizza parlor, you may smell the pizza ("Now I am aware of the scent of pizza"). You may observe the movement of a cat ("Now I'm aware of a running cat"). The clouds in the sky might change ("Now I'm aware of changing pictures in the clouds"). When you are not listening to yourself, your ears can pick up sounds that otherwise might have gone unnoticed. Your sense of smell sharpens. How does a flower smell? You can find new ways to stimulate your taste buds. What do rose petals taste like?

Becoming more engaged in your surroundings is an antidote to self-absorption and inhibition.

Substitute Assertion for Inhibition

Alfred Adler thought that, for many people, every change of situation brings up apprehension and fears. The fear was the result of how we weigh and evaluate the change. His solutions involve recognizing how you suffer interpretation errors that can lead you into tragedy. Education is the key to removing these errors (Adler 1927).

The conditioned-reflex therapist, Andrew Salter, took a more behavioral approach to defeating inhibition. He recommended disinhibiting yourself by expressing yourself, even if you must insult others. He believed such actions are preferable to an obsequious, inhibited manner (Salter 1949). Salter went on to say that if you take extreme positions that oppose your inhibitions, you are eventually likely to strike a balance. Salter is credited with starting the assertiveness movement.

Assertiveness, in the sense that Salter suggests, is roughly the same as aggressiveness. That view is currently out of vogue. Psychologists Robert Alberti and Michael Emmons (2001) describe *assertiveness* as self-expression directed toward equalizing relationships with others. Empathy, honesty, straightforwardness, and omitting needlessly harmful statements characterize a healthy assertive style.

If you think you can benefit from correcting a social inhibition through self-assertion, here are two start-up tips:

1. Behaviorally inhibited people often display a half smile as they gaze away from the eyes of others. You can block this automatic motor pattern by doing the opposite. Make a point to glance (not stare) at the other person. As you do, think of something pleasant. Smile if you can. By projecting a warm smile, you can make yourself feel good. You can encourage pleasant feelings between yourself and others.

2. Break the ice. Share an observation with someone else. Say you are checking out at the supermarket. You have a natural opportunity to observe to the cashier, "It looks like a busy day at the supermarket." Comments like this can initiate a pleasant dialogue.

Do these and the other suggested exercises, and you will be well on your way to defeating your inhibition.

KEY IDEAS AND ACTION PLAN

What key ideas from this chapter can you use to rid yourself of your parasitic anxieties and fears? What's your action plan? Write it down. Test it out. Record what happened.

Key Ideas

1.

2.

3.

Action Plan

1.

2.

3.

Results from Actions Taken

1.

2.

3.

POSTSCRIPT

If you were once a shy or inhibited person and have since broken free from needless inhibitions, you may still find yourself a tad quieter in a group than most. You are likely to feel more comfortable within your own skin knowing that you can express yourself with impact when it is in your interest to do so. If you experience yourself feeling too inhibited, there is a gap between this point in time and a point in the future where you may feel free of needless inhibitions and more natural. It's what you do during this time that will tell a tale about shedding inhibitions or carrying them forward. In the long run, shedding inhibitions requires less effort than continuing to carry them.

CHAPTER 15

Addressing Self-Worth Fears

Seventeenth century French philosopher René Descartes doubted the existence of everything. The one thing he could not doubt was the fact that he was doubting. He concluded with the famous observation, "I think, therefore I am." Here's a question that Descartes did not consider: Is who you are based on who you think you are?

Certainly, your core sense of self is central to your sense of well-being. But is this self a bundle of mercurial changing beliefs? Does it reflect attitude? Can you define yourself by your values? Is your definition of self an illusion that would vanish without the use of language?

This chapter will look into the world of the self. You'll see how your perception affects your sense of who you are. You'll see how to unknot yourself from parasitic anxieties and fears through building a strong and realistic self-concept.

AVOIDING THE CONTINGENT-WORTH TRAP

Psychologist Arnold Lazarus quips, "Western cultures put too much emphasis on success. This is one of my pet peeves—the ubiquitous emphasis on competition, on winning, of being number one, and so forth. ... Johnny is told his parents are ashamed of him for his lower than expected grades" (Knaus 2000, 48). These pressures can affect a child's sense of worth by cobbling personal value to achievements.

How do you judge your worth? Do you assess it by your physical appearance? By your athletic prowess? From what you value? By being able to "beat the system"? Does your sense of self-worth come from your accomplishments and from what other people think of what you do?

However you judge your personal value, this is your *theory of worth*. Many in achievement-oriented cultures base their theory of worth on successes and what others think of them. This makes for a contingent-worth theory.

A *contingent-worth* theory can have an "I am not enough" emphasis: "I'm not smart enough." "I'm not confident enough." "I'm not attractive enough." With a tarnished sense of worth, you are likely to feel inadequate. This raises your sense of vulnerability, lowers your threshold for feeling threatened, and elevates your risk for parasitic anxieties and fears. If your solution for feeling worthy and gaining freedom from fear is to become something other than what you are, how can you feel good about yourself and escape your fears? Your solution is impossible.

Contingent-worth theories reflect either-or dichotomous thinking. You're either one thing or its opposite: a success or a failure. You think, "I'm worthy because I look beautiful," "I'm worthy because I contribute to my society," or "I'm worthy because I'm wealthy." But what happens if the source of your self-esteem becomes unavailable?

A young actress client named Carol routinely played the parts of teenagers. She got her self-worth from her youthful and beautiful appearance. When I first saw Carol, she was thirty years old. Used to playing the part of a much younger woman, she identified herself with those roles. But now the roles were no longer available to her.

Carol freaked when she saw her first wrinkle. Coupled with her loss of acting roles, she felt anxious and devastated. She believed she had lost her identity. As you might suspect, Carol stopped looking for acting jobs. She fell into a slump.

Carol based her worth on having the appearance of a teenager. And this worked well for many years. But the time came when what she found worthy about herself was no longer available. Now she had a conflict between reality and fantasy.

Fortunately, Carol began to accept the reality that she had a broad range of talents and was much more than a pretty face. She adapted to changing times and roles. She put her efforts on auditioning for dramatic adult parts.

Once Carol saw her worth as extending beyond her appearance, she felt relieved. The idea of a pluralistic self put things into perspective for her.

I first saw Carol in the early days of my career. Over the years, I happily saw that she continued to develop as an actress and to grow as a self-accepting person.

The Pluralistic Self

You can choose to accept a contingent-worth definition. This definition can include basing your worth on your values, family, or anything else about yourself. However, if your theory of worth is not working in your favor, exploring a pluralistic theory of self can give you a different perspective.

A *pluralistic theory of self* is the proposition that you are much more than your collected traits, qualities, aptitudes, and abilities. From a pluralistic view, you can't be only one way: an anxious person. Rather, you have thousands of attributes, abilities, feelings, experiences, and memories. You have the ability to learn. Otherwise, you wouldn't be able to read this book. You have a broad range of skills. You can think, express yourself, visualize the future, and profit from past experiences. You have social sensitivities. In a nutshell, you have a lot going for you. But there is more.

The roles you take are part of your self-view. They include father, daughter, teacher, executive, cook, or gadfly. Values add another dimension to the mix. These are your guiding principles on what is important and how to lead your life. Values can include responsibility, integrity, and persistence. Your beliefs, such as pluralistic or contingent-worth beliefs, strongly influence how you interpret experience. Your cardinal attributes stand out. They can include being shy, extroverted, persistent, creative, witty, mathematical, musical, forceful, flexible, spiritual, grounded, autocratic, dominant, passive, compassionate, thoughtful, anxious, athletic, and so forth. You possess at least eighteen thousand of these attributes. But there is more than that.

You have habits, routines, and expectations that characterize you. Your self-view can include your body image, intelligence, innovativeness, will, health, appearance, and how you get along with others. You likely have seven primary emotions, such as fear, sadness, and happiness. These spin out into about five hundred secondary emotions, such as angst and exuberance. Experiences and accomplishments add to the mix of what is a self. Your friendships count. So, are you who you think you are?

From a pluralistic perspective, it is hard to overgeneralize about yourself based on a single characterization or label. By developing a pluralistic view, you are less likely to feel weighted down by contingent-worth thinking and accompanying anxieties. Free from surplus stress, you are less likely to feel anxious about yourself. You are more likely to take responsibility for your own change program by using your talents in positive ways.

EXPANDING AN INCONGRUITY BETWEEN WORTH AND SELF

Compare your theory of worth to your theory of self. In completing this exercise, list your accomplishments and attributes that figure into your sense of worth. This may include personal initiatives you have taken or what you have contributed to others, in addition to any other potential criteria.

To build a theory of self, you can start with a collection of your beliefs and experiences. Who knows? You may quickly run out of space describing what you know about your self.

Theory of Worth	Theory of Self

If you hold on to a contingent-worth view, where your self-worth is measured by what you do, and you also believe that the self is too broad and complex to measure, you have a contradiction to resolve. If you are a complex human, how can you be only one way, say, a failure or a success? It is here where any contingent-worth theory is in jeopardy. For example, suppose you defined yourself on the basis of a noteworthy feature. You label yourself an anxious person. But how can a complex, pluralistic, evolving self be only one way: anxious? When you experience a lot of anxiety, that label can seem to fit. However, acting anxiously does not define you. Rather, it marks a recurring experience.

Looking Beyond Contingent Worth

Once free from needless anxiety about your self, does this mean you are free to follow an "anything goes" outlook? If you wanted the money in your neighbor's bank account, would you forge a check? After all, you might reason, you are a complex self that cannot be globally judged. But you're living in the real world. Such immature thinking leads to antisocial behavior that carries consequences.

The pluralistic theory of self includes acting responsibly and ethically. Indeed, once freed from a limited and punitive self-worth agenda, you are more likely to operate on the basis of higher-order values. Why? From a self-observant view, it is normally in your enlightened self-interest to do so.

Is there anything to salvage from a contingent-worth theory? Instead of defining your worth based on contingencies, you can turn some contingencies into goals. If you have made your worth contingent on your grades in school, improving your grades can remain a goal.

Improving skills and making achievements represent worthwhile goals. This becomes part of what you can direct your efforts to do. From a pluralistic perspective, the fruits of your efforts don't define you. They benefit you.

You can adopt a pluralistic theory of self and yet find yourself surrounded by people operating with contingent-worth theories who define you by what you do. So, if someone called you a green mongoose, would that make you one?

KELLY'S ROLE CONSTRUCTS

Transactional analysis (TA) pioneer Eric Berne thought that negative ideas and actions follow scripted patterns. A distressed lifestyle is the result of self-limiting life plans that govern how you live. If you script your life as an anxious person, you are likely to play out the script without questioning the authorship. The goal of TA is to change the script from a self-defeating to a self-enhancing one (Berne 1964).

In the 1950s, personal-construct theorist George Kelly mapped out how we construct reality through the scripts we follow. If the script links to problems, we can edit the script (Kelly 1955).

Kelly would view you as having the ability to anticipate what will happen to you next. These anticipations may give you a big advantage. Your abilities include asserting self-control, acting to control the environment, responding to changing events, and initiating changes. Throughout this process, you actively construct meaning for the events and realities that you perceive and are in a better position to influence the events around you. Kelly notes that "the world keeps on rolling on and revealing these predictions to be either correct or misleading. This fact provides the basis for the revision of constructs" (Kelly 1955, 14).

When you leave your home to go to the grocery store, you expect to see certain things along the way: vehicles in traffic, stoplights, trees, and eventually the faces of people in the store. But what if there were no traffic, store, or person? You anticipated one thing and saw another. What might this mean? You'd probably try to figure out what happened.

Kelly thought that most people act like scientists. They have theories about themselves, others, and the world around them. They make observations. They gather facts. They generalize. They make predictions. But the process can be naive and flawed.

What you expect will shape your response. Anticipate meeting friendly people, and this anticipation shapes your initial response. Anticipate meeting judgmental people, and you are likely to experience a threat and possibly anxiety. So what happens if you repeatedly anticipate threats that do not exist? Kelly suggests a reconstruction of these anticipations. Reconstruction can come from reflection. It also can come from testing your expectations.

Kelly thought that changes in perception come about through experimenting with new behaviors. He emphasized risk-taking, adventure, and creativity. He saw personal development as a process of extending your capabilities and reorganizing based upon results.

Establishing a New Character

Practically everyone can find scripted patterns that promote disharmony within themselves. Kelly would say that we would wisely change these patterns. His idea was to rewrite the script, practice the new script, and keep what works. In this way, you create a new set of reality-tested anticipations.

When you follow anxious scripts, you default to a dire prediction over a positive, objective one. Suppose your major fear script was to get tongue-tied around people in positions of authority. As a result, you typically take the blame, whatever it may be. To avoid conflict, you allow yourself to get bullied into doing other people's work for them.

It takes extra awareness and extra steps to interrupt this sequence and to substitute a healthier way of thinking, feeling, and behaving. But you can do it by rewriting the script.

To start changing your script, create a *pretend person*. Give the person a name. Keep it to yourself. This pretend person can do what you've seen others do effectively in similar circumstances; such actions are likely to have a positive impact and are potentially within your ability to do.

Your pretend person is the character in your script who addresses your life issues. Through this pretend person, you will shift from deficit scripting (repeating negative habits) to how you'd prefer to act.

Design your new script so that it describes measurable and achievable changes in your behavior that are consistent with reasonable goals. These behavior changes can be the opposite of what you usually do or a minor adjustment in what you usually do. For example, instead of being tongue-tied around authority, the pretend person may speak naturally, as if talking to anyone. Instead of taking the blame, the pretend person assesses situations to determine where the bulk of the accountability lies. The pretend person accepts conflict and deals with it. If it's someone else's job, the pretend person declines to do it.

As you write the new script, give directions in reasonable detail. Break down how the pretend person will act your part. This can include tone and volume of voice, body language, and clothing style to use. It can include how to make a positive impact on others without compromising your own rights. It can involve dealing with pressures toward conformity. If a coworker bullies you into doing his or her work, the pretend person refuses.

The bully will want the pretend person (you) to go back to acting like a rug. So plan for how you'll stick to your guns. Perhaps a simple question, "Whose job is this?" can get the point across. If that doesn't do it, then continue, "That's your job. Why do you want me to do it?" If necessary, the pretend person flatly says no. If your pretend person's role involves facing conflict, especially against unreasonable demands, then the pretend person accepts emotional discomfort as part of the behavioral change process.

The following framework will help you write your new script.

YOUR KELLY ROLE-CHANGE FRAMEWORK

Here is your framework for behaving like a scientist, taking charge of your own development, and creatively testing a new script by playing the role of the pretend person.

1. Before creating this script, create a new name for yourself. Keep the name a secret. (This is like an actor assuming a new identity and name for the purposes of playing a part.)

2. Describe the basic theme that is the thesis of your experiment. Describe how you tend to anticipate acting in certain situations when you feel driven by parasitic fears. This is what you want to change. Write this in the third person (that is, use he or she).

3. Draft the new script to include the changes that you want to make. Describe what your pretend person does in targeted situations. Consider how your pretend person would act without the burden of fear: how would this person think, feel, and act differently? Describe your pretend person's approach.

4. When writing the script, define how you can have a positive impact on other people as well as advance your own interests.

5. Consider how your pretend person will project his or her voice, use body language, determine types of risks, decide the manner of expressing ideas and feelings, and so forth.

6. Now that you have a new script, try it out. Play the role of the pretend person. For how long should you do it? As a rule of thumb, test the script for about two weeks. At the end of that time, you'll likely have figured out what to drop, what to modify, and what to maintain that feels right. If part of the role seems especially promising from the start, extend it. If part of the role might do more harm than good, modify it or drop it.

SCRIPTING EMPATHIC THINKING

Telling people to stop being afraid is rarely fruitful. Angry confrontations don't work any better. Both approaches suggest a lack of empathy. There's a more humanistic approach.

The humanistic psychology movement started in the 1960s. It helped make a shift away from the autocratic and then-dominant Freudian psychology and radical behaviorism methods that were control oriented. This person-centered approach focused on individuality, human potential, and self-directed change.

Psychologist Abraham Maslow (1962) described humanistic psychology as the "third force." The first was behaviorism. The second was Freudianism. A powerful part of the third force came from George Kelly's work and that of Albert Ellis.

The core builders, such as Maslow, Rollo May, and Carl Rogers, gave an impetus and respect to this movement. They collectively emphasized genuineness, acceptance, and empathy as basic conditions for human development. There is significant research to support these value-oriented approaches.

Empathy is a bedrock concept, especially in the work of Carl Rogers and his client-centered therapy. *Empathy* is the ability to understand and share the feelings of others.

You can also have self-empathy. More often than not, you probably don't feel empathy for yourself when you are stricken by parasitic anxieties and fears. Nevertheless, by causing a shift from self-absorbed fears to a self-observant view, you can decide to see yourself through more empathetic eyes.

When bugged by fear, your sense of self is under pressure. Inadequacy thinking distorts your global self-concept. You could stand empathic relief.

By treating yourself like your best friend, you can take a more empathic view toward yourself. If your friend had foibles and faults, would you reject your friend, or would you accept your friend and empathize with his or her difficulties?

You are likely to get farther by taking a pluralistic, empathic, and accepting view of yourself than by chastising yourself and creating stress. Predictably, if you feel respected and understood, you'll feel less pressured by cognitive-evoked fears. You'll have more free energy to make self-directed changes, using cognitive, emotional, and behavioral approaches. Focus your thinking in an empathic direction and see what results.

YOUR EMPATHY SCRIPT

To help make this shift toward self-understanding, write an empathy script for yourself, giving reasons for having empathy for yourself. Make use of the following thoughts:

1. You have a right to achieve self-acceptance and a place in this world.

2. You have many talents and positive qualities that are vital parts of your pluralistic self.

3. You can accept the existence of even those feelings that you don't like. They are part of your self-experience.

These and other self-views can feed into a feeling of understanding, or empathy. Use the following space to write your empathy script.

An empathic approach is not a wimpish one. You can remain tough on your problems while still being kind to yourself.

DEVELOPING SELF-EFFICACY

You are more likely to create and sustain a positive new direction if you can assign the change to your own efforts rather than to medications, the fates, or luck. Self-efficacy is a self-directed way to attain and sustain inner control through your own efforts. Developed by Stanford professor and psychologist Albert Bandura, *self-efficacy* is the belief that you have the power to organize, regulate, and direct your actions to achieve mastery over needless anxiety as well as over posttraumatic stresses (Bandura 1994; Benight and Bandura 2004).

You can build self-efficacy by showing yourself that you can take steps to overcome negative patterns. For example, decide how to organize your resources to achieve the results you seek. Activate these resources. Acknowledge the results of your efforts. Doing so will add credibility to the belief that you can carry through with a constructive plan to decrease fearful thinking and sensations and to achieve positive results.

KEY IDEAS AND ACTION PLAN

What key ideas from this chapter can you use to rid yourself of your parasitic anxieties and fears? What's your action plan? Write it down. Test it out. Record what happened.

Key Ideas

1.

2.

3.

Action Plan

1.

2.

3.

Results from Actions Taken

1.

2.

3.

POSTSCRIPT

The self may be an illusion, but how you think and feel about your self is real. This feeling rarely exists apart from your social world and your thoughts of what you think others think of you.

Chapter 16 will present another challenge that relates to your self-view: addressing social-evaluation fears. This is an especially good area to carry over knowledge of building a pluralistic self-concept, devising and practicing different scripts, expressing self-empathy, and practicing self-regulatory actions to boost your social self-efficacy.

Addressing Social-Evaluation Anxieties

Parasitic social anxieties and fears are far more intense than the normal jitters and butterflies in your stomach before you give a talk or meet with strangers. Social anxieties and fears can be among the most brutal kind of tension. Expecting to be evaluated, disapproved of, and rejected, you are likely to experience unpleasant physical and emotional sensations. Your heart may pound, you may sweat, and you may feel flushed, stiff, or rigid. Those thoughts and feelings can make you feel as if you're living in a torture chamber.

Fear of disapproval puts a freeze on the quality of your expressions, constructive assertions, and communications. Since significant parts of our lives involve other people, a generalized fear of disapproval can put a pall over the possibility of establishing and enjoying a range of relationships consistent with your social interests.

If you suffer from social-evaluation anxiety, you're hardly alone. About 11 million Americans suffer from severe social anxieties and fears that cause them to feel petrified by social contacts. Perhaps as many as 30 million more fall below that threshold, yet feel socially awkward more often than most people. Members of this latter group will sometimes feel crippled by parasitic social fears. But often, these ordinarily silent fears can get swept under the rug or played down. Feared locations can be avoided, anxieties can be masked with a few drinks or drugs, or coping can be sidetracked through workaholism.

Can you change a pattern of social anxieties and fears? You can defeat parasitic social anxieties and fears by implementing a prime solution emphasized in this book: face and resolve your fear in the context in which it occurs. This chapter will look at how to uncouple yourself from your fears.

DIRECTIONS FOR SOCIAL FEARS

Social contacts are inescapable. People are all around. We live and work in groups. We contact each other through multiple social channels. But social anxieties and fears can fall within select life areas, such as going to parties, attending formal social events, or giving public talks. With crippling impact, parasitic anxieties and fears also can generalize to practically every part of your social life.

Aside from the subjective feelings of stress, terrifying social-threat thinking can strongly influence your choice of mate, work, recreational opportunities, and the general quality of your life. Males with social phobias tend to marry later and artificially limit their occupational opportunities. Social phobias can place limits on a woman's career and often the selection of a mate: a woman with social phobias tends to settle rather than select.

When do parasitic social anxieties and fears start? Parasitic social fears typically start around adolescence, but they can begin earlier or later. They are equally prevalent between men and women (Beesdo et al. 2007; Beidel and Turner 2007).

What are general signs of a parasitic social anxiety? When anticipating social experiences or interacting with other people, you tend to feel self-consciousness. You fear being evaluated and judged. You expect that most others won't like you. You dread feeling uptight, having your heart pound, and being unable to think straight. The thought of speaking in front of groups, for example, can stir intense anxiety months before the event.

What are general signs of a parasitic social fear? You have trouble making small talk, shy away from public view, or tense up when meeting people in positions of authority. You normally hide when you hear the doorbell ring. Sweating, trembling, and blushing are common. When you think to make a comment in a group, you clam up and lose the opportunity.

Do parasitic social anxieties and fears exist in pure form? You will rarely find a pure social fear. They practically always have coexisting complications. Depression is common (Ingram et al. 2005). Perfectionism is common (Ashbaugh et al. 2007). Alcohol and drug abuse are common (Baillie and Sannibale 2007). However, by effectively addressing social fears and stripping away coexisting conditions, you can gain relief.

Can parasitic social anxieties and fears be overcome? Social anxieties and fears can be so inhibiting and costly that many of those absorbed in these fears would do practically anything to overcome them if they knew how. You can effectively address these parasites. Cognitive behavioral therapy approaches for social anxiety disabilities are highly effective (Butler et al. 2006; Gould and Johnson 2001; Gil, Carrillo, and Meca 2001). Through applying these techniques, not only can you find ways to decrease these fears; you can also add rewarding social dimensions to your life.

PUTTING A FACE ON SOCIAL FEARS

Even the most confident people can experience stage fright in some social situations. But when social anxieties and fears rise to a level of concern, they are more than the jitters. Parasitic social fear is a persistent fear of getting tongue-tied, socially fumbling, turning red, boring people, or looking like a fool. Here are some examples:

Tom attended a New Year's party with his friend Bob. Neither felt comfortable about striking up conversations with women. But they were quite comfortable communicating with each other.

Tom saw Sally in animated talk with a group of women. He thought about going over to her. To boost his courage, he slugged down a few drinks. Then he did a hesitation waltz while commiserating with Bob about why women like Sally make themselves unapproachable. At the end of the evening, as he and Bob left the party, they were entangled in an inebriated conversation about why women should approach men.

June has a warm personable quality and feels at ease meeting new people. Despite her comfort with meeting and talking to people, June has an extreme public-speaking anxiety. Because she is afraid to speak before staff and customer groups, she refuses job promotions. She imagines herself feeling flushed and tongue-tied and then running from the stage in disgrace. She says she'd rather spend a year in a dungeon than deliver a talk.

Don and Ellen have an intimate date at their favorite restaurant. Ellen feels happy about the occasion and is animated and expressive. Don finds her too loud. He believes that she must be disturbing the other patrons. He sternly criticizes Ellen for her loudness. Ellen suggests that he has a warped sense of values: she's the one he's going home with, not the strangers at the next table.

What do Tom, Bob, June, and Don have in common? Each acts self-consciously. Each expects to be evaluated. Each expects rejection. Each gets self-absorbed in fearful thinking and behaves as if they dread experiencing the feeling of fear.

Peering into the Looking Glass

Social fear reflects a self-absorbed process. Despite fearing evaluation, your social fears are mostly about you and what you think about your fears and public image. But sometimes you can project your fearful inner imagery onto others.

By peeling away a few layers of the parasitic fear onion, you might find that you tend to believe that others will think about you just as you think they will (Cooley 1902). But to affirm this *looking-glass* view requires mind-reading abilities that humans don't possess.

If you project fearful inner imagery onto others, there is a quick solution. Behave the way you would like to see yourself behave. The odds favor that you will come to see yourself in the manner in which you behave. But if you interpret such a change in your behavior as faking it, your self-view will tend to be governed by this interpretation.

TAKING A SOCIAL-FEARS INVENTORY

Do you have social anxieties and fears that merit working to correct? Use the following inventory to check. You may recognize some conditions in yourself that you can go on to address. If you are largely free from fear in social areas, you may still gather ideas from this chapter for addressing your nonsocial fears. Many techniques that prove effective with social fears also apply to the nonsocial variety.

This social-fears inventory uses a sampling of thoughts, feelings, and actions commonly experienced by people with parasitic social anxieties and fears. The inventory is not a standardized measure, but it shows some of the restraints people with social anxieties often have.

The inventory serves a triple purpose:

1. It suggests a broad range of social-fear experiences.

2. It boosts awareness of your personal involvement with these fears.

3. It identifies high-ranked items that point to areas that you can profitably work to correct.

WHAT'S YOUR FEAR?

Instructions: Rate each situation according to how you generally feel by circling the number that describes your reaction: 1 = never, 2 = rarely, 3 = sometimes, 4 = often, 5 = habitually.

1.	"I feel uptight before approaching someone I don't know."	1 2 3 4 5
2.	"I'm afraid of making a fool of myself in public."	1 2 3 4 5
3.	"I have very little to offer others."	1 2 3 4 5
4.	"Others are more sociable than I am."	1 2 3 4 5
5.	"If people really knew me, they wouldn't like me."	1 2 3 4 5
6.	"When someone looks in my direction, I look away."	1 2 3 4 5
7.	"I'm afraid to make a mistake in front of other people."	1 2 3 4 5
8.	"I feel insecure about my social abilities."	1 2 3 4 5
9.	"My conversations feel strained."	1 2 3 4 5
10.	"I am poor at making small talk."	1 2 3 4 5
11.	"I worry about upcoming social events."	1 2 3 4 5
12.	"I feel intimidated in the presence of authority."	1 2 3 4 5

13. "I believe that others think I'm weird or stupid."   1 2 3 4 5

14. "I feel self-conscious."   1 2 3 4 5

15. "I'm afraid to answer the telephone."   1 2 3 4 5

16. "I worry about what others think about me."   1 2 3 4 5

17. "I'm afraid of feeling fear in a social setting."   1 2 3 4 5

18. "Even if I extend an invitation, I fear that people won't visit me."   1 2 3 4 5

19. "I feel very ill-at-ease around people I don't know well."   1 2 3 4 5

20. "I fear others noticing that I'm afraid."   1 2 3 4 5

21. "I feel insecure about my appearance."   1 2 3 4 5

22. "I feel uncomfortable eating alone in restaurants."   1 2 3 4 5

23. "I feel anxious entering a room where people are already seated."   1 2 3 4 5

24. "I fear criticism."   1 2 3 4 5

25. "I feel embarrassed when I get attention in a group."   1 2 3 4 5

26. "I freeze up when I'm around attractive people."   1 2 3 4 5

27. "Before I talk, I rehearse what I will say."   1 2 3 4 5

28. "I fear being the center of attention."   1 2 3 4 5

29. "I fear going to formal social events."   1 2 3 4 5

30. "I have more courage after a few drinks [or getting high]."   1 2 3 4 5

31. "I don't match up to other people's standards."   1 2 3 4 5

32. "I fade into the background in group settings."   1 2 3 4 5

33. "I stumble over my words when talking to people I don't know well."   1 2 3 4 5

34. "I'll cross the street to avoid saying hello to an acquaintance."   1 2 3 4 5

35. "I experience extreme stage fright about speaking before a group."   1 2 3 4 5

36. "I want to hide if people I'm with draw attention to themselves."   1 2 3 4 5

In reviewing your inventory responses, questions where you circled 4 or 5 suggest a problem area. If you endorsed ten or more items with 4 or 5, you could have a general social phobia. So, instead of many problems, you have many variations of the same problem.

In fact, the inventory identifies clusters of conditions linked to social anxieties and fears. As you review your answers, you may find that they reflect such issues as emotional intolerance, negative social self-concept, and avoidance behaviors, such as ducking opportunities to speak before groups or not answering the phone.

If you are like practically everyone else, you can find at least one zone in your life where you feel socially anxious about one thing or another. You are into sales and feel rejected if you don't make the sale. Expecting rejection, you tense up before meeting a sales prospect. An acquaintance walks by without acknowledging you. You wonder what you did wrong. You feel awkward about approaching someone you know, lest you "intrude" on him or her. So you may have zones in your life where you are socially anxious that don't appear on the inventory.

Using this personal information as well as the results of the inventory, what is your most significant parasitic social anxiety or fear?

_____

_____

Then use the following three levels of intervention to help yourself quell this social fear.

THREE LEVELS OF INTERVENTION

After identifying a social fear or pattern of social fears, you can confront your fear at multiple levels: practical, empirical, and core-problem solving. The *practical level* involves taking commonsense actions. The *empirical level* involves examining your perceptions and beliefs, and scientifically debunking the ones that are parasitic. At the *core level*, you get down to parasitic thoughts about yourself and other deeply held negative views that, upon examination, don't jibe with reality.

As an example of how to use these three levels of intervention, consider the fear of speaking in public. This fear is the second most common fear, after snake phobias; public-speaking anxieties generally carry greater consequences, however.

Public-speaking anxieties revolve around how you evaluate your ability to express yourself and your public impact. When your self-evaluation is parasitic, it tends to weave negatively through many parts of your social life.

Fear of public speaking shows up in many ways: when talking before a group, asking a question, stating an opinion, fearing to offend, or remaining silent when you have something to say. Here's a way to address this complex fear at practical, empirical, and core levels of intervention.

The Practical Level

Practical interventions involve applying behavioral actions and commonsense ideas to reduce your fears. Examples might be to quit drinking caffeinated beverages when this substance elevates your risk for anxiety. Or to engage in moderate exercise to help reduce depression and anxiety, boost your immune system, provide added energy, improve concentration, and give you other benefits of fitness.

Here are some practical tips for overcoming a public-speaking anxiety:

Have a clear goal of what you want to accomplish. This can help you shift to a self-observant point of view. Ask yourself what it is that you want to accomplish. Is it to dispense information? Is it to inspire action? Is it to deliver an uplifting message? Is it to share a passion? For example, your passion is gardening, and you've been asked to give a talk about gardening. Is your goal to desensitize yourself to speak in front of groups? Your goal suggests a practical approach to your public-speaking fear challenge.

Engage what you fear through behavioral exposure exercises. This means practicing and receiving feedback to improve. You can create many practice opportunities. Ask one question in a class that you attend. Volunteer to give an announcement. Read a news item that interests you to your luncheon group. Join a Toastmasters International group where you get practice speaking under graduated and supportive conditions. Teach a class.

Videotape a mock presentation. This will help you hear, see, and iron out any wrinkles you might discover. Common wrinkles include hesitation statements, such as "uh" and gestures such as scratching your nose. Video feedback is a useful way to iron out such wrinkles.

Don't sweat the opening. You may struggle with an opening statement: "Should I tell a joke? Should I start with an attention-grabbing statement?" Your opening statement doesn't have to be profound. Telling an audience what you are going to say and then saying it is often sufficient.

Keep it simple. For shorter presentations, build your talk around one to five main points. Palming a three-by-five index card that lists the main points can help you stay on track.

Avoid overpreparation. You may concern yourself about not having enough to say. That's legitimate. But consider the opposite. Overpreparation is more likely to prove defeating. Flooding your mind and notes with details taxes your memory, and juggling too much information can distance you from your audience. However, if you are making a presentation on a complex topic or research, a computer slide-show presentation can help keep you organized. You can use the visuals to outline the main points. You fill in the details.

Rehearse using the *main point method*. Rehearse by presenting the main points you plan to make. Start with saying the main points. Repeat the exercise and expand on each point. Then add a new detail each time you rehearse until you've reached your allotted time.

When speaking, look at your audience. But focus your attention on those who appear most attentive.

Don't expect perfect retention from your audience. Audiences consist of people with fallible memories, biases, and diverse opinions. Few—if any—will remember all you had to say. Research shows that college students will leave a lecture and forget about 70 percent of what they heard within hours or days. What do you want your audience to remember? Focus on communicating that part.

The Empirical Level

Empirical interventions involve applying methods of scientific inquiry to defeat parasitic fears. Applying this method can cause a noteworthy shift from self-absorbed parasitic thinking to a self-observant approach. The following questions and answers show how to address a common demand that people with public-speaking fears often place upon themselves.

What are common cognitive signatures for public-speaking anxieties? Parasitic public-speaking anxieties can come from "have to" beliefs, such as the following: (1) You have to express yourself perfectly well. (2) You have to make infallible statements. (3) You have to impress and amaze your audience with your knowledge and intellect. (4) You have to be perfect or you'll be a failure. Redefine your "have to" statements as guesses or hypotheses. Now you are in a position to move from "have to" expectation to an evaluation of the expectation. For example, "I hypothesize that an audience expects that I'll give a perfect speech." "I hypothesize that unless I'm perfect, I'm a failure." Scientists seek to disconfirm hypotheses. They temporarily accept what can't be disconfirmed. Act as your own scientific authority. What loopholes can you find in "have to" hypotheses that you hold? Can you find a more accurate operating hypothesis?

What conclusions extend from a "have to" view? When you hold "have to" expectations, your mental associations can spread like wildfires. If you assume that you will not do well enough to meet your expectations, this can extend to a looking-glass view: you project that your audience will evaluate your presentation and deliver a failing grade. Now, how can you tell in advance that an audience, if polled, would think as you think about your upcoming talk?

What dire predictions can come from "have to" predictions? Anxiety about public speaking often involves dire predictions, such as getting booed off the stage. One question puts this matter into perspective: where is the evidence that this will occur? Unless you are an arch conservative speaking before an extremely liberal audience, or vice versa, dire predictions are dire predictions and no more than that.

How valid are fears of failure? Occurring before the fact, failure is a prediction. Predictions are not the same as facts. But how likely is your prediction that you will fail? If you are predicting failure based on an expected audience response, think again. It's not possible to predict every person's response with perfect accuracy. If you assume that everyone in your audience will come to the same conclusions about you, this belief suggests that you plan to speak before members of a brainwashed cult of programmed thinkers. If you speak before a normal audience, you are likely to be on safer ground by assuming variability between audience members in their degree of attention and interest.

If you think you have to make an infallible presentation, does this jibe with reality? What are the chances of getting a 100 percent positive rating from an audience consisting of people of diverse views, interests, and motives? Not very high. You'll rarely satisfy all members of your audience. You may have an arch perfectionist or two in the audience who like to exercise their defect-detection skills by finding fault with others. Since no one is perfect, they never run out of defects to gripe about. Some will have quibbles even if your speech is perfect.

Do you have to perfectly maintain the attention of all of your audience? If you fear losing some of your audience to their meandering minds, do you plan to take the blame? For example, can you legitimately blame yourself if some people came up with new ideas inspired by your speech and then drifted away into this new train of thought? They may have been temporarily lost to you while making gains for themselves. Others might have gotten a rotten night's sleep the night before and would have slept through an artillery attack. Others might feel genuinely bored. Your topic doesn't interest them. How do you know what's what?

CHALLENGING "HAVE TO" THINKING

Use the following space to identify and challenge "have to" thinking in public speaking, dating anxiety, fear of intruding, or whatever other form your social anxieties and fears might take.

"Have to" Demands	Empirical Challenges

Core Interventions

With *core level interventions*, your focus is on your self-concept, your ability to accept and tolerate discomfort and adversity, and your personal attitudes, philosophies, beliefs, and values. Core factors include how you habitually interpret and handle setbacks. If you tend to magnify them, you could end up with double troubles, such as blaming yourself for not being strong enough to manage your stresses. An intervention would be to ask yourself, if you think you can't stand what you don't like, are you not already standing a tension that grows from a negative evaluation of your ability to withstand stress?

A common secondary distress is the tendency to magnify the onerousness of a situation. Sometimes this magnification reflects a core sense of vulnerability and self-doubts about your coping resources. Here, the core challenge is to create a nonmagnifying perspective.

You see your situation as awful beyond measure. You can address this view at a core level. Typically. the word "awful" means something unpleasant or bad. It's part of everyday discourse: "The hurricane was awful." But in the world of core secondary distresses, "awful" can represent an exaggeration that ignites parasitic anxiety and fear.

Albert Ellis uses the term *awfulizing* to describe a human tendency to turn a bad situation into something worse (Ellis and Harper 1997). When you awfulize, any situation rises to a tragic level. Discomfort is intolerable. Failure is magnified. Nothing can seem worse. Sometimes the situation is not even that bad, but you make a tempest out of a teapot. On the other hand, you may experience a legitimate tragedy. Experiencing a loss, inconvenience, discomfort, or fear is bad enough without an add-on awfulizing double trouble.

An awfulizing double trouble is a core issue worth noting and contesting for at least three reasons:

1. Sometimes a situation will turn sour. This is not imaginary.

2. Taking a bad situation and making it worse detracts from solving the problem or accepting reality.

3. A double-trouble misery can feel several times worse than warranted by the original unfortunate situation.

To address awfulizing about a substandard public-speaking performance, you can use Ellis's ABCDE model.

AN ABCDE RESOLUTION FOR AWFULIZING A SUBSTANDARD PERFORMANCE

The sample situation is giving a poor presentation as measured by an audience survey rating of 2 out of 5, where 5 is excellent and 1 is poor.

Adversity or activating event: Making a below-average presentation.
Reasonable beliefs about the happening(s): "I'd like to have done better, but you can't win them all."
Potential emotive and behavioral consequences of the reasoned belief: Disappointment and unhappiness with the result. Reviewing feedback and taking advantage of the information to improve future performances.
Parasitic beliefs about the happening(s): "This is awful. I'm a failure. People hate me. I'll never live this down."
Potential emotive and behavioral consequences of the parasitic beliefs: Self-loathing, anxiety, avoidance of future talks.

Disputing problem-related parasitic beliefs: This starts with an assumption: it is beneficial to give above-average rather than below-average talks.

The following disputation addresses the four parasitic beliefs listed above:

1. Is the situation as awful as you think? Answer: If you take a standard dictionary definition, "awful" means unfortunate or bad. This situation can fit the definition. But "awfulizing" means more than that. If "awful" means 100 percent bad, can you imagine a situation that would be worse? Probably. You could have gone blind during the presentation. Your local newspaper could have carried a front-page headline saying that you did a miserable job. Recognizing that worse things could have happened can give you some much-needed perspective. Perhaps your situation may be tough to swallow but it's not worth double-troubling yourself over.

2. Does your belief that you failed have validity? Answer: The conclusion that you failed is an extension of "have to" thinking where, based upon a single performance, you are either a success or a failure as a person. Making this claim is ludicrous. It suggests that this one event marks you one way forever.

3. Does your belief that people hate you for your performance have validity? Answer: Your relationships with others are likely to be varied. Taking a looking-glass approach and believing that all others share the same views as you do about yourself suggests that you have extraordinary powers, which you probably don't have. A poor rating on a talk doesn't define you any more than would a substandard grade on a test.

4. Does your belief that "I'll never live this down" seem reasonable? Answer: Concluding that you'll be remembered for your talk for as long as you live suggests that what you said or did was so memorable that, thirty years later, someone might approach you to say, "Aren't you the one who gave that below-average talk?" What are the odds of that happening?

Effects from the disputation: Disappointment over the results of the talk. A strong reduction in double-trouble awfulizing thinking. A willingness to use specific feedback and try again with an improved plan.

The above disputation can be augmented by Ellis's three dimensions of acceptance: unconditional acceptance of self, others, and life. Assuming that your talk got a poor rating, at the core level you can still unconditionally accept yourself. This is partially accomplished by separating an evaluation of your global worth from an evaluation of your performance. You can evaluate your performance. But how does one public-speaking performance define you for all time? By choosing self-acceptance over self-debasement, you've come a long way to drop a parasitic anxiety about your worth.

You may feel angry at your audience for not giving you glowing accolades. Accepting others' rights to make their own evaluations, even if they have no recognition of what went into the development of your talk, helps to eliminate a second double trouble.

The third dimension is unconditional life acceptance. This simply means that there are many aspects to life that you can't control.

These three acceptances help put the vicissitudes of daily living into perspective. With this perspective, you can see that many things go well, others can turn sour, and there is much more that happens in between. The art is in giving short- and long-term weighting to events that compel attention without making more of them than they deserve.

Now it is your turn to use the ABCDE method to address a core parasitic social fear.

YOUR ABCDE RESOLUTION FOR A SOCIAL FEAR

Use this ABCDE worksheet to challenge and resolve a target fear. First describe the activating event; then examine your beliefs about the event and the consequences for those beliefs. Then dispute the parasitic beliefs and write down the effects of the disputation.

Adversity or activating event:
Reasonable beliefs about the happening(s):
Potential emotive and behavioral consequences of the reasoned belief:
Parasitic beliefs about the happening(s):
Potential emotive and behavioral consequences of the parasitic beliefs:
Disputing problem-related parasitic beliefs:
Effects from the analysis and disputation:

KEY IDEAS AND ACTION PLAN

What key ideas from this chapter can you use to rid yourself of your parasitic anxieties and fears? What's your action plan? Write it down. Test it out. Record what happened.

Key Ideas

1.

2.

3.

Action Plan

1.

2.

3.

Results from Actions Taken

1.

2.

3.

POSTSCRIPT

A crow doesn't worry about intruding on other crows, nor does it distress itself about whether fellow crows will expel it from crowdom. Unlike the crow, socially fearful people see themselves as scorn-worthy intruders. Fearing to displease, members of this group make unobtrusive entries and exits. When you learn to act more self-observant and receptive, your level of tolerance can radiate to others with reciprocity. Instead of viewing yourself as intrusive, you may see more opportunities for being inclusive.

CHAPTER 17

Vanquishing Panic

There is no mistaking the dread you can experience when your heart suddenly races and you gasp for breath, tremble, start to sweat, and feel numb and unreal. In that moment of terror, you feel extremely vulnerable and dizzy. You fear fainting, losing control, and going crazy. You may think you are going to die, and your fear of death escalates the panic. You might feel so frightened that you cry. You may call 911. What's going on? You are having a panic reaction.

Panic does not need to be an all-or-nothing event. It can exist with more or fewer symptoms and with varying degrees of intensity. But at whatever level panic occurs, it is among the worst experiences of fear. You may view yourself as crippled and in a state of collapse. This vulnerability can feel enormously threatening.

From 3.5 to 10 percent of people between the ages of fifteen and sixty have persistent or isolated panic reactions (Barlow 1988; Katerndahl and Realini 1993). Even if panic were rare, however, you would have no more need to feel humiliated about experiencing a panic reaction than a person with diabetes would about that condition. But all too often, humiliation is what you feel.

Self-blame for panic does no good. The responsible thing to do is to address and abate panic. The experience is controllable and preventable. And you can gain a double benefit. Many techniques for abating panic also apply to coping with other forms of parasitic terrors and dreads.

Although panic can seem as uncontrollable as a sudden rainstorm, it is definable, addressable, and abatable. Understanding your panic is a prime step toward quelling or ably coping with this equivalent of a psychological and biological cloudburst.

UNDERSTANDING PANIC

The physical symptoms of panic can feel so severe that you may think you have a medical problem. But panic is normally psychologically addressable. You can often successfully manage panic through applying psychological techniques designed for that purpose. A prime technique is education. You can start that learning process now.

How long does panic last? If you've experienced a panic reaction, you've suffered a sudden and intense fear that can range from a short, unpleasant jolt of tension to a wave of pure terror that can last ten minutes or more. Panic symptoms go away usually between two and thirty minutes. In rare instances, panicked feelings can last an hour or more. But even a few minutes of panic can seem like an eternity of misery.

Is panic different from high anxiety? The physical sensations that go with panic are different from anxiety. When anxious, you are more likely to experience muscle tension, headaches, or a nervous stomach. You are absorbed in a world of inner troubles. But you normally don't think that you are about to die or go crazy. This anxiety is on a time dimension. Panic is an in-the-moment reaction. This sudden surge of tension can feel so extreme that you experience a loss of control.

Can panic be made worse? Panic can start with active catastrophic anticipations. For example, you have a fear of being trapped in an elevator, and an upcoming interview for your dream job is on the twenty-fifth floor. The only reasonable way you can get to that level is by taking the elevator. You don't have time to locate and climb the stairs. Rather than give up on this job opportunity, you decide to face your panic. As you approach the elevator, you are mindful that you fear entrapment. You imagine the elevator cables snapping and not being able to escape as the elevator plunges. As you get closer to the elevator, fear storms. Your heart starts pounding. You feel chest pain. You think you are having a heart attack. You gasp for breath. Dizziness engulfs you. You then begin to feel self-conscious that others around you might think ill of you if you start sweating from fear. This secondary fear escalates your panicked feelings.

How do cognitive, emotional tolerance, and behavioral techniques apply to panic? To cope with a state of panic, you would start with self-observant thinking. Continuing with the elevator example, perhaps you would remind yourself that in your most recent physical checkup, you got a clean bill of health. You would then remember that you've had the same thoughts and sensations before, and they usually go away in about three minutes. You would remember statistics you've gathered on the odds of elevator cables snapping with you in the elevator: you'd have a far better chance of being hit by lightning. As this self-observant thinking takes shape, your perspective shifts. From an emotional-tolerance perspective, you recall that you have a goal of living through the tension of panic until the sensations subside. From a behavioral perspective, you recall that you can train your brain to switch off fear by facing what you fear and habituating to the situation. You have a preliminary plan. You sit down. You read a sheet of instructions for engaging behavioral techniques. They include taking your pulse rate. So, you take your pulse and find you are at 125 beats per minute. This is comfortably within a safe area. You concentrate on breathing slowly in and out. You check your watch to measure how long the panic takes to subside. You decide that this panic will soon subside and that you can survive. Armed with cognitive, emotional-tolerance, and behavioral coping tools, you determine to go for the job. You force yourself to get onto the elevator. You notice that you still feel tense and panicky, but you also feel more in control. Your panic subsides.

What results can you anticipate from using cognitive, emotional-tolerance, and behavioral methods with panic? Using cognitive, emotional-tolerance, and behavioral techniques strongly boosts the odds in favor of your learning to quell panic. While there are no guarantees that applying these methods will immediately quell panic, there is a high probability that self-absorbed panic thinking and avoidance will help maintain a panic perspective.

BIOLOGY AND PANIC

Most people with panic suffer from a psychological condition and do best with psychological solutions. But panic can be associated with a variety of physical factor, as well, including a suffocation response, mitral-valve prolapse, and other physical conditions. If you know that any of these conditions coexists with your panic, you will be less likely to jump to conclusions about the origin of your panic.

Suffocation Theory

Some research suggests that panic is caused by a biologically based *suffocation response*. According to suffocation-alarm theory, the oxygen monitors in the brain may sometimes misread the carbon dioxide content in your blood. When the carbon dioxide level is off, you get a false suffocation response that results in physical symptoms associated with a panic reaction. You won't suffocate, but it can feel as though you might. This type of panic can seem to come out of the blue.

According to the suffocation theory, oxygen binding to hemoglobin reduces levels of carbon dioxide in the blood. This condition affects the speech centers in your brain, and you are likely to experience yourself as inarticulate. Such changes in blood chemistry are temporary; the symptoms of suffocation go away once your chemistry returns to equilibrium.

Unfortunately, suffocation theory does a poor job in predicting panic responses. How do you know when you are going to have a suffocation-alarm reaction?

In situations where you believe you will suffocate, try holding your breath for thirty seconds. This can help alter the biochemistry of panic. However, if you fear you will stop breathing, you may understandably be reluctant to take this step. As an alternative, breathe in and out with your hands cupped over your nose and mouth. If the carbon dioxide sensor is off, this will help recalibrate it.

Mitral Valve Prolapse and Panic

A link between a *mitral valve prolapse* (a faint heart click or murmur) and panic is well established. About 34 percent of those with panic have a mitral valve prolapse (Liberthson et al. 1986).

Most medical authorities define a mitral valve prolapse as benign, not lethal. But if you interpret the sensation of a heart murmer as the start of a heart attack, you could panic.

You should see a medical specialist if you are concerned about your heart. Only a doctor can credibly make the diagnosis of a mitral valve prolapse or other underlying condition. If you know that you have a heart murmur, you can use this information to avoid panicking over this type of heart irregularity.

Other Panic-Related Physical Conditions

Some experience panic following taking medications for nonmental health conditions. In rare situations, for example, Accutane (isotretinoin, an acne treatment) can increase your vulnerability to panic following stress situations or can evoke serial panic episodes. This form of panic subsides when you stop taking the medication. Overproduction of norepinephrine, one of the neurotransmitters released by the brain in emergencies, may be the result of irregularities and heighten your risk for panic. Amphetamines, caffeine, and cocaine can promote these irregularities and set the stage for panic. Other factors that can link to panic include alcohol abuse, hypoglycemia, fluctuating sex hormones, and magnesium deficiency.

If your vulnerability for panic has a physical basis, cognitive, emotional-tolerance, and behavioral methods can still be effective in reducing panic symptoms. While the sensations of panic may not be all in your mind, panicked thinking about panic surely is. Defusing this thinking is strongly associated with a significant reduction in panic.

THREE FORMS OF PANIC

Physical feelings of weakness, coupled with catastrophic thinking, can escalate a sense of panic that seems to come out of the blue. This is an unpredictable or *uncued* panic. *Cued* panic occurs when you panic only under specific situations, such as entering areas that you view as dangerous because you can't escape once there. Elevator phobia is an example. It is also common that people have *mixed* panic: you may link certain conditions to your feelings of panic, such as lights, tone, and touch (Davis 1998).

If you heard a distant shrill voice when you experienced an uncued panic, hearing a similar voice later may remind you of terror with panic sensation, and this association may cause you to fear feeling panicked. The voice is a conditioned stimulus. But conditioned stimuli can be anything you associate with panic, including a change in your heart rate or a specific air temperature you associate with danger. One client associated the sound of a helicopter with a near-death experience in a war zone and hid in panic whenever he saw or heard a helicopter. Another client associated temperature over 80 degrees with a terrifying death camp experience. He refused to leave his apartment in summer months at times when the temperature shot up.

Conditions you associate with uncued and cued panic can evoke panic thinking and feelings of uneasiness. You may prevent the feeling of panic by avoiding situations you are afraid will bring it on. Most cues for panic are imaginary dangers, however. Learning to face rather than avoid situations that you fear can bring long-term relief.

Coping with Uncued Panic

Panic can come about without any visible reason and as a surprise. However, there probably are early and subtle panic signals. The founder of behavior therapy, Joseph Wolpe, found that 83 percent of the time, people who experienced panic reactions had significant tension the day before. He suggested a connection between a panic response and recently elevated stress hormones (Wolpe 1967). Some studies have shown that higher than normal levels of epinephrine (a stress hormone) increase the risk for panic (Van Zijderveld et al. 1999).

Even though uncued panic may be unpredictable, you have four things within your power to do:

1. Think about your thinking and refuse to accept panicked thinking as fact. Thinking you are going crazy, for example, is a proposition, not a fact. Remind yourself of that.

2. Exercise emotional tolerance through an acceptant attitude. Acceptance can take this form: "If I panic, I panic. Tough. There is worse."

3. Engage behavioral measures such as breathing exercises, measuring the length of time that panic lasts, or making a mental note of the physical symptoms.

4. Rehearse beforehand what you'll do if panic returns by practicing applicable cognitive, emotional tolerance, and behavioral methods.

Coping with Cued Panic

With cued panic, you know what kicks off your fear: elevators, crowds, open spaces, and unfamiliar places are some common examples. Looking down from a cliff can create a sense of dizziness that triggers panic. Meeting new people in a social situation can trigger an intense parasitic fear followed by panic. After being in a minor vehicle accident, you later panic when nearing the intersection where the accident occurred.

You can also panic in situations that remind you of a traumatic episode. You may have had a near-death experience. Cues from the event can include time of day, a special date, air temperature, a color, a smell, or a screeching sound. Any of these cues can cause panic.

The good news is that you can predict what cues will cause a panicked reaction. Knowing the situations that you associate with panic, you can prepare to deal with specific panic responses. You can expose yourself to the dreaded situation in a graduated way and use the occasion to change your thinking, build emotional tolerance, and overcome the panic.

Coping with Mixed Panic

It doesn't take long for people with uncued panic to connect the panic to specific situations, to be hyperalert to physical sensations that precede panic, to negatively interpret the cues associated with panic, and to panic over the possibility of panic. Once you've experienced an uncued panic, subsequent panic can follow identifiable cues associated with the earlier panic, such as a mild feeling of weakness. Panic can build from an awareness that panic is impending. The script can start like this: "Oh, no, here it comes again." This awareness of this type of triggering cognition can start a chain of panicky thoughts, which escalates the panic. Catastrophic thoughts about the sensations of panic can happen in an instant, and panic builds from there.

You may have a specific situation, such as a formal gathering, when you first felt panic. As a result, you now associate formal social gatherings with panic. So you may make up excuses not to attend weddings. You don't attend graduations. You call a friend to say you can't get to his birthday party because you are ill. You know, of course, that you are physically well. Still, fear can dominate your outlook, and you'll go out of your way to avoid situations you connect with panic.

Similarly, if you are prone to panic, you may also be prone to develop phobias for places where you've panicked before. For example, you may avoid restaurants if you once panicked while eating out.

Realizing that conditions like sounds, air temperature, and places, such as a restaurant, are not dangerous rarely eradicates the fear. For example, restaurants are ordinarily safe places. So if you fear entering a restaurant, logically what is there to fear?

From a logical view, there is no meaningful danger in dining at a restaurant. But your amygdala is not your seat of logic. It is a primitive survival mechanism. To show the amygdala that there is no danger, you have to prove to this brain region that eating in a restaurant is not dangerous. This involves building emotional tolerance through behavioral exposure.

A complex panic doesn't happen in a vacuum. You'll likely have cognitions that connect to the fearful situation: you believe you'll look foolish; you think people will think you are crazy if you show signs of panicking. The panic thoughts merit questioning: where is the evidence that all restaurant patrons will see you in the same way? Might some view you with sympathy because they've also experienced panic? What is the likelihood that you won't be noticed? Here, applying logic to a psychological distress can help shift your perspective from overgeneralizing to specifying. But a big part of the goal is to stop the amygdala from overresponding. So when it comes to dealing with phobia and panic conditions, the prime solutions usually are doing exposure, developing emotional tolerance, and thinking straight about the problem.

EXPLANATION SEEKING

When you first experience panic, you may look for a physical explanation and seek medical assistance. Believing that you are having a heart attack can cause you to speed to the emergency ward. That can be a good idea. The first time panic happens, you want to rule out a physical condition, such as coronary heart disease. However, if tests show no evidence for coronary heart disease, you may experience a state of disbelief. Perhaps the physician missed something. For this reason, it sometimes happens that people with panic have consulted with over fifty different physicians to diagnose a physical ailment that can't be found.

If something is wrong with you physically, it's important to know what it is and address the problem. But what if panic is from combined psychological, social, and biological factors, and is not a disease?

Accurate explanations can help quell panic. If you know the triggers, signs, and causes of panic, self-observation can replace a panicky self-absorbed reaction, which is what so many have as they focus on their symptoms and interpret what they experience as a heart attack or that they are going crazy and look foolish.

When panicked, do you think you are incapable of surviving? Performance tests given during high fear arousal show that we can manage basic survival operations effectively. When you panic, blood flow actually increases to the right cerebral hemisphere, which enhances survival. At the same time, the blood supply to the left hemisphere is reduced. The resulting imbalance impedes your reasoning abilities, but you can still reason.

In uncued and cued panic, the threat is the panic, and a primitive survival reaction is misplaced. To change this response, try shifting from right-brain survival back to left-brain reasoning functions. You can take these self-observant actions: check your watch to see how long the reaction lasts; make mental notes of the various aspects of the reaction, including your thoughts, feelings, and behaviors.

Through shifting from a self-absorbed perspective about panic to a self-observant perspective, you are less likely to panic over the panic. Accepting what you are experiencing moderates the intensity and duration of panic. The art is to get from panicking over panicking to acceptance and emotional tolerance of what you can honestly view as a highly unpleasant experience.

In situations where you experience a panic reaction for the first time, here is a useful question: what is different in your life situation? Stress accompanies life changes, including those that are positive. Have you gone on a diet? Have you started taking a new medication? Have you had a recent trauma?

A CASE OF MANAGING PANIC

Perhaps one of the best ways to understand panic and what to do about it is to look at how a knowledgeable professional encountered and coped with this condition. Here's what Donna, a psychologist, did to address her own state of panic.

Donna experienced a panic reaction following the recent deaths of three people she felt close to. When her panic started, she first felt sudden disturbing symptoms in her body. She described them as "waves of hot and cold spreading through my chest and down my arms and legs, tingling in my limbs, my heart beating fast, feeling as if I couldn't breathe, and sudden sweating. It hit me seemingly out of nowhere. Bam! My body was on red alert, and it felt awful."

She first thought she was having a heart attack: "I felt a new spurt of hot and cold pour through my skin. I took my pulse, and it was fast but steady. I have a home blood-pressure kit and took my blood pressure. It was a little high but still normal. I did a symptom check. I found no pressure in my chest, or pain in my chest, arm, or jaw. The symptoms were on the surface, on my skin. I'd experienced such feelings before from adrenaline overload. I told myself I was likely having an anxiety attack, not a heart attack. If I couldn't abate the symptoms with a couple of minutes of rational thinking and relaxation, I'd call an ambulance, just in case it was a heart attack. But I was pretty certain it wasn't.

"My first step was to attend to my breathing. It was shallow and fast. I spent sixty seconds taking slow, deep breaths. Since the symptoms lessened when I breathed correctly, I became more certain it was anxiety and not a heart attack. What had I been thinking? Then I tried to uncover the thoughts that had triggered the physical symptoms.

"The first thoughts that came to mind were that Tim was dead, Lou was dead, and my brother had died two years ago. Everyone was dead, leaving behind relatives whom I was supposed to support and help through their grief. That grief went on for months and months. It took so much out of me. I heard myself say 'This was awful. I can't stand it anymore.'

"As I thought about the people around me, I thought, 'I've had enough. They should not make any more demands on me. I should not have to deal with any of this awful stuff. They won't leave me alone to attend to my own life. All this death has been awful. My husband has had some health problems lately. He could be next. I can't stand the idea of being without him.'"

Donna recorded her thoughts as she sat by her computer. Then she started to reflect on her thinking. "The thought of my husband dying (when in fact he's no closer to dying than any of us) and me as a young widow was the trigger for my anxiety attack. I realized that the thought had streaked through my mind like a meteor in daylight. I almost didn't register it consciously. But that was the final straw. It had triggered a fight-or-flight panic reaction in my body. My physical symptoms of anxiety were still intense but slightly less so than a few minutes earlier.

"While still attending to my breathing, making sure I was not edging toward hyperventilation, I proceeded to rationally dispute each of my irrational beliefs. The 'I can't stand it' thoughts seem to be an especially strong trigger for me. My physical symptoms began to abate within seconds of identifying and then disputing this irrational self-talk.

"I continued to monitor my breathing and my thinking, disputing my awfulizing and catastrophic thinking and ending with a more rational view. True, things were bad. True I had pressures on my time. But I could clearly see that taking a bad situation and making it worse, and then getting myself anxious by catastrophizing about my husband's condition, escalated my sense of terror. Fortunately knowing what cognitions to look for and how to challenge them came easily. I have practiced this in calmer times, and that gives me a repertoire of rational self-talk to use in times of stress.

"After the worst symptoms left me, I went to the kitchen and made myself a high-protein drink and drank it slowly. Adrenal overload can cause severe fluctuations in blood sugar. This can cause more physical symptoms. A healthy drink with protein and complex carbs can prevent that. I took extra doses of B-complex vitamins. Maybe it was a placebo, but I believe that my fight-or-flight reaction used body stores of thiamine, pantothenic acid, and other B vitamins.

"I could smell myself. Anxiety sweat has a pungently bad odor. I took a shower, making an effort to enjoy the feeling of the hot water and the fragrance of my lavender soap. I told myself that even in the midst of loss and grief, I could still enjoy simple pleasures.

"While feeling the pleasantness of the hot shower, I continued disputing my awfulizing and catastrophizing. I reassured myself that although I did not like dealing with loss and the grief that goes with it, I could stand it. By then, most of my symptoms were gone. I did continue to feel a little jangly inside, down in my abdomen. My chest felt fine. I told myself that the jangly feeling was the result of the sudden rush of adrenaline, a natural symptom. I could stand it. It was an inconvenience, not a catastrophe.

"I slept well that night. The next day, I had gastrointestinal distress, a normal symptom of the fight-or-flight response. Recognizing what was going on, I spared myself another bout of awfulizing and catastrophizing about my physical sensations. I also spent the day doing important tasks that I wanted to do and had put off due to my feeling that I must live up to my responsibilities to others. Instead, I engaged in behaviors to make my life better. I stacked another cord of firewood, took care of my garden, mowed the lawn, and went to the gym to work out—all things that I actually enjoy and that make my own life more manageable."

In dealing with her panic reaction, Donna did the following:

1. She assessed her symptoms and came up with a plan for dealing with them.

2. She made a rational effort to distinguish anxiety from a more serious heart ailment.

3. She monitored her breathing, using a breathing technique to prevent an escalation of more unpleasant symptoms that can be brought on by shallow, fast breathing and/or hyperventilation.

4. She identified the irrational self-talk that had triggered the fight-or-flight response, and she replaced the irrational statements and beliefs with rational statements.

5. Because she had practiced recognizing and challenging anxiety-evoking beliefs in calm circumstances, she found it easier to automatically use Albert Ellis's ABCDE system in a stressful circumstance.

6. She engaged in self-care: eating, bathing, and comforting herself.

7. She accepted that her body would need several days to fully recover from the adrenaline overload.

8. When she suffered gastrointestinal distress the next day, she accepted it as a normal consequence of adrenal overload. She did not make a federal case over a minor discomfort. Thus, she avoided rekindling her panic.

9. She actively engaged in behaviors that made her life more enjoyable and manageable.

10. She continued to monitor herself for shallow breathing and took a metacognitve approach to monitor her thinking for signs of irrational self-talk.

In life, there are times when multiple pressures can get to even those who know better. But the real message from Donna's experience is that through knowledge and know-how, she brought a panic reaction to a relatively quick end. She also acted to prevent panic from coming back. Her efforts prevented a recurrence.

You can employ the same techniques in overcoming panic reactions.

GOALS FOR OVERCOMING PANIC

Most people with panic reactions have one of two goals: to avoid panic or to overcome panic. When the goal is to avoid the experience of panic, the normal response is to stay away from uncomfortable situations that you associate with panic. That's the self-absorbed solution.

If your goal is to directly face a panic situation to rid yourself of the fear, you'll approach this in a self-observant way.

Assuming that your goal is to rid yourself of this fear, you can find many ways to face it. Your approach will likely depend on the type of panic you experience. For example, with uncued panic, you can focus on accepting that certain life events are unpredictable. You'll deal with them as they occur. With cued panic, you can profitably attend to terrorizing cognitions by taking a self-observant approach in which you refuse to capitulate to panic thinking. You apply methods of scientific inquiry to challenge panic thinking. But whether the panic is uncued, cued, or mixed, here are some general ways to set the stage for positive change.

Exercise. Exercise leads to greater cardiac efficiency, greater lung capacity, buildup of endorphins (the natural feel-good brain chemical), physical confidence, improved body image, and higher serotonin levels, which is associated with calmness. Exercise will normally take several weeks or months to show effects. So, the sooner you start, the sooner you'll arrive at a point where you gain the benefits.

Practice breathing from your diaphragm. Panic reactions can cause you to breathe about twice as rapidly as normal. As you use the muscles of the chest and neck, your body's carbon dioxide level can drop. This can result in apprehension and a quickening heartbeat. By assuring that your breathing patterns are from the diaphragm, you can increase your chances for relief from panic reactions. To practice diaphragmatic breathing, pretend that your stomach is a balloon. When you breathe in, your stomach expands. When you breathe out, it contracts.

Change how you label panic. Call it a "temporary psychological and biological reaction." Tell yourself that this experience is time limited. This relabeling can make the physical symptoms of panic seem less oppressive and durable.

PANIC-CONTROL SIMULATION TECHNIQUES

Panic-control simulation techniques are growing in popularity as a way to deal with each major physical part of panic. With this exposure method, you try to simulate the symptoms of panic to show yourself that you can survive them. Common physical symptoms of panic include dizziness, difficulty breathing, and a quickened heartbeat. When these symptoms are separated, panic can seem manageable. When combined, panic can feel worse.

Take dizziness as a panic factor. If you feel dizzy, you may believe that you are about to faint. If you fear fainting, now you have a double trouble. But is the trouble factual? When you are panicked, dizziness doesn't predict fainting. Fainting occurs with a slow heartbeat. When you are panicked, your heart rate has increased. Panic protects you against fainting. Besides, you have to have some confidence in the wisdom of the body. If you fainted when panicked, you would be unlikely to survive in the wild.

Dizziness is easily simulated. Here is a common technique. Spin yourself enough times in a chair to show yourself that however dizzy you get, you won't faint. You may even conclude that fainting is preferable to dizziness.

The quickened heartbeat of panic is only dramatic when compared to a resting heart rate. If you were panicked and took your pulse rate, you would probably discover it to be about what you'd expect if you were exercising. The dramatic change is the alarming factor.

A quickened heartbeat is easy to simulate. Do moderate exercise to bring your heart rate to between 120 and 140 beats per minute. However, check with your physician to be sure the increased heart rate you get when you panic is a benign kind.

Hyperventilation is the attempt to breathe in air beyond the metabolic need, and it commonly occurs in panic. Panicking over your breathing difficulties can add to the torment of panic.

Hyperventilating is easily simulated. For example, breathing through a straw with your nose pinched shut can simulate a panic symptom of gasping for air. You'll feel forced to return to normal breathing within a short time.

Using the simulation techniques described above to intentionally experience aspects of a panic reaction, you can show yourself that the symptoms of panic are not overwhelming. This knowledge can help quell panicked thinking about dizziness, heart rate, and breathing.

PROCRASTINATION AND PANIC

Procrastination is the act of putting off, postponing, or delaying relevant and timely activities until another day or time. In procrastination over panic, you avoid facing the fear by doing something that seems safer.

Avoidance sequences are a common part of the panic process. This involves an often elaborate but predictable pattern of ideas and activities that are part of avoiding situations associated with panic. These are sometimes called *safety behaviors*. The most basic avoidance sequence involves an interaction of negative self-talk about the situation, automatically diverting from the feared situation, and gaining a specious reward for the retreat.

Diversionary activities come in many forms. Some people will say prayers to distract themselves. Doing so can be helpful, but it also can have a paradoxical effect. If you believe you are powerless to act on your own, you can experience a form of learned helplessness that, when routinely repeated, can lead to depression. Another common response is to use alcohol or drugs to inhibit stress. Some people rely on prescriptive medications to alleviate panic. Both of these diversions are normally self-defeating and do more harm than good.

Some diversions, while palliative, can be temporarily helpful. Humming a "merry tune" can distract you from a panic situation. People will play and listen to music to distract themselves from tension. When these palliatives are used to "catch your breath" before taking a positive corrective action, they can serve their purpose well. A planned retreat with the intent of coming back soon to address the anxiety or panic can be productive. You go for a brisk walk, then come back to work out the problem. You count to a hundred and then come back to the problem. You take a warm bath and then come back to work on the problem. The idea is to divert yourself to reduce tension as a prelude to working to resolve the problem.

But if you use diversions to avoid a panic situation, they are temporary safety behaviors that do not substitute for facing and solving the problem. Guided exposure to certain feared situations is more likely to prove productive over the long run. An illusion that a long-term fear will disappear if you find a way to avoid it can cause you to duck beneficial situations in the service of avoiding the fear. You can use cognitive skills, build emotional tolerance, and use behavioral techniques to face your fears and boost your sense of self-efficacy.

On the other hand, if done with the intent of establishing control over panic, some diversionary techniques can have a positive long-term effect. For example, in the midst of a panic reaction, you might go for a fast walk. You may find that you soon calm down. This diversionary technique can be useful when you show yourself that you can establish some control over your panic.

By identifying and facing procrastination ploys that you associate with panic, you position yourself to directly face your fears. By addressing collateral issues, you can increase your self-efficacy. That is a real confidence boost!

USING THE ABCDE METHOD FOR DEALING WITH PANIC THINKING

In a storm of panic distress, our emotions, sensations, and panic thinking seamlessly interplay. Catastrophic thinking is a common part of this drama. With practice, you can take a double trouble from the interplay when panic occurs.

The following ABCDE method describes a prime way to take catastrophic thoughts out of panic. This method helps you shift from a self-absorbed process to a self-observant one. When you find yourself in a storm of panic, making such a shift is challenging. By knowing how to do this, and practicing what you know, you can put yourself in charge of what you do when panicked. And because you know you can do this, you are less likely to panic.

What follows is one way to approach the challenge of taking catastrophic thinking out of panic. Following that, you can fill in the blanks and customize your own program to cope with panic.

AN ABCDE METHOD FOR ADDRESSING PANIC

ACTIVATING event (experience): Experiencing physical sensations you associate with the onset of panic.

Rational BELIEFS about the event: "I've experienced these sensations before. They'll remain the same for a while, escalate, or diminish and disappear. The outcome is whatever the outcome is."

Emotional and behavioral CONSEQUENCES of the rational beliefs: A sense of emotional acceptance and tolerance about the experience. Possibly making adjustments in breathing or breathing into cupped hands to help recalibrate the CO_2 sensor in the brain.

Irrational beliefs about the event: "Oh my god, it's happening again. I can't stand it. I'm about to die."

Emotional and behavioral consequences of the irrational beliefs: A swelling of panic associated with the catastrophic fear of dying. Frenzied behavior. A 911 call.

DISPUTES for irrational beliefs:

1. What is the "it" that is happening again? Sample response: The likely "it" is both the fear of the feeling and the catastrophic anticipation that emotions and sensations of panic are intolerable. Now, why can't you stand what you don't like? The answer is, you can stand what you don't like.

2. If panic is happening again, and you think you're going to die, then how is this view any different from before? Sample response: This experience is similar to panic you've experienced before, including the idea that you're about to die. You did not die that time. You just thought that you would. So, if you have a past history of surviving panic, why would you think that you won't survive this time? The answer is, you're highly likely to survive this experience. The threat is found in your catastrophic thoughts, not in reality. You can use your self-observant skills to refocus on what you can control, which is refusing to cave in to this form of dramatic thinking.

EFFECTS of disputes: The effects involve decreasing the intensity of a panic by changing the interpretation of the experience. This can help reduce intensifying panic due to catastrophizing about the symptoms and outcome. Following survival from panic, new conclusions are reasonable:

1. The fact that you can start to think differently when an uncued panic starts shows you are not helpless.

2. Defusing catastrophic thinking decreases the intensity of panic and its durability.

3. The hormone storm passes without any durable ill effects.

4. You still don't like feeling panicked for unknown reasons–who would? But you now have more compelling evidence that the catastrophic prediction of dying is no more than a mental myth attached to panic sensations.

Now, it is your turn to fill in the blanks. If the above sample approach fits, use what you wish. If you have a different self-observant approach you prefer to put into play, record it and test it.

YOUR ABCDE METHOD FOR ADDRESSING PANIC

Use the ABCDE method for addressing a panic response. First describe the activating event; then examine your beliefs about the event and the consequences for those beliefs. Then dispute the parasitic beliefs and write down the effects of the disputation.

ACTIVATING event (experience):
Rational BELIEFS about the event:
Emotional and behavioral CONSEQUENCES of the rational beliefs:
Irrational beliefs about the event:
Emotional and behavioral consequences of the irrational beliefs:
DISPUTES for irrational beliefs:
EFFECTS of disputes:

KEY IDEAS AND ACTION PLAN

What key ideas from this chapter can you use to rid yourself of your parasitic anxieties and fears? What's your action plan? Write it down. Test it out. Record what happened.

Key Ideas

1.

2.

3.

Action Plan

1.

2.

3.

Results from Actions Taken

1.

2.

3.

POSTSCRIPT

Panic has a beginning, a middle, and an end. Panic follows a process that includes an awareness phase, a cognitive trigger phase, a panic escalation phase, and a resolution phase. The good news is that you can attack negative panic thinking at any stage or phase of the panic cycle.

Correctly labeling the physical sensations of panic can help put the pattern into perspective. You can simulate each sensation and see that you have control over the process. This exposure method can help reduce the fear of panic. Identifying and labeling catastrophic thinking adds to this perspective.

CHAPTER 18

Preventing Anxieties and Fears from Coming Back

Once you come to grips with your parasitic anxieties and fears, you can begin to concentrate on maintaining what you gained by using the techniques you found helpful in defeating your anxieties. You use maintenance strategies to reduce the risk of their returning and to limit their duration should they return. This chapter will look at steps you can take to stop needless fears from coming back or shorten their tenure if they do.

QUICK STEPS TO RESTORE BALANCE

Anxiety and fear have survival value. They may recur. At times, you may experience parasitic anxieties but probably less often than before you took measures to defeat them. And you now have many techniques for addressing these anxieties if they do recur.

Any parasitic habit can creep back. Such an event gives you a chance to hone your cognitive, emotional-tolerance, and behavioral skills. But you don't have to wait. You can practice these skills to keep in shape. Indeed, practicing anti-anxiety skills is a means of preventive maintenance.

Practicing your cognitive, emotional-tolerance, and behavioral skills is similar to doing daily physical exercise. The more you practice, the stronger you get.

Getting in good physical condition involves an effort to get in shape, maintain your gains, and improve. Maintaining your gains to contain needless anxieties is also a process that takes effort. But you can also strengthen your cognitive, emotional-tolerance, and behavioral skills when you act to advance your positive interests in life. You can create positive new challenges to practice what you've learned. If you want to start your own business, actively explore this possibility. If you want to travel, plan to travel and execute the plan.

When you focus your attention on a meaningful mission, you'll tend to brush aside barriers, such as fear. By engaging in growth activities, you can decrease the impact of fears that creep back or are newly hatched.

However great your progress, parasitic anxiety thinking is unlikely to entirely disappear. Thus, you'll have occasion to retest your new coping skills and strengthen them.

Here are four quick steps to rally yourself:

1. Reviewing the key ideas, action plans, and exercise sections in each chapter of this book is a quick way to access what you found most important among this book's resources. As a tune-up measure, you can review this written record each month to remind yourself about what worked, what didn't, and what fell in between.

2. Practiced parasitic anxieties can creep back. But now you know more about detecting this foe. With the onset of a parasitic anxiety, use your ABCDEs and challenge parasitic logic (see chapter 7). As you practice the ABCDE system, you will get better at its use. As you get more skilled in the method, you will find less need to use it for that purpose.

3. Do a BASIC-ID (see chapter 5 for review). You can use this method for diagnostic, prescriptive, and maintenance purposes: What's going on with each of the modalities? If there is a modality hot spot, what can you do about it? Arnold Lazarus, the system's pioneer, recommends a monthly BASIC-ID review as an early warning system (1997).

4. You can address parasitic anxieties and fears through PURRRRS (see chapter 7). This technique gives you a reflective approach for organizing information about your fears and staging and executing a plan that you can sustain and change as needed. When you invoke PURRRRS, you engage your self-observant abilities. When you control the fear process through PURRRRS, you position yourself to control the outcome (Knaus, 2002).

DEALING WITH THE MYTH OF PERFECT CONSISTENCY

A big part of maintenance lies in dealing with false expectations. If you expect to keep parasitic anxieties and fears out of your life, you'll feel let down. We're all fallible. If you expect to experience discomfort and occasional stress from fear, you are less likely to feel disappointed when anxieties make a cameo appearance. You use what you've learned or invent to address the expected "unexpected."

Armor-plating yourself against parasites or nipping every parasite in the bud would involve perfect consistency. If you believe you can do this, you're likely to wage a quixotic battle against windmills. Instead, you might find the phrase "it is what it is" helpful when you assess an unpleasant situation.

As a first measure, dispense with the impossible dream of a bulletproof maintenance program where you'll never have to struggle with another parasite. Don't expect yourself to be able to monitor and counter every parasitic thought that crosses your mind.

You can't have perfect consistency in keeping parasitic ideas away. But you can commit to make self-growth a continuing part of your life plan. You can continue to educate your reason with reasonable consistency. You can persist in doing what you want to accomplish over your lifetime. You can improve in what you do.

Consider lapses as manageable hassles, and you're less likely to be troubled by them.

ACCEPTING LAPSES

If you assume that change is a process and not an event, it is easier to accept the ups and downs of growth. This acceptance can feel less taxing than thinking that you must have a lasting solution or everything you've done is worthless.

From time to time, parasitic thoughts will make a cameo appearance. A cameo appearance does not qualify as a lapse and is certainly not a relapse. A *lapse* is like taking a step back. A *relapse* involves the same level of persistent worries, anxieties, and fears that originally disturbed you. You can reverse both lapses and relapses using techniques that you have already learned in this book. You can find new applications for what you have already learned and develop new techniques to strengthen your maintenance skills. The next sections review techniques for addressing recurring parasitic thoughts and accompanying double troubles, circular thinking, and self-doubt.

A Mindfulness Intervention

You can use an idea from cognitive behavioral mindfulness therapy to remind yourself that the thoughts that go with parasitic anxieties and fears are passing thoughts. They are part of how you are thinking at the moment. They do not define the global you. If you decide to define yourself by negative thoughts, you face another peril. That view typically opens more chances for misery.

Atlanta psychotherapist Edward Garcia (personal communication) suggests that the harder you try to avoid fear, the more fear can dominate your life. Garcia suggests that you consider this question: rather than view fear as something to get rid of, what if you welcomed fear and invited it along in your journey through life? Think of parasitic thoughts as passengers, not as permanent fixtures.

Beef Up Your Attack Against Double Troubles

When parasitic anxieties and fears return, double troubles come too. This secondary distress blooms in different forms: blaming yourself for backsliding, worrying about worrying, feeling disturbed about feeling disturbed, and getting depressed about feeling depressed.

By recognizing and effectively dealing with double troubles, you can do much to reduce added distress and prevent this form of distress from coming back. You have at least four ways to contest double troubles:

1. Label any instance of distressing yourself over distresses a form of double trouble. Accurate labeling can make the process more understandable, controllable, and correctable.

2. Buffer yourself with unconditional self-acceptance. This pluralistic view expands your self-view so that you see that you are more than your fears. Remind yourself that it's okay to be fallible. You can conclude that double-trouble thinking is part of that fallibility but doesn't come close to reflecting the essence of you.

3. Buffer yourself by practicing a nonjudgmental view. True, parasitic anxieties and thoughts have consequences. Still, judging your parasitic beliefs without judging yourself is a path for taking responsible actions.

4. Actively challenge double-trouble views through incongruity questioning: if you are a loser for backsliding, does that mean that everyone else is also a loser for having human failings? If so, why? If not, why not?

Break Circular-Thinking Patterns

Circular thinking surfaces in most forms of parasitic anxieties. You engage in circular thinking when you support a parasitic view by using similar ideas to say the same thing: "There is a ghost under my bed. I feel its presence. Because I feel its presence, there is a ghost under my bed." Using a feeling to validate a belief is wide open to dispute.

Parasitic circular thinking magnifies distress. Learning to break the circle is a useful preventive maintenance skill. Break circular thinking once, and you'll be better prepared the next time to recognize and dispense with it.

Circular thinking may elude detection until you make it conscious. Making it conscious often involves recognizing the root idea and expanding it through the simple word "because." If you think, "I am a weak person," adding the word "because" opens opportunities to see if there is circularity present. If you add the word "because," you might conclude the following: "I am a weak person because I am fearful." Now you have evidence that you're tumbling about in a circle: "I'm weak because I'm fearful. Because I'm fearful, I'm weak."

To prove that such a definition of yourself fully represents the essence of you, you'd have to show its merit in practically everything that you do. When you fail to prove that this definition fully applies, consider dropping the definition. By dropping the definition, you act to break the circle and prevent its return.

Also remember that you have plausible alternative ways of viewing yourself: your life is pluralistic and ongoing. What happens at one time changes at another.

Anxiety and fearful feelings don't make an event awesome, catastrophic, or uncontrollable. They may, however, accurately represent what you think. Prefacing a circular thought with the phrase "I assume" can strip away the appearance of the absolute assurance projected in the circular process. You might say, "I assume that I am a weak person." Such a shift in thinking can change your feeling.

The presence of circular thinking gives you an opportunity to take steps to prevent parasitic anxiety from creeping back. Pausing to recognize the circle helps to prevent it from widening and you from tightening. Refusing to use one word to validate another takes the magic from the emotional logic. Prefacing the circle with the phrase "I assume" can prevent the idea from becoming an uncontested conviction.

Use Productive Imagery Buffers

Although it is possible to feel confident and to engage in self-doubt at the same moment, this incongruity is unlikely. As a preventive maintenance measure, practice *productive imagery*, which is using images that are incongruous with parasitic thinking.

1. Construct a picture in your mind where you are free from parasitic anxieties and fears. For example, view yourself as steady on your feet when facing adversity. Under adverse conditions, imagine asking yourself, "What is the problem here that I can solve?" Imagine yourself solving the problem.

2. Imagine yourself surrounded by your anxieties and fears. Give each a name. Introduce yourself to each one. Tell each one that you are the master of your fate. Then quell any debate on the topic by describing why this is so. You can change your thinking. You can tolerate tension. You can act in your best interest. You might ask each fear, "Why would you desire to prevent positive change and progress?" Rebut answers that are based on parasitic logic.

3. Imagine your voice of fear reading from a script in an ongoing television series. Write out the script. What is the beginning, the middle, and the end? What is the main theme? Now, think of yourself as a playwright. Rewrite the script. Make your voice of reason the hero. In changing the script, what does your main character think that's different? What does your character feel that's different? What does your character do that's different? Evoke the image of the main character when you experience a stirring of parasitic fear.

4. Give your voice of anxiety and fear a new voice. The voice is that of someone you tend not to respect. Can a shift in tone make your voice of fear sound unappealing?

5. Use your imagination to dispense with an imaginary terror. Visualize yourself in a dark cave looking out toward the light. Imagine a giant scorpion blocking your exit. Then imagine you discover the scorpion is an illusion. Is it possible for you to pass through this portal of fear, even though the scorpion looks real? Now, use this technique when you experience the return of an anxiety and fear. Can you create an image of that fear that looks real but that you can still pass through?

SUSTAINING LIFESTYLE CHANGES

You can view keeping parasitic anxieties and fears away as a healthy lifestyle change that, like any other lifestyle change, has its challenges. Here's a look at some of the factors that go into changing your lifestyle for the better.

What is a healthy lifestyle change? A healthy lifestyle change involves getting rid of harmful habits by developing and sustaining healthy new habit patterns. For example, you lose weight and keep it off. You exercise and sustain the effort. You quit drinking and smoking to maintain health benefits and to save money. You make such lifestyle changes to improve your chances for long-term health.

Can you make lifestyle changes to prevent parasitic anxieties and fears from coming back? The idea of reducing needless fears and preventing them from coming back is very much in the tradition of making a classic lifestyle change. As part of this effort, you gather information about parasitic fears, educate your reason, and build emotional tolerance through cognitively and behaviorally facing your terrors. Over your lifetime, you persist with this plan. But there are a number of conditions that increase your risk for parasitic tensions: excessive alcohol consumption, smoking, ingesting excessive amounts of caffeine, working at a boring job, recurrent heated interpersonal conflicts, inadequate exercise, and a poor diet are some examples. It's important to address these conditions as well.

What barriers commonly stand in the way of sustaining meaningful lifestyle changes? A lifestyle change typically includes enduring short-term deprivations to achieve a long-term goal of improved health or greater happiness. Few enjoy deprivation. A change process that involves denying yourself some relief or pleasure often evokes psychological reactance, or resistance. This resistance, such as avoiding the feeling of fear, can be a powerful barrier. As you avoid the uncomfortable feeling, you may enjoy a specious sense of relief, which, in turn, rewards further avoidance and procrastination. By looking at trade-offs, you are more likely to focus on the long-term benefits of stretching your resources to actualize healthy interests to boost your self-efficacy.

What progress can you reasonably anticipate? When you make a lifestyle change, you normally act to eliminate a self-sabotaging habit or habits. You quit drinking or smoking. You change your sedentary practices by exercising. But gains in these areas are often hard to sustain unless you know how. You probably have a better chance of sustaining an anti-anxiety lifestyle change than a weight loss or exercise program. However, weight loss and exercise programs can serve as a buffer against anxiety.

Boosting Your Chances for Health and Happiness

Parasitic anxieties and fears are nothing to brush off lightly. If you persistently experience anxieties and fears, they can affect your happiness as well as your health.

Psychiatrist Tom A. Williams (1923) noted that fear, if prolonged or excessive, wears on the body, causing disease. He cited experimental evidence from his day in support of that assertion. In the 1930s, Hans Selye, a Canadian endocrinologist, demonstrated that the body's adaptation to persistent stress includes a sensory system that remains excessively vigilant and promotes a higher metabolic rate for the more vulnerable organs, which may eventually fail to function properly. He predicted that gastrointestinal disorders, coronary heart disease, and cancer may result from stress. He named the condition of stress leading to fatigue the *general adaptation syndrome* (Selye 1975).

Persistent stress and disease are linked. A higher incidence of thyroid diseases, respiratory diseases, gastrointestinal disorders, arthritis, allergies, and migraines is associated with depression and anxiety (Sareen et al. 2006). Anxiety adds to a decline in adaptive functioning, poor health, and more sick days from work (Stein et al. 2005).

You can reverse the wear and tear on the body resulting from parasitic anxieties, however. You can do so by developing and strengthening your ability to cope with real and imagined threats and adversity (Holden 1991). Indeed, developing and applying effective problem-solving and coping skills is a way to assert control over key parts of your life.

Lightening the Allostatic Load

Normal conditions of daily living involve stresses and adjustments to stresses. When you jump into the ocean for a swim, your body adjusts to the change. When you are stuck in traffic, and running behind schedule, you feel frustrated. Your body adjusts to the frustration and then to relief when traffic suddenly starts to move and you can make your appointments. You have a meeting with a surly colleague. You experience stress in anticipation of an unpleasant encounter. When your colleague surprisingly acts cordial, you feel relief. These changes and adjustments are what Rockefeller professor Bruce McEwen calls *allostatic load factors* (McEwen and Wingfield 2003). The *allostatic load* is the cumulative wear and tear on your body from repeated changes and readjustments to various stressful social, personal, and environmental events.

A persistent but inefficient turning on or shutting off of adrenaline and other stress responses increases your risk for disease, such as hypertension, coronary heart disease, and diabetes (McEwen 1999). The allostatic load theory has some preliminary support. Poor coping skills are a major factor predicting a higher allostatic load (Glei et al. 2007).

Activities to lighten the allostatic load, such as exercise and diet, are prevention strategies that support maintenance. These stress-reducing activities can balance temporary stresses that normally come from taking positive initiatives.

Patterns of parasitic thinking and pessimism suggest poor coping skills. These conditions of mind predictably contribute to the allostatic load. But at this point in your reading, you likely will have a sound awareness of cognitive, emotional tolerance, and behavioral coping techniques to address these conditions. The question then becomes, what can you do to reduce general stress factors to further drop your risk of parasitic anxieties and fears from coming back?

Stress exposure increases with poor sleep and exercise patterns, overeating, smoking, high caffeine intake, excessive alcohol consumption, impoverished living conditions, recurring interpersonal conflicts, a pessimistic outlook, and an above-average biological tendency toward anxiety. But active efforts to exercise and maintain a healthy weight reduce cardiac risk up to 79 percent (Völler 2006). Exercise is an evidence-based way to reduce anxiety and depression (Berk 2007). Weight loss appears to improve health across the board (Foreyt 2005).

Corrective activities to reduce stress and improve health involve engaging in a healthy form of stress (Edwards and Cooper 1988; Nelson and Cooper 2005). This healthy type of stress results from efforts to solve problems. I call this form of stress *propellant stress*, or *p-stress* (Knaus 1994).

Physical and Environmental Factors and Anxiety

The following actions all involve increasing p-stress to lower other forms of unhealthy stress.

What coping actions help reduce the risk of anxiety returning? The BASIC-ID, PURRRRS, and ABCDE methods are tested ways to address stressful thinking and associated conditions. You can use these methods as an intervention and for preventive maintenance. But it is one thing to learn mentally to stop making a bad situation worse and another to change an ongoing source of distress. You may need to address the latter if you want to keep anxieties and fears at bay.

What preventive maintenance changes can you make to reduce your vulnerability for anxiety? Physical factors include your diet, exercise routines, and sleep patterns. The abuse of tobacco, alcohol, coffee, and amphetamines raises your risk for having anxiety-like sensations and adds to the allostatic load. You can buffer yourself against stress and anxiety sensitivity by building toward a healthy lifestyle: get adequate sleep, eat healthily, exercise regularly, and drop addictive habits. (Substance abuse is a pernicious way to medicate yourself to snuff out tensions. Abuse can readily become a destructive additional problem.)

What types of environmental stresses increase your vulnerability for anxiety? Environmental stresses include working a boring or stressful job, living in poverty, or residing with an abusive family member. If you live in a northern climate and are at risk for winter depressions, you may experience depression reappearing as the days grow short. Reducing the environmental factors that cause you stress, in whatever way you can, will make you less vulnerable to anxiety.

The thirteenth century Dominican monk, theologian, and philosopher Thomas Aquinas is credited with saying the following: "Let me control what I can, accept what I can't, and know the difference between the two." Recognizing what you can control opens options. Although you can't stop ocean waves from pounding the shore, you can still build sand castles or take a swim.

Reducing your allostatic load through lifestyle changes starts with creating healthy priorities. Priorities are important for one obvious reason and for a less obvious one, as well. You probably can't do everything at once. That's the obvious reason. The less obvious reason is that even positive change increases strain in the short run (Holms and Rahe 1967). Taking on one major challenge at a time can help level out the stress until the positive benefits take hold.

Spring Free from Procrastination Traps

Lifestyle changes are both a challenge to make and to maintain. While most people know what to do, they normally face obvious and subtle barriers. A major barrier is the procrastination barrier.

When you procrastinate, you face the two-agenda problem. You want the benefits of a change, but you want something else more. You want to avoid the hassle involved with making and sustaining the change.

Sure, you'd like to lose twenty pounds. But you say you are under too much stress now to think about that. You'd like to exercise, but your schedule is too hectic and you don't have the time. You'd like to clear negative thinking from your mind, but you are too overwhelmed to try. Each excuse shows a preference for a second agenda.

"But" thinking shows your intent to avoid short-term discomfort. Refuse to accept "but" thinking, and you have another challenge: how to achieve your primary agenda. This can be the shortest path to prevent parasitic anxieties from coming back. Second-agenda thinking is the path to frustration over lapses and relapses. To work your way past procrastination barriers, look for incentives to support your primary agenda.

Beware of the procrastination-reactance connection. If you think of your second agenda as a privilege or benefit, think again!

A simple cost-benefits analysis of the short- and long-term advantages and disadvantages of supporting your primary agenda can show that there is no meaningful privilege lost by prioritizing it. (For more information on addressing procrastination, see my book *The Procrastination Workbook* under Suggested Reading).

DESIGN A PREVENTIVE MAINTENANCE PLAN

A basic theme throughout this book is that of applying cognitive, emotional tolerance, and behavioral methods to overcome parasitic anxieties and fears. Intellect, ingenuity, and will overlay this process. Using these complementary processes, you can establish a maintenance plan, such as the following:

A PREVENTIVE MAINTENANCE PLAN

Prevention Factor	Intellect	Ingenuity	Will
Cognitive	Recognize anxiety-and-fear thinking when it first starts to kindle. Apply one or more of the following: the PURRRRS, BASIC-ID, and ABCDE approach. Supplement with other cognitive, emotional tolerance, and behavioral methods to put parasitic thinking into perspective so that you can disable this default reaction.	Consider how to maintain a healthy perspective through recognizing and questioning incongruities. Be alert for double trouble and circular reasoning and for new ways to address these responses by applying your educated reason to meet the challenge.	Will is not something you can dial up. But you can create conditions for strengthening it. Focus on your prime incentives for preventing anxieties and fears from coming back. How much do those incentives matter?

Emotional Tolerance	Identify discomfort-dodging urges that accompany parasitic thinking. If you have an urge to retreat, can you think of a better way to manage your thinking?	Look for adaptive ways to accept the existence of discomfort. Create a positive coping image of you managing the problem signaled by the discomfort. Then, build in accepting discomfort as part of your plan to translate the coping image into action.	The will to avoid discomfort can be strong. What other emotions can you mobilize to balance this will with an incentive to live through discomfort so as not to fear discomfort? Imagine a new emotion, say, a sense of forcefulness. Pit forcefulness against the will to retreat. Can you imagine yourself forcefully nipping anxiety in the bud by squarely facing the fear?
Behavioral	What behaviors extend from parasitic thinking? What actions can counter them? For example, rather than retreat out of fear of defeat, use assertive ways to respond by moving to conquer the fear.	What creative actions can you take to support maintenance? For example, can you write a poem extolling the benefits of prevention? Can you give creative flair to a "to do" list of preventive maintenance techniques?	What benefits do you get from consistently asserting your will to review and renew behavioral techniques to stop parasitic anxiety-and-fear reactions from coming back? How can you continue to directly or gradually expose yourself to the parasitic anxiety or fear condition?

Now it is your turn to design your own preventive maintenance plan.

YOUR PREVENTIVE MAINTENANCE PLAN

How can you bring your intellect, ingenuity, and will to maintain your gains and reduce the risk of anxieties returning? Customize this prevention maintenance plan to make it work for you.

Prevention Factor	Intellect	Ingenuity	Will
Cognitive	Apply the PURRRRS, BASIC-ID, and ABCDE approach to disable default parasitic reactions.	Use ingenuity to prevent and quell needless anxieties and fears.	Create conditions and incentives for asserting will over anxieties and fears.
Emotional Tolerance	What are your discomfort-dodging urges that accompany parasitic thinking? What techniques can you use to manage discomfort-dodging urges?	What are some adaptive ways to accept discomfort? How can you solve the problem that caused the discomfort?	What emotions can you mobilize to balance discomfort? How can you balance a will to retreat from discomfort with a will to solve the problem?
Behavioral	What behaviors extend from parasitic thinking? What actions can counter them?	What actions can you take to support preventive maintenance?	What benefits do you get from behaving with consistency to stop parasitic anxiety-and-fear reactions from coming back?

Self-administered primary intervention and maintenance measures against anxiety can be effective with or without individual therapy. However, you don't have to travel the road alone if you find parasitic anxieties and fears formidable.

You can use the ideas and exercises in this book to help yourself promote a happier and healthier life. What you learn through self-help efforts can produce favorable results. But know your limitations (Menchola, Arkowitz, and Burke 2007).

KEY IDEAS AND ACTION PLAN

What key ideas from this chapter can you use to rid yourself of your parasitic anxieties and fears? What's your action plan? Write it down. Test it out. Record what happened.

Key Ideas

1.

2.

3.

Action Plan

1.

2.

3.

Results from Actions Taken

1.

2.

3.

POSTSCRIPT

A professor held up a drinking glass to his students. He filled it with pebbles. He asked them if it was full. The students said that it was. He added dirt and shook the glass. He asked if it was full. The students said that it was. He added water. He asked if it was full. The students said that it was. He asked what the demonstration meant. One student responded, "Stick with the big issues. Don't get bogged down in details. Avoid getting stuck in the mud."

It comes down to this: Stay focused on the prize, the enjoyment of your life. In the process, maintain a self-observant perspective and look for opportunities where you can contribute to the welfare of others.

Suggested Readings

Edmund Bourne. 2005. *The Anxiety and Phobia Workbook*. 4th ed. Oakland, CA: New Harbinger Publications.

Edmund Bourne and Lorna Garono. 2003. Coping *with Anxiety: 10 Simple Ways to Relieve Anxiety, Fear, and Worry*. Oakland CA: New Harbinger Publications.

Jeffrey Brantley. 2007. *Calming Your Anxious Mind: How Mindfulness and Compassion Can Free You from Anxiety, Fear and Panic*. Oakland CA: New Harbinger Publications.

Martha Davis, Elizabeth Robbins Eshelman, and Matthew McKay. 2008. *The Relaxation and Stress Reduction Workbook*. 5th ed. Oakland CA: New Harbinger Publications.

Michael Edelstein and David Steele. 1997. *Three Minute Therapy: Change Your Thinking, Change Your Life*. New York: John Wiley and Sons.

John Forsyth and George Eifert. 2007. *The Mindfulness and Acceptance Workbook for Anxiety: A Guide to Breaking Free from Anxiety, Phobias, and Using Acceptance and Commitment Therapy*. Oakland CA: New Harbinger Publications.

William Knaus. 2002. *The Procrastination Workbook: Your Personalized Program for Breaking Free from the Patterns That Hold You Back*. Oakland CA: New Harbinger Publications.

William Knaus. 2000. *Take Charge Now: Powerful Techniques for Breaking the Blame Habit*. New York: John Wiley and Sons.

References

Adler, A. 1927. *Understanding Human Nature*. New York: Garden City Publishing.

Alberti, R., and M. Emmons. 2001. *Your Perfect Right: Assertiveness and Equality in Your Life and Relationships*. Atascadero, CA: Impact Publications.

Ashbaugh A., M. M. Antony, A. Liss, L. J. Summerfeldt, R. E. McCabe, and R. P. Swinson. 2007. Changes in perfectionism following cognitive-behavioral treatment for social phobia. *Depression and Anxiety* 24:169–77.

Baillie, A., and C. Sannibale. 2007. Anxiety and drug and alcohol problems. In *Clinical Handbook of Co-Existing Mental Health and Drug and Alcohol Problems*, edited by A. Baker and R. Velleman. New York: Routledge/Taylor and Francis Group.

Bandura, A. 1994. Self-efficacy. In vol. 4 of *Encyclopedia of Human Behavior*, edited by V. S. Ramachaudran. New York: Academic Press.

Bar-Haim, Y., D. Lamy, L. Pergamin, M. J. Bakermans-Kranenburg, and M. H. van Ijzendoorn. 2007. Threat-related attentional bias in anxious and nonanxious individuals: A meta-analytic study. *Psychological Bulletin* 133:1–24.

Barlow, D. H. 1988. *Anxiety and Its Disorders*. New York: Guilford Press.

———. 2000. Unraveling the mysteries of anxiety and its disorders from the perspective of emotion theory. *American Psychologist* 55:1247–63.

Barlow, D. H., and L. A. Campbell. 2000. Mixed anxiety-depression and its implications for models of mood and anxiety disorders. *Contemporary Psychiatry* 41 (2), Suppl. 1:55–60.

Barrett, L. F., E. Bliss-Moreau, S. L. Duncan, S. L. Rauch, and C. I. Wright. 2007. The amygdala and the experience of affect. *Social Cognitive and Affective Neuroscience* 2:73–83.

Baum, L. F. 1960. *The Wonderful Wizard of Oz.* Mineola, NY: Dover Publications.

Beck, A. T. 1976. *Cognitive Therapy and the Behavioral Disorders.* New York: New American Library.

Beesdo, K., A. Bittner, D. S. Pine, M. B. Stein, M. Hofler, R. Lieb, and H. U. Wittchen. 2007. Incidence of social anxiety disorder and the consistent risk for secondary depression in the first three decades of life. *Archives of General Psychiatry* 64:903–12.

Beidel, D. C., and S. M. Turner. 2007. Prevalence of social anxiety disorder. In *Shy Children, Phobic Adults: Nature and Treatment of Social Anxiety Disorders,* edited by D. C. Beidel and S. M. Turner. 2nd ed. Washington, DC: American Psychological Association.

Benight, C. C., and A. Bandura. 2004. Social cognitive theory of posttraumatic recovery: The role of perceived self-efficacy. *Behaviour Research and Therapy* 42:1129–48.

Berk, M. 2007. Should we be targeting exercise as a routine mental health intervention? *Acta Neuropsychiatrica* 19:217–18.

Berne, E. 1964. *Games People Play: The Basic Handook of Transactional Analysis.* New York: Ballantine Books.

Bishop, S. R. 2007. What we really know about mindfulness-based stress reduction. In vol. 2 of *The Praeger Handbook on Stress and Coping,* edited by A. Monat, R. S. Lazarus, and G. Reevy. Westport, CT: Praeger Publishers.

Blascovich, J. 2000. Using physiological indexes of psychological processes in social psychological research. In *Handbook of Research Methods in Social and Personality Psychology,* edited by H. T. Reis and C. M. Judd. New York: Cambridge University Press.

Buhr, K., and J. Dugas. 2006. Investigating the construct validity of intolerance of uncertainty and its unique relationship with worry. *Journal of Anxiety Disorders* 20:222–36.

Burton, R. 2001. *The Anatomy of Melancholy.* New York: Review Books Classics.

Butler, A. C., J. E. Chapman, E. M. Forman, and A. T. Beck. 2006. The empirical status of cognitive-behavioral therapy: A review of meta-analyses. *Clinical Psychology Review* 26:17–31.

Campbell, J. 1967. *The Hero with a Thousand Faces.* Cleveland, OH: The World Publishing Company.

Carleton, R. N., D. Sharpe, and G. J. G. Asmundson. 2007. Anxiety sensitivity and intolerance of uncertainty: Requisites of the fundamental fears? *Behaviour Research and Therapy* 45:2307–16.

Carlson, J., R. Watts, and M. Maniacci. 2006. *Adlerian Therapy: Theory and Practice.* Washington, DC: American Psychological Association.

Castaneda, C. 1968. *The Teachings of Don Juan: A Yaqui Way of Knowledge.* Berkeley, CA: University of California Press.

Choy, Y., A. J. Fyer, and J. D. Lipsitz. 2007. Treatment of specific phobia in adults. *Clinical Psychology Review* 27:266–86.

Clara, I. P., B. J. Cox, and M. W. Enns. 2007. Assessing self-critical perfectionism in clinical depression. *Journal of Personality Assessment* 88:309–16.

Coelho, H. F., P. H. Canter, and E. Ernst. 2007. Mindfulness-based cognitive therapy: Evaluating current evidence and informing future research. *Journal of Consulting and Clinical Psychology* 75:1000–5.

Cooley, C. H. 1902. *Human Nature and the Social Order*. New York: Charles Scribner's Sons.

Darwin, C. 1965. *The Expression of Emotions in Man and Animals.* Chicago: University of Chicago Press.

Davey, G. C. L., F. Eldridge, J. Drost, and B. A. MacDonald. 2007. What ends a worry bout? An analysis of changes in mood and stop rule use across the catastrophising interview task. *Behaviour Research and Therapy* 45:1231–43.

Davis, M. 1998. Are different parts of the extended amygdala involved in fear versus anxiety? *Biological Psychiatry* 44:1239–47.

Dollard, J. 1942. *Victory over Fear*. New York: Reynal and Hitchcock.

Dubois, P. 1908. *The Psychic Treatment of Nervous Disorders: The Psychoneuroses and Their Moral Treatment*. New York: Funk and Wagnalls Company.

Dugas, M. J., P. Savard, A. Gaudet, J. Turcotte, N. Laugesen, M. Robichaud, K. Francis, and N. Koerner. 2007. Can the components of a cognitive model predict the severity of generalized anxiety disorder? *Behavior Therapy* 38:169–78.

Edwards, J. R., and C. L. Cooper. 1988. The impacts of positive psychological states on physical health: A review and theoretical framework. *Social Science and Medicine* 27:1447–59.

Egan. S. J., J. P. Piek, M. J. Dyck, and C. S. Rees. 2007. The role of dichotomous thinking and rigidity in perfectionism. *Behavior Research and Therapy* 45:1813–22.

Ellis, A. 2000. Rational emotive behavior therapy. In *Current Psychotherapies*, edited by R. J. Corsini and D. Wedding. Itasca, FL: Peacock.

———. 2003. *Ask Albert Ellis: Straight Answers and Sound Advice from Americas Best-Known Psychologist*. CA: Impact Publishers.

Ellis, A., and R. A. Harper. 1997. *A Guide to Rational Living*. 3rd ed. North Hollywood, CA: Wilshire Book Company.

Engels, A. S., W. Heller, A. Mohanty, J. D. Herrington, M. T. Banich, A. G. Webb, and G. A. Miller. 2007. Specificity of regional brain activity in anxiety types during emotion processing. *Psychophysiology* 44:352–63.

Evans, S., S. Ferrando, M. Findler, C. Stowell, C. Smart, and D. Haglin. 2008. Mindfulness-based cognitive therapy for generalized anxiety disorder. *Journal of Anxiety Disorders* 22 (4):716–21.

Felmingham, K., A. Kemp, L. Williams, P. Das, G. Hughes, A. Peduto, and R. Bryant. 2007. Changes in anterior cingulate and amygdala after cognitive behavior therapy of posttraumatic stress disorder. *Psychological Science* 18:127–29.

Festinger, L. 1957. *A Theory of Cognitive Dissonance.* Stanford, CA: Stanford University Press.

Festinger, L., and J. M. Carlsmith. 1959. Cognitive consequences of forced compliance. *Journal of Abnormal and Social Psychology* 58:203–11.

Flett, G. L., P. L. Hewitt, K. R. Blankstein, and D. Pickering. 1998. Perfectionism in relation to attributions for success or failure. *Current Psychology: Developmental, Learning, Personality, Social* 17: 249–62.

Foreyt, J. P. 2005. Need for lifestyle intervention: How to begin. *American Journal of Cardiology* 96 (4A): 11E–14E.

Frankl, V. 1959. *Man's Search for Meaning.* Boston: Beacon Press.

Franklin, B. 1986. *Benjamin Franklin: The Autobiography and Other Writings.* New York: Penguin Classics.

Gil, P. J. M., F. X. M. Carrillo, and J. S. Meca. 2001. Effectiveness of cognitive-behavioural treatment in social phobia: A meta-analytic review. *Psychology in Spain* 5:17–25.

Glei, D. A., N. Goldman, Y. Chuang, and M. Weinstein. 2007. Do chronic stressors lead to physiological disregulation? Testing the theory of allostatic load. *Psychosomatic Medicine* 69:769–76.

Glover, D. S., G. P. Brown, C. G. Fairburn, and R. Shafran. 2007. A preliminary evaluation of cognitive-behaviour therapy for clinical perfectionism: A case series. *British Journal of Clinical Psychology* 46: 85–94.

Goossens, L., S. Sunaert, R. Peeters, E. J. L. Griez, and K. R. J. Schruers. 2007. Amygdala hyperfunction in phobic fear normalizes after exposure. *Biological Psychiatry* 62:1119–25.

Gould, R. A., and M. W. Johnson. 2001. Comparative effectiveness of cognitive-behavioral treatment and pharmacotherapy for social phobia: Meta-analytic outcome. In *From Social Anxiety to Social Phobia: Multiple Perspectives,* edited by S. G. Hofmann and P. M. DiBartolo. Needham Heights, MA: Allyn and Bacon.

Hardy, T. 1979. *Tess of the D'Urbervilles.* New York: W. W. Norton and Company.

Henderson, L., and P. Zimbardo. 1998. Shyness. In the *Encyclopedia of Mental Health,* edited by Howard Friedman. San Diego, CA: Academic Press.

Herbert, F. 1965. *Dune.* Philadelphia, PA: Chilton Books.

Hirai, M., and G. A. Clum. 2006. A meta-analytic study of self-help interventions for anxiety problems. *Behavior Therapy* 37:99–111.

Holden, G. 1991.The relationship of self-efficacy appraisals to subsequent health related outcomes: A meta-analysis. *Social Work in Health Care* 16:53–93.

Holle, C., and R. Ingram. 2008. On the psychological hazards of self-criticism. In *Self-Criticism and Self-Enhancement: Theory, Research, and Clinical Implications*, edited by E. C. Chang. Washington, DC: American Psychological Association.

Holms, T., and R. Rahe. 1967. The social re-adjustment scale. *Psychosomatic Research* 11:213–18.

Ingram, R. E., W. Ramel, D. Chavira, and C. Scher. 2005. Social anxiety and depression. In *The Essential Handbook of Social Anxiety for Clinicians*, edited by W. R. Crozier and L. E. Alden. New York: John Wiley and Sons.

Jacobson, E. 1938. *Progressive Relaxation*. Chicago: University of Chicago Press.

Kagan, J. 2000. Inhibited and uninhibited temperaments: Recent developments. In *Shyness: Development, Consolidation, and Change*, edited by W. R. Crozier. New York: Routledge.

Katerndahl, D. A., and J. P. Realini. 1993. Lifetime prevalence of panic states. *American Journal of Psychiatry* 150:246–49.

Kelly, G. 1955. *The Psychology of Personal Constructs*. New York: Norton.

Kessler, R. C., P. Berglund, O. Demler, R. Jin, K. R. Merikangas, and E. E. Walters. 2005. Lifetime prevalence and age-of-onset distributions of DSM-IV disorders in the National Comorbidity Survey Replication. *Archives of General Psychiatry* 62:593–602.

Knaus, W. 1979. *Do It Now: How to Stop Procrastinating*. Englewood Cliffs, NJ: Prentice-Hall.

———. 1982. *How to Get Out of a Rut*. Englewood Cliffs, NJ: Prentice-Hall.

———. 1994. *Change Your Life Now: Powerful Techniques for Positive Change*. New York: John Wiley and Sons.

———. 2000. *Take Charge Now: Powerful Techniques to Break the Blame Habit*. New York: John Wiley and Sons.

———. 2006. *A Cognitive Behavioral Workbook for Depression: A Step-by-Step Program*. Oakland, CA: New Harbinger Publications.

Lazarus, A. A. 1997. *Brief but Comprehensive Psychotherapy: The Multimodal Way*. New York: Springer Publishing Company.

———. 2008. *Multimodal therapy*. In *Current Psychotherapies*, edited by R. J. Corsini and D. Wedding. 8th ed. Belmont, CA: Thomson.

Lazarus, R. S. 1991. *Emotion and Adaptation*. New York: Oxford University Press.

LeDoux, J. 1998. Fear and the brain: Where have we been, and where are we going? *Biological Psychiatry* 44 (12):1229–38.

Lee, D. 2005. Maladaptive cognitive schemas as mediators between perfectionism and psychological distress. Paper presented at the American Psychological Association Convention, Washington DC. Record identifier: 526232006-001.

Lewis, M. D., and R. M. Todd. 2007. The self-regulating brain: Cortical-subcortical feedback and the development of intelligent action. *Cognitive Development* 22:406–30.

Liberthson, R., D. V. Sheehan, M. E. King, and A. E. Weyman. 1986. The prevalence of mitral valve prolapse in patients with panic disorders. *American Journal of Psychiatry* 143:511–15.

Lieberman, M. D., N. I. Eisenberger, M. J. Crockett, S. M. Tom, J. H. Pfeifer, and B. M. Way. 2007. Putting feelings into words: Affect labeling disrupts amygdala activity in response to affective stimuli. *Psychological Science* 18:421–28.

Ma., S. H., and J. D. Teasdale. 2004. Mindfulness-based cognitive therapy for depression: Replication and exploration of differential relapse prevention effects. *Journal of Consulting and Clinical Psychology* 72:31–40.

Mahon N. E., A. Yarcheski, T. J. Yarcheski, and M. M. Hanks. 2007. Relations of low frustration tolerance beliefs with stress, depression, and anxiety in young adolescents. *Psychological Reports* 100: 98–100.

Maslow, A. 1962. *Toward a Psychology of Being*. New York: Van Nostrand.

Mayszczak, K., T. Pawowski, A. Pyszel, and A. Kiejna. 2006. Correlation between depressive and anxiety symptoms, distress, and functioning. *Psychiatric Policy* 40:269–77.

McEvoy, P. M., and P. Nathan. 2007. Effectiveness of cognitive behavior therapy for diagnostically heterogeneous groups: A benchmarking study. *Journal of Consulting and Clinical Psychology* 75:344–50.

McEwen, B. S. 1999. Protective and damaging effects of stress mediators. *New England Journal of Medicine* 338:171–79.

McEwen, B. S., and J. C. Wingfield. 2003. The concept of allostasis in biology and biomedicine. *Hormonal Behavior* 43:2–15.

Menchola, M., H. S. Arkowitz, and B. L. Burke. 2007. Efficacy of self-administered treatments for depression and anxiety. *Professional Psychology: Research and Practice* 38:421–29.

Mineka, S., and R. Zinbarg. 2006. A contemporary learning theory perspective on the etiology of anxiety disorders: It's not what you thought it was. *American Psychologist* 61:10–26.

Murray, C. J. L., and A. D. Lopez, eds. 1996. *The Global Burden of Disease: A Comprehensive Assessment of Mortality and Disability from Diseases, Injury, and Risk Factors in 1990 and Projected to 2020.* Cambridge: Harvard University Press.

Nelson, D., and C. Cooper. 2005. Stress and health: A positive direction. *Stress and Health: Journal of the International Society for the Investigation of Stress* 21:73–75.

Pavlov, I. P. 1941. *Lectures on Conditioned Reflexes.* Vol. 2 of *Conditioned Reflexes and Psychiatry*, translated and edited by W. H. Gantt. London: Lawrence and Wishart.

Perkins, A. M., S. E. Kemp, and P. J. Corr. 2007. Fear and anxiety as separable emotions: An investigation of the revised reinforcement sensitivity theory of personality. *Emotion* 7:252–61.

Perls, F., P. Goodman, and R. Hefferline. 1951. *Excitement and Growth in Human Personality.* New York: Julian Press.

Popper, K. 1963. *Conjectures and Refutations.* London: Routledge.

Posner, M. I., and M. K. Rothbart. 2007. *Educating the Human Brain.* Washington, DC: American Psychological Association.

Rector, N. A., K. Szacun-Shimizu, and M. Leybman. 2007. Anxiety sensitivity within the anxiety disorders: Disorder-specific sensitivities and depression comorbidity. *Behaviour Research and Therapy* 45:1967–75.

Riccio, D. 2008. *Everyday Commitments: Choosing a Life of Love, Realism, and Acceptance.* Boston: Shambhala.

Riley, C., M. Lee, Z. Cooper, C. G. Fairburn, and R. Shafran. 2007. A randomised, controlled trial of cognitive-behaviour therapy for clinical perfectionism: A preliminary study. *Behaviour Research and Therapy* 45 (9):2221–31.

Robinson, J. L., J. Kagan, J. S. Reznick, and R. Corley. 1992. The heritability of inhibited and uninhibited behavior: A twin study. *Developmental Psychology* 28:1030–37.

Saboonchi, F., and L. G. Lundh. 2003. Perfectionism, anger, somatic health, and positive affect. *Personality and Individual Differences* 35:1585–99.

Salter. A. 1949. *Conditioned Reflex Therapy.* New York: Creative Age Press.

Sareen J., F. Jacobi, B. J. Cox, S. L. Belik, I. Clara, and M. B. Stein. 2006. The functional impact of anxiety disorders with physical conditions in the community. *Archives of Internal Medicine* 166:2109–16.

Schachter, S., and J. Singer. 1962. Cognitive, social, and physiological determinants of emotional states. *Psychological Review* 69:397–99.

Schienle, A., and A. Schäfer. 2006. Neural correlates of exposure therapy in patients suffering from specific phobia. *Verhaltenstherapie* 16:104–10.

Schmidt, L. A., N. A. Fox, K. H. Rubin, and E. M. Sternberg. 1997. Behavioral and neuroendocrine responses in shy children. *Developmental Psychobiology* 30:127–40.

Selye, H. 1975. *Stress Without Distress.* New York: Signet.

Siev, J., and D. L. Chambless. 2007. Specificity of treatment effects: Cognitive therapy and relaxation for generalized anxiety and panic disorders. *Journal of Consulting and Clinical Psychology* 75 (4):513–22.

Smith, M. L., and G. V. Glass. 1977. Meta-analysis of psychotherapy outcome studies. *American Psychologist* 32:752–60.

Stein M. B., P. P. Roy-Byrne, M. G. Craske, A. Bystritsky, G. Sullivan, J. M. Pyne, W. Katon, and C. D. Sherbourne. 2005. Functional impact and health utility of anxiety disorders in primary care outpatients. *Medical Care* 43:1164–70.

Taylor, S., ed. 1999. *Anxiety Sensitivity: Theory, Research, and Treatment of the Fear of Anxiety.* Mahwah, NJ: Lawrence Erlbaum Associates.

Teasdale, J. D., Z. V. Segal, J. M. G. Williams, V. Ridgeway, M. Lau, and J. Soulsby. 2000. Reducing risk of recurrence of major depression using mindfulness-based cognitive therapy. *Journal of Consulting and Clinical Psychology* 68:615–23.

Tomaka, J., J. Blascovich, J. Kibler, and J. M. Ernst. 1997. Cognitive and physiological antecedents of threat and challenge appraisal. *Journal of Personality and Social Psychology* 73:63–72.

Toneatto, T., and L. Nguyen. 2007. Does mindfulness meditation improve anxiety and mood symptoms? A review of the controlled research. *The Canadian Journal of Psychiatry* 52:260–66.

Van Zijderveld, G. A., D. J. Veltman, R. van Dyck, and L. J. P. Doornen. 1999. Epinephrine-induced panic attacks and hyperventilation. *Journal of Psychiatric Research* 33:73–78.

Völler, H. 2006. Significance of changes in habits followed by risk reduction. *Clinical Research Cardiology* 95, Suppl. 6:V1.6–11.

Von Clausewitz, C. 1982. *On War.* New York: Penguin.

Weekes, C. 1979. *Simple, Effective Treatment of Agoraphobia.* New York: Bantam.

Williams, T. 1974. *The Glass Menagerie.* Ontario, Canada: New Directions.

Williams, T. A. 1923. *Dreads and Besetting Fears.* New York: Little, Brown, and Company.

Wine, J. 1971. Test anxiety and direction of attention. *Psychological Bulletin* 76:92–104.

Wolpe, Joseph. 1967. Lecture given at Temple University, Philadelphia, PA.

William J. Knaus, Ed.D., is a licensed psychologist with more than forty years of clinical experience in working with people suffering from depression. He has appeared on numerous regional and national television shows including the **Today Show,** and over 100 radio shows. His ideas have appeared in national magazines such as *U.S. News and World Report* and *Good Housekeeping,* and major newspapers such as the *Washington Post* and the *Chicago Tribune.* He is one of the original directors of training at the Albert Ellis Institute. He is the author of twelve books including *Overcoming Procrastination* and *Do it Now.*